THE MORNING OF OUR LIVES
Growing up with popular culture

Steve Cooke

First published in Great Britain in 2017
Copyright © 2017 Steve Cooke

Steve Cooke has asserted his right under the Copyright, Designs and Patents Act 1988 to be identified as the author of this work.

Every effort has been made to obtain the necessary permissions with reference to copyright material, both illustrative and quoted. We apologize for any omissions in this respect and will be pleased to make the appropriate acknowledgements in any future edition.

ISBN: 9781522043058

Cover photo: the author and his mother. *Photographer*: unknown but almost certainly the author's father or sister.

1 Watch With Mother

2 The Green, Green Grass Of Home

3 Glory, Glory, Hallelujah

4 Set The Controls For The Heart Of The Sun

5 Journeys Without Maps

6 Hearing Secret Harmonies

7 Sherlock And Verloc

8 The Dean And I

9 God Save The Queen

10 Police And Thieves

11 A New Career In A New Town

12 The Band That Time Forgot

13 Groovy Times

14 Temporary Kings

15 Ashes To Ashes

Watch With Mother

The body lay slumped in the corner, limp and motionless, like a discarded rag doll. There was no flicker of life from the inert shape. The left of its torso was covered by a large dark burn patch. It was a horrific sight. As soon as my eyes fell upon it, I let out an involuntary scream, dissolving into hysterical, convulsive sobbing. My gaze remained fixed upon the charred body, even as I backed away in fear. A crowd gathered to drag me away from the scene of the carnage.

It was only my teddy bear, but at the age of two, this was a massively distressing experience. It is also the earliest memory of childhood that I can recall. I can't exactly remember what my teddy bear was called. Probably teddy. My mother had given stern warnings about the dangers of going near the fire and getting burnt. I had it in my head that fire and burning were the most scary things imaginable. So to see teddy disfigured in this way was at that point the most major trauma of my life. It took a good hour to calm me down. Teddy was swiftly removed from the room and taken to the soft toys remedial centre and re-appeared a few hours later with a patch. To my two-year old mind, the incident seemed to have taken its toll on teddy and he never recovered his joie de vivre. I didn't fancy hanging out with this bipolar bear, so he was swiftly replaced in my affections by a small girl's doll called Sophie. This didn't seem remotely strange to me at the time. It was only later that I realised that boys were not meant to be in touch with their feminine side so early in life. I was trying to think of a more dramatic opening for this memoir, like *"My first act on entering this world was to kill my mother"*[1], but there was no such drama right at the beginning, so the trauma of the disfigurement of my cuddly toy must suffice.

I was born in March 1959, 33 days after Buddy Holly died and during the recording of *Kind of Blue*. Although born with a shock of black hair, this soon disappeared to be replaced by lustrous wavy blond hair. Since both of my parents had black or brown hair, this must have caused some alarm in much the same way as one of the blond devil spawn from *The Midwich Cuckoos*. Fortunately, I never intoned *"they must be taught to leave us alone"* whilst scouring their cerebral cortex with my mind probe and, no doubt to their relief, my blond waves gave way to a more familiar black mop of hair. We lived in Emerson Park in Hornchurch, Essex. Well, our postal address said Essex, but we were officially in a London Borough called Havering. Havering was an appropriate name - the district of dither, somewhere that couldn't make up its mind if it was in Essex or London.

---

[1] *From William Boyd's "The New Confessions".*

Emerson Park was destined to become synonymous with well-off arrivistes, with huge vulgar houses with faux palladian pillars and monogrammed front gates, home to the first generation of West Ham footballers to earn decent wages, but in the early sixties a relatively unspoiled suburban outpost. We were an unsurprising nuclear family, father, mother, sister, brother and cat. Bob, Barbara, Laura and me, Stephen. The cat, which followed us home one day and adopted us, was black and was therefore obviously named Blackie. Stephen is not the best name in the world. It could have been worse. My school teemed with Kevins, Waynes and Carls. I would have preferred Ed but most of my friends called me Steve, which didn't seem so bad. It was Captain America's real name, after all. My mother resolutely refused to contract Stephen down to Steve, clearly believing it to an unacceptable compromise of the dignity of the name she had chosen for me. Laura was in fact my sister's middle name, promoted to be her primary moniker when her first name, Virginia, was jettisoned at an early stage. The suggestion that I might adopt my middle name and become Johnny, after the Human Torch, was summarily dismissed.

The television ranked comfortably ahead of the fireplace as the centrepiece of our living room. In our current world of multiple televisions and other screens, it is easy to forget that then nearly all houses had just one television. The sole visual entertainment portal was, of course, strictly controlled by the parents. Once permission had been obtained, you could settle down to some channel surfing. This was not the experience we have nowadays, flipping through the EPG from the comfort of the sofa. Firstly, you didn't get to hang five for very long, in order to surf through three channels - with generally one showing the test card, which could sometimes be relatively compulsive viewing compared with the offerings of the other two. Secondly, there were no remote controls, so your surfing had to be done a foot away from the set, turning the circular dial. I remember looking in wonderment in the mid-seventies at one of my friends' parents' televisions, which had a remote control. It was, of course, connected to the set by a huge wire, which the viewers kept tripping over.

I had a regular appointment each day with *Watch With Mother*. Early 60s domestically produced children's television has not aged well. In *The Flowerpot Men*, Bill and Ben, two cheaply produced puppets, would emerge from underneath their flowerpots to commit some minor potting shed accident, aided by their hapless accomplice, Little Weed, who in fact looked more like a sunflower, but it would be another six or seven years before people were called Sunflower. Seconds away from discovery by the gardener, they would scuttle back to the sanctuary of their flowerpots. This happened in every episode. A DVD box set of *The Flowerpot Men* is probably not high up the release schedules, but back in 1962 it was riveting viewing. The limited production values of two men working flowerpots by strings did not trouble the mass of viewers. Sadly, these did not improve much in the next 15 years, and viewers (including me for old time's sake) were still being treated in the late seventies to the sight of a man's hand in a sock with two buttons sewn onto it as Ramsbottom the snake in *The Sooty Show*. The rest of the *Watch With Mother* stable, *The Woodentops* and *Andy Pandy*, did not benefit from any higher budget, more complex plotting or character development, but at the time satisfied all but the most sophisticated toddler.

Foreign imports soon took things to the next level, with actual humans talking, and children like you and me doing impossibly exciting things. Whilst we played with Blackie the cat, children in Australia were stopping time during the circular flight of a boomerang in *The Magic Boomerang*. I eventually acquired a boomerang but couldn't even make it come back to me, let alone stop time. Blackie harboured feelings of inferiority, as intelligent animals on television were regularly saving children who were stuck down wells or disused mine shafts and confounding criminal enterprises – from horses (*Champion the Wonder Horse*) through dogs (*Lassie*) to dolphins (*Flipper* – although he did struggle with those mine-shaft rescues).

The Singing Ringing Tree bore the packaging of a benign children's programme but its contents were more sinister – had I been aware of mind altering substances at this point in my life, I might have assumed that my mother had been lacing my orange squash with acid, such was its surreal and disturbing story arc: a truly scary and malign dwarf, coupled with a bizarre menagerie of talking animals, made for a genuinely uncomfortable half hour. It transpired that the programme was made in East Germany in the late fifties and was no doubt replete with subliminal messaging as part of some Communist plot to subvert the consciousness of the youth of the decadent west.

There were two police programmes that we would all regularly watch. *Dixon of Dock Green* was on early Saturday night and had a welcoming homely feel. You just knew that nothing horrible was going to happen. Jack Warner, with his assuring fireside manner, wouldn't let it. The fact that his character, PC George Dixon, had already died in a previous film – *The Blue Lamp,* shot by vicious young hoodlum Dirk Bogarde – seemed to have been forgotten. These days, the twittersphere would be agonizing over whether the Dixon series was in fact a prequel – *"but if it was a prequel, how come that PC Dixon gets promoted to sergeant when he died as a constable? or whether it was occupying a parallel world to the film – a subtle Schrodinger's cat theory demonstration for early evening television - or maybe the film is non-canonical and not part of the Dock Green televisual universe?"* – or an absurd or convoluted explanation would be required – the entire earlier series was a dream (*Dallas*), a duplicate pieced together from DNA fragments (*Alien Resurrection*) or reborn in exactly the same form by a convenient reanimating MacGuffin (*Star Trek: The Search For Spock*). Genetic reconstruction technology was sadly not available to the late fifties Metropolitan Police Force and, more importantly, in those days we just didn't care. We just accepted it as the new reality. PC Dixon would end each show with a short speech about bad apples or how crime never paid. It was deeply comforting. At the end of each series, PC Dixon would mention that he was going to be on holiday for a few weeks, lest viewers become alarmed at his absence, fearing that Dirk Bogarde's bullet might have finally caught up with him and that bad apples would be allowed to fester unchecked on our streets.

Z Cars was meant to be grittier and more realistic than other police series. To this end, there were no characters walking around who had previously died. It was set in a fictional new town called Newtown, which was a suburb of a seaport called Seaport. The writers were obviously saving their powers of imagination for the scripts. I didn't know where Newtown was but didn't want to live there, as all that ever seemed to happen there was that Colin Welland and Brian Blessed would sit in the front of a police car, with a really bad backdrop of the road behind them, chatting to each other. Colin Welland spoke in a Yorkshire accent, then rarely heard on primetime television, which probably accounted for its gritty reputation.

"This is the BBC Home Service. Here is the news read by Frank Phillips. C.S. Lewis, Dr Clive Staples Lewis, has died at his home in Headington, Oxford. He would have been 65 next Friday. Thousands of teenagers who had been waiting for more than 12 hours to book for a Beatles show in Liverpool were disappointed. At one time the queue stretched for over a mile and the police had to seal off side streets to traffic. When the tickets ran out, many young girls burst into tears. More rain is forecast for most of Scotland, Northern Ireland and western districts of Wales and the West of England.............We interrupt this broadcast for some news from Washington.........Hello, London, this is Leonard Parkin, calling radio newsreel from Washington. President Kennedy and Governor John Connolly of Texas were shot today from an ambush as President Kennedy's motorcade left the centre of Dallas, where the President was on a speaking tour. People screamed and lay down on the ground as shots were heard. An Associated Press photographer, it is reported, a man called Olgins, said he saw blood on the President's head."

I don't remember where I was on the day President Kennedy died. I was only four. I certainly didn't know who C. S. Lewis was, although I would come to love him. I do, however, remember where I was on the following day. I was watching the debut of *Dr Who*. There was no doubt a subdued atmosphere in our house, reflecting the death of JFK, and to a lesser extent, C. S. Lewis. Had we then known that Aldous Huxley had also died that day, it might have been even more subdued. The release of *With The Beatles* the same day also went completely unnoticed in our household. I do remember Mum announcing that a new television series was starting which we ought to watch. Although I was apparently transfixed from then on and never missed it, I have little memory of the first few episodes. What I do remember is that the following Saturday, the first episode, *An Unearthly Child,* was repeated before the second. This led me to asking Mum and Dad, after every single episode for about two years, 'isn't there going to be another one?'

'No, Stephen, that was just for the first one,' Mum would reply, through gritted teeth.

The first episode that I really remember was a year later, when the truly frightening and shocking sight of a Dalek emerging from the post-apocalypse Thames embedded itself into my consciousness in a way that almost no image has done since. I faithfully followed the Doctor through time and space for another ten Earth years. First stop was the cinema – where I was disconcerted to find a different actor playing him (although that was a harbinger of things to come), a Tardis full of wires and tubes from a child's chemistry set and not looking remotely like the egg box chic of the Tardis I knew and loved and Daleks who sprayed dry ice at their victims rather than turning them black and white negative when their death rays were deployed. This disturbing lack of continuity with the TV *Dr Who* canon, keenly felt by a five year old, was dialled back on the much better follow up, *Dalek Invasion Earth,* where a really impressive Dalek space ship (benefitting from an upgrade from the upturned paper plate flying saucer with visible strings from the original series) and an in colour rerun of the amphibious Dalek emergence, mollified rebellious fans. There were many memorable scary moments over the course of the journey – from Cybermen gradually waking and emerging from their honeycomb of frozen cocoons when someone left the fridge door open to giant maggots and later a giant fly (although these two were strangely not related).

Gerry Anderson was an inevitable accompaniment to Saturday mornings for most of the sixties. His trademark *Supermarionation* made puppetry exciting in a way for which no-one reared on Shari Lewis with Lamb Chop and Charlie Horse was prepared. My first recollection is of the long take-off ramp with an upturned bit at the end, from which *Fireball XL5* would launch. I'm not sure that I had identified that Steve Zodiac and Venus were in fact puppets, such was the woodenness of acting in competing foreign import live acting programmes. *Stingray* swiftly followed. James Garner was recreated in puppet form and christened Troy Tempest, hero of the World Aquanaut Security Patrol (WASP), nemesis of amphibious baddie, the Mighty Titan, and love interest of both mermaid Marina and WASP commander's daughter Atlanta (voiced by future Miss Moneypenny, Lois Maxwell). Maverick and The Rockford Files were never this good. The programme would open with WASP boss Commander Shore barking *"stand by for action!"* and announcing portentously that *"anything could happen in the next half hour".* In reality, usually the same thing happened in the next half hour every week, generally involving lots of explosions.

Major excitement in Z Cars as Colin Welland reports that the screen wash isn't working. Were steering wheels really this big?

The stuff of which a lifetime of nightmares is made.

By the time of *Thunderbirds,* half an hour had been extended to an hour, such were the breadth and complexity of the adventures. For most people these days, International Rescue is an organization led by the eldest sibling of a well-known family, with their robotic, marionette-like movements and stilted speech - but enough of the Milliband brothers. The International Rescue of the sixties operated from their secret tropical island to be at the scene of an emergency anywhere on the globe before the first commercial break. You didn't ring 999 for these guys.

Technology was needlessly but thrillingly deployed throughout the island. Rather than a more remote silo, Thunderbird 1 was launched from its bay beneath the Tracy Island swimming pool, which slid back to allow launch. It is not known whether any unsuspecting bathers were caught in the pool during this manoeuvre, necessitating rescue nearer to home. Similarly, Thunderbird 3 is the only known example of a deep space rocket to be launched from the centre of a living room, providing an interesting diversion during cocktail hour. Thunderbird 2 would trundle down a long driveway but had been designed so that its wing tips were a couple of feet too wide for the thoroughfare, necessitating cutting edge innovation which enabled the fringing palm trees to flip back automatically on the approach of the craft.

Applied science in the outside world was similarly breath-taking but somehow flawed, as if to invite disaster requiring the intervention of the Tracy boys. In the first episode, *Trapped In The Sky*, we are told that although the hypersonic airliner *Fireflash*, with its nuclear engines, could stay up in flight for six months, the reactor shielding will only last two hours, after which all the passengers will die of radiation poisoning, rendering a diversion to Leeds Bradford on account of fog at Manchester a more stressful journey than normal. In the second episode, the US Army have eschewed the use of tried and trusted caterpillar tracks for their latest rough terrain vehicle, Sidewinder, in favour of long spindly legs which can easily fall into a hole, which they inevitably do, the eponymous *Pit of Peril.* A series of ludicrously unstable high towers (including a doomed attempt to move the Empire State Building), transmission masts, oil rigs and bridges ensues, ensuring that Thunderbirds are go. To take up the slack when badly designed tall buildings are not toppling over, nihilistic proto-terrorist the Hood busies himself setting bombs and sabotaging nuclear installations, where only International Rescue can save the day. Communications between the Thunderbirds team were, like their technology, unnecessarily complicated. "F.A.B." was the Thunderbirds catchphrase and was used to signify assent. It didn't actually stand for anything, but captured the zeitgeist of the groovy sixties, which seemed to still be going on a century later in the Thunderbirds world of 2067. It was also was two syllables longer than "yes", which would have been an equally satisfactory way of connoting agreement.

Thunderbirds was the most successful Gerry Anderson series and, like *Dr Who*, made the transition to the big screen. *Thunderbirds Are Go* again featured the twin threats of the Hood and unnecessary defective tech. The new Mars space vehicle, Zero X, is downed first by the Hood's footwear and then by the ridiculously complicated arrangements for re-entry, which involve engagement with two predictably defective flying supports, resulting in Zero X levelling an entire town in Florida (fortunately evacuated before the Anderson model makers could show off their destruction chops). *Thunderbird 6* saw all the familiar dangers of the year 2068 manifest themselves. Ignoring the precedent of the R101 and the Hindenburg, it was decided to dust off the airship concept for passenger travel. To tip the odds of a successful maiden flight further against the airship, the Hood's crack team of moustachioed foreign sounding terrorists had secreted themselves aboard with malevolent intent. International Rescue agent Lady Penelope manages to outwit the Hood, but not the predictably positioned high radio mast on which the airship becomes precariously perched.

The half hour format returned for *Captain Scarlet and the Mysterons*. The Mysterons are powerful unseen Martians who have the power of retro-metabolism (in brief, recreating things under their own control); but first, as the scary opening sequence ominously intones, they must destroy. As per most science fiction programmes where the sinister aliens have the ability to recreate exact duplicates of humans, the duplicates walk around with fixed glazed expressions and have had their sense of humour expunged. Conflict is triggered by a Mars expedition, via Zero X, which unaccountably manages to take off without technological incident or sabotage by the Hood, leading to interplanetary conflict. Their first victim is Captain Black, trigger-happy captain of the expedition, who is reconstituted with deathly pallor, heavy five o'clock shadow and a voice five octaves lower than his human counterpart. Captain Scarlet is the next victim but fortunately has had a shave, retains his tan and has the voice of Cary Grant. Fate takes a hand when the Mysteronised Scarlet takes a tumble from the extremely high and unstable London Carview tower (presumably a left over from a Thunderbirds stock of buildings) and frees himself of Mysteron control, although his sense of humour never returns.

Captain Scarlet is in the employ of the Spectrum organization, a global police force now dedicated to fighting the menace of the Mysterons. National interests have been subjugated and sovereignty ceded to Spectrum, the sort of supra-national monolithic organization that would have UKIP raging. The age of austerity also seems to be over, and European financial deficits eliminated, as Spectrum seems to have a massive budget, enabling hi-tech luxuries such as their headquarters, Cloudbase, a flying aircraft carrier, and a fleet of vehicles secreted across the world, from which any Spectrum agent never seems to be more than ten minutes away. The most popular of these is the Spectrum Pursuit Vehicle, otherwise known as the

SPV, a tasty set of wheels in which the Spectrum boy racers tear around the countryside. Continuing the Thunderbirds tradition of needlessly complex technology, the designer of the SPV eschewed a simple windscreen, favouring instead a computer monitor viewed by the driver who, it was decided, would be facing the rear. One hopes the electrics are more reliable than my car, or Captain Blue might find himself having more to moan about than having to tune manually to Radio 4 every time he gets in his vehicle. In this age of profligate expenditure on technology, some savings have, however, been made. Signage throughout the world has been standardized to a single 1960s Letraset font, whether it be the *"Frost Line Outer Space Defence System"*, a chain of high security space missile defence bases or *"Stone Point Village"*, a hamlet of five houses.

The two round green circle Mysteron "eyes", playing over their victims, when combined with the sinister four-note musical motif, remains one of the most disturbing memories of my children's television years. The atmosphere of tension and drama of *Captain Scarlet* would however be entirely dissipated by the shockingly poor end credits sequence, featuring equally bad music and visuals. Accompanying the pictures of the good Captain in a series of unlikely scenes that never appeared in the actual programme (such as attempted drowning by being attached to a massive rock whilst sharks circle him hungrily or manfully wedged between two constricting walls of spikes which threaten to perforate our hero) was an attempt at a groovy song presumably perpetrated by some lumbering out of touch session musicians. With words like *"Captain Scarlet - he's the one who knows the Mysterons' game, Captain Scarlet – to his Martian foes, a dangerous name"*, it sounded like the Tremeloes after someone had spiked their Horlicks with acid.

The visions of the future that programmes like *Captain Scarlet* presented were always way adrift. They either thought that major advances would happen more rapidly than they actually did – witness the multiple films that equipped the end of the 20th century with Metropolis-style flying cars zipping round 350 storey buildings – or failed to anticipate changes and were hopelessly outdated by the time you reached the time period in question. *Captain Scarlet* fell firmly into the latter category. I certainly won't be around in the year 2068 but I feel sure that video tapes and computers with large plastic buttons and lots of flashing lights to signify the CPU hard at work will not have made a comeback, unless retro kitsch is back big time.

In an era prior to my first contact with James Bond, spy series like *The Saint* and *The Man From U.NC.L.E.* seemed the real thing. In *The Saint*, future Bond Roger Moore developed his full range of quizzical expressions, whilst steadfastly refusing to carry a gun or pick up any armament dropped by a bad guy, much to the frustration of the audience. In *The Man From U.N.C.L.E.,* Napoleon Solo and Ilya Kuryakin had no such scruples, wearing shoulder holsters and glamorous guns with silencers, such was the viciousness of the struggle with T.H.R.U.S.H., their adversary. T.H.R.U.S.H stood for the *'Technological Hierarchy for the Removal of Undesirables and Subjugation of Humanity'*, lofty aims which any lesser criminal organization might have defined more narrowly in order not to lose their focus. They did, however, regularly step up to the plate with imaginative ways of carrying forward their precepts, such as mass delivery of mind altering gasses to place whole populations under their control, combined with more routine ruthless cold blooded killing of people they didn't like.

My father grew up in Coventry, the youngest child of eight. His mother, known to us as Grandma Cooke, lived to the age of 100 and was the subject of hugely unpopular (as far as Laura and I were concerned) visits to her nursing home in Leamington Spa in her declining years. Rather disappointingly, the telegram she received when she turned 100 was not from the Queen, but Sir Keith Joseph. I didn't know who Sir Keith Joseph was at the time, but knew he wasn't as important as the Queen and could legitimately join in the feeling of disappointment. Dad fought in the Second World War in the Eighth Army in the Western Desert and then Italy, including Monte Cassino, but passed on few stories of his experiences. He developed throat cancer in 1965 and, although successfully treated, it returned in 1989. He had to have a tracheotomy and then had seven years of terrible suffering, when he was in reality just biding his time for the end, what Keats would have called his 'posthumous life'.

 He was a brilliant but flawed man. Clever and funny, he held jobs ranging from advertising through selling musical instruments to management consulting. He could have reached for the stars but satisfied himself with the top of the stairs. He finally settled for being a self-employed consultant and worked for himself, a perfect arrangement, as it meant that his goals and targets could be set by a boss who was perfectly aligned with his limited aspirations. He was also a chronic sleepwalker. Family legend has it that his brother Tom once woke up to the sight of my father standing over him with a pillow poised above Tom's head, as my father intoned 'It's alright, it won't hurt.' He bequeathed this habit to both Laura and me. I once managed to dress myself perfectly for school, come downstairs and start preparing my breakfast, entirely asleep, before my parents heard the midnight stirrings and came to investigate. Laura and I once held an entire conversation in our sleep. We had no idea what we were talking about, but both remembered it the next morning.

 My mother would be enraged by his lack of ambition. When he felt like it, he could be the life and soul of the party and hold a room with his wit. These moments were, however, rare and his usual bearing was a solitary one, listening to the test match on the car radio on holiday, whilst Mum, Laura and I were at the beach. He would spend hours fiddling with some newly-acquired, and generally useless, piece of technology, which, having been found wanting, would spend a long period in storage fruitlessly waiting for the verdict of history on its utility to be reversed, before it was eventually released to the next generation of eager users (me). The eight-track cartridge and Apple Newton were just made for my father. Any innovation that he introduced into the household was generally a complete disaster. His announcement in the summer of 1973 that we would be scrapping our coal burner, and replacing it with an oil-fired boiler, was followed, with tragic inevitability, by the oil crisis and a massive increase in our heating bills. Mum was not impressed and he was never again allowed to make any important decisions. The badly letrasetted piece of cardboard (which warned "DANGER – 10,000 VOLTS!") visible from the study window, that was his attempt to produce a fake burglar alarm, was a constant source of amusement to Laura and me. He had lots of inspired ideas, but was just like the man who almost invented the vacuum cleaner – who narrowly missed by producing a device which blew rather than sucked and just redistributed the dust around the room.[2]

Mum and Dad, both in their early twenties, before they met.

---

[2] *This was spotted by the man who actually did invent the vacuum cleaner, Hubert Cecil Booth, who, inventing the original blow job, observed that it should suck, not blow.*

He seemed to spend an inordinate amount of time in the summer sitting in front of the television, watching the test match. It was a multi-media experience, with the television sound turned down so that Dad could listen to the Johnners and Trevor Bailey commentary on Radio 3. Occasionally, I would sit with him, slightly frustrated that this rather long programme, which seemed to last an entire day, was precluding access to more interesting fare. It just seemed to be some people dressed in white running randomly around a field. It was scarcely more interesting than the test card. Maybe the two were related, and the test match was a dynamic version of the test card. Gradually, I got more into the cricket and, even more surprisingly, Dad would sometimes even talk to me about the match. He was a distant parent and the rare shared moments away from the test match still stick in my mind - a trip to White Hart Lane to see Spurs play (but only after constant entreaties borne out of my football obsession finally permeated his bubble), the odd visit to Chelmsford or Ilford to watch Essex play cricket and a solitary bout of cricket practice in the garden. I didn't really think it odd at the time and maybe it wasn't. Or maybe it was.

Laura and I were effectively brought up in a single parent family. My mother had grown up in Grimsby in Lincolnshire. Her mother, Christina (known to us as "Nanny"), was a MacBeath from Thurso in Caithness, but no trace of Scottishness remained. Her husband, Jack, was a lovely man whom I remember distinctly for his warm heart and illicit ice cream purchases for me. His early death at the age of 65 in 1965 was a huge blow to my mother, who adored him. The double blow of his death and my father's throat cancer meant that 1965 was not an easy year for her. My mother was a wireless operator for a Lancaster squadron in the war and then travelled with the forces to Singapore and Hong Kong, before meeting and marrying my father in the late fifties.

When my father's diagnosis with cancer threatened the continuation of his employment and our financial security, she trained herself in shorthand and business studies and began a career as teacher and lecturer, whilst continuing to raise us pretty much single-handed. She was truly liberated and it was her, not my father, who schooled me in traditional male skills like DIY. I spent a whole summer at the age of 11 making and putting up a set of slatted shelves in our airing cupboard. Her explicitly stated ethos was simple: either I would get to love DIY, and become a useful addition to any household, or hate DIY and become determined to have the sort of well remunerated job where I could pay someone else to do it, again becoming a useful addition to any household. The conditioning worked - I went down the latter route and I still go into a cold sweat in the proximity of a hammer or saw. She also had a refreshing antipathy to the hoarding of junk, and taught me this by example. It was an expensive lesson, as amongst the junk that was first despatched to the temporary holding pen of our attic, and then trashed in one of her ruthless purges, was a large pile of imported early sixties Marvel editions ('just silly comics, Stephen'), now changing hands for stupendous sums.

She had a formidable taste for adventure and new experiences. A new hobby would pop up each year. No-one ever knew where the inspiration had come from. She just seemed to wake up and decide that was what she was going to do. One day, a beehive appeared in our garden. No-one commented on it until a man arrived and installed a swarm of bees in it. I'm not sure Dad even noticed until his lawnmower collided with it. Mum certainly didn't seek his approval for her apiculture adventure. That was simply not the way it worked in our house. It was a comedy episode each time she needed to tend to her flock. She would appear completely covered in her protective clothing, sealed comprehensively inside, with her head shielded by an impenetrable cowl, resembling someone preparing to work with some highly radioactive substances in a nuclear installation. We would be giggling, as this golem waddled its way robotically down the garden. In contrast, the gentlemen who came to assist her in coaxing her recalcitrant bees back into the hive when they had swarmed in one of the apple trees, was clad in a t-shirt and shorts and suffered no apparent injury. She would then attempt to sedate the bees by blowing smoke with a bellows into the hive. This always seemed to have the opposite effect, with the inhabitants of the hive angrily buzzing around the garden looking for the fire. Mum would beat a hasty retreat before they spotted the arsonist. We giggled even more, but swallowed our pride when some honey was produced and swallowed that too. Wine-making followed. Her product never resembled wine as most people would recognise it, but undeniably had an alcoholic component that would come in useful in later years and be at the scene of some minor social solecisms.

Laura was two years younger than me. Talented in all sorts of ways, her greatest expertise lay in getting me into trouble and winding me up. Her modus operandi was generally to frame me for some minor misdemeanour and, once I'd been told off by Mum, to emit a very subtle sibilant noise, a fast repeated "ss ss ss ss ss ss ss". This was barely audible, other than to the dogs in the neighbourhood and, critically, me. Roughly translated, it meant "ha ha, I've outwitted you again". Mum was oblivious to it and it was absolutely infuriating. This would generally drive me to greater righteous anger, probably including a physical assault on Laura. This would in turn lead to greater punishment and further delivery of "ss ss ss ss ss ss ss" and the cycle continued.

It was a house where something was always going on. There was usually some prank being played or something else causing us to be laughing uncontrollably. Mum and, in those rare moments of participation when he got into the groove, Dad, both had a huge sense of fun. Mum would often tell the story, from the years before Laura and I arrived, of when they were

Mum and Dad in the mid-fifties, before my arrival. They appear to be talking to a ventriloquist and his dummy.

invited to a séance. As usual, my father had acquired a new piece of technology. A tape recorder. That may not seem very remarkable now, other than on account of the curiosity that people were then still recording things on tape, but tape recorders were apparently still not common as a household item. My father deployed it to embody the spirit of the one of the departed relatives of a participant in the séance, and, later, her pet parrot. I am told this got the séance moving along nicely. Not being there, I can't attest to how funny this was, but what I can say is that every time my Mother told the story, it reduced her to tears of laughter.

    Mum and Laura would often combine to play some prank on me. One Christmas, this centred around a tin of *Quality Street*. *Quality Street* was devised by Harold Mackintosh in 1936 in the midst of the depression to cheer people up. I doubt that, if I was starving and unemployed and had just marched down from Jarrow, a caramel swirl or strawberry delight would mollify me. He named it after the J. M. Barrie play of the same name, using two characters from the play, Miss Sweetly and Major Quality, for the illustrations on the tin. Famously, Saddam Hussein was reported to like them and offered one to George Galloway when Gorgeous George was visiting him to salute his courage, strength and indefatigability. I don't know whether Saddam favoured the purple ones and had tasked a unit of the elite

Republican Guard with separating them all out but, like many, I did and, although, if pressed, would accept a green triangle, wasn't that keen on the rest of the tin. Laura and Mum were keenly aware of my Christmas confectionery preferences and had doctored the tin, so that all of the purple ones had been removed. They would offer me the tin – which in itself aroused suspicion, as it was generally every man for himself where chocolate was concerned in our house, but when combined with the fake saintly expression that had been adopted by the two Miss Sweetlys, my antenna was firmly up. I rooted around in the tin but could find no purple ones.

'Where are all the purple ones?' I grumbled, reluctantly picking out a green triangle.

'Oh, aren't there any left?' Mum said, summoning up all her thespian skills.

An equity card was surely on the way. They then both made a big show of rooting around in the tin and amazingly finding a purple one, having palmed one. It was skilfully done and had me fooled for a while, if deeply suspicious. Such was the dedication to family pranks, I suspect they had practised the palming of purple ones extensively. When this was repeated later the same afternoon, I was on their scent. This time they had under-estimated my counter-insurgency espionage capabilities. By close observation of the evil pair, I had soon tracked down where they had hidden the stash of purple ones and removed them to my own hiding place.

'I think I'll have another Quality Street,' I announced about ten minutes later, inserting my hand into the tin and, to their consternation, pulling out a purple one.

At this point, they obviously thought that their scouring of the tin had not been up to the rigorous prank standards adopted in the Cooke household. When I repeated this, their alarm bells were ringing and they were scurrying off to examine the stash. Imagine their dismay to find that it had been covertly appropriated by the enemy. These were the years before you could buy packets consisting wholly of purple ones, so I thanked them for their service in being so kind as to diligently separate out all my favourite chocs and went on to enjoy my Christmas. I doubt if anyone would have dared to mess with Saddam's soft centres.

I spent long hours in the kitchen under Mum's culinary tutelage. There was no gender stereotyping in our house. My mother's cooking, however, was not her strong point. My father was wholly incapable of preparing any sort of food. His sole contribution was rather sweetly to make my breakfast for my ludicrously early start for Saturday morning school. His speciality was Weetabix with hot milk poured over it, the results of which were a breakfast disaster that even my mother could have foreseen – a tasteless sludge which made me yearn for weekday school starts.

Sunday lunch was a particular low point. It was traditional roast beef with all the trimmings. Well, roast beef, Jim, but not as we know it. It was only when I was about 16 that I realised that roast beef, like BBC2, was also available in colour. This grey desiccated spccimen was usually accompanied by roast potatoes, which had been cooked for a similar length of time and consequently formed a unyielding carapace which could not be penetrated without recourse to professional cutting equipment. Any attempt to cut them with table cutlery risked dangerous starchy shrapnel fragments flying off and maiming unfortunate members of the family. The roast beef was invariably followed by rice pudding ("to use up the space in the oven") which had also been subjected to the same unitary cooking timetable as the beef and potatoes, reducing it to a substance which would certainly merit trial by the military as the ballast for flak jackets, such was its robust yet repellent composition. Jam was generally added as a palliative, but could not usually be absorbed by the rubbery mass. Her curries were similarly ill-starred, being simply a runny beef stew into which she had tipped some curry powder, sultanas and apple slices. The watery mass was only contained on the plate by a levee of tightly packed starchy rice, which came from the same stable of consistency as the pudding version. Again, the realization that this catastrophe bore little relation to the real thing only came with the advent of post-pub dining in my later teens.

My mother was a child of the dawn of the convenience food era and this always influenced her culinary choices. Semolina and pilchards were a feature of the menu in our house long before John Lennon chanced upon the combination. There was, in her view, no recipe which couldn't be improved by the substitution of some tinned or packeted analogue of a key fresh ingredient – 'I've tried my own version of ratatouille today,' she would say, presenting some grey courgette slices topped with a smear of tinned tomato puree, as the hapless diners pleaded full stomachs or searched desperately for a pot plant in which to deposit the misbegotten mess.

To be fair, this sort of cooking was par for the course in that time: this was the era of the vol au vent – a white concoction resembling (in both visual and, I am assured, taste terms) cat sick, ladled into appallingly dry flaky pastry. To date, no retro cookbook of which I am aware has even considered rehabilitating this abomination. I would also say, in her defence, that her summer pudding and trifle have never been bettered and her plucky attempts at Baked Alaska eventually brought success, once the beta version design flaws around the insulating properties of the meringue crust had been overcome and the ice cream core thus did not emerge in liquid form during the cooking process, forming a strange Fanny Craddock style version of Iles Flottantes.

It was a blessed relief when cooking was outsourced, as was traditional on Friday evenings, when we would settle down to the finest entertainment that television could offer, viz *The Virginian* followed by *Hawaii-5-0,* accompanied by fish and chips, Ski hazelnut yoghurt and a bar of Galaxy chocolate. When my father introduced his latest new gadget, a Sparklets soda syphon, into the equation in the early seventies, it became a banquet that seemingly could not be bettered. Fortunately my mother never tried to replicate yoghurt. I can't even begin to imagine what ingredients she might have selected for her version, but I have a vision of a festering curdled mélange. Ski yoghurt arrived in the UK in the mid-sixties with a slick continental veneer, masquerading as a luxury item. '*Ski – the full of fitness food, for all the family,*' chirped the inane advert, giving the impression that if you ate a single pot it would counteract the effect of the fish and chips and chocolate and you wouldn't have to go to the gym for a week. Whatever, it was certainly the most popular culture in our household. Its health-giving properties were far from our thoughts and by the time that Steve McGarrett barked '*book him Dano – murder one,*' as he inevitably did in each episode, we were basking in contentment. The hangover came on Saturday, with the knowledge that Sunday lunch was just around the corner.

In August 1964, I knew something was amiss, as I was taken to Horne's the outfitters in Romford, to be fitted for what was called a blazer. I needed this, my mother explained, because I would be going to school.

Langtons state primary school on Westland Avenue, Hornchurch was a forbidding looking Edwardian building but was a happy place. The original headmistress, Miss Church, was a well-respected central casting spinster headmistress who seemed to be about 90 but was probably in no more than her late fifties or early sixties. I am still incapable of visualizing her as anything other than Alastair Sim in drag. The teachers were friendly and had some genuinely inspiring educators amongst them. My strongest memory is of Mr. Halliwell, a jovial Welshman, Cardiff City fan and a jack of all trades, moving effortlessly from the football pitch to the history book. Aside from his misplaced over-estimation of the worth of Cardiff City striker John Toshack, he was one of the wisest teachers I would have for many years. Given the possible choices of other state schools in the area at that time, I was very lucky to go to Langtons.

The most repellent feature of the daily school regime was probably the mandatory dosing with school milk. Whilst I appreciate the theory behind regular calcium supplements for growing children, one would have hoped that a less vile delivery system could be devised. The crates containing the hated one-third pint bottles would be delivered first thing and dutifully placed by the radiator so that by the appointed milk consumption hour of eleven, they were well into the curdling process. The resulting brew made school custard a delight in comparison. Some more prescient and indulged children had their own personal supply of banana Nesquik to soften the blow. If only we had had a Tory government and milk snatcher Thatcher had been able to abolish school milk seven years earlier, there would then have been one thing I could thank her for.

I drifted through the Langtons years generally without incident, neither an alpha male in the playground, nor a target for the bullies. My sole moment of serious conflict came when Simon Horswell stole my chair in a French lesson. I'm not sure why this was such an issue, but it clearly touched a nerve and before I knew it I had offered Horswell out for a fight in the mid-morning break.

As soon as the words came out of my mouth I regretted them. I had cried havoc and let slip the dogs of war and was now wondering how I might coax them back into their kennel before they bit me. It was probably as a result of the two bits of advice Mum had given me before packing me off to school. First, don't let your mouth touch the spout of the drinking fountain – you don't know what germs lurk there. Second, don't let yourself be bullied. To assist me with the latter, she had bought me a pair of boxing gloves and attempted to tutor me in self-defence, but it never really captured my imagination. This was to be my maiden bout and sure to end in tears. Were I to be writing a lightly fictionalized account of my life, this would be a David and Goliath encounter, with a heavily tattooed and studded opponent carrying three or four stone more than me, carrying a concealed flick knife or a sock containing billiard balls. After a series of bruising strikes, each of which felled me mercilessly, and close to defeat, I would use his weight against him and topple him with a well-aimed blow. In truth, we were relatively evenly matched. I had no fighting pedigree so was generally thought to be a pussy, whilst he had an air of confidence and was assumed to be a bit tasty. I don't have much of a memory of the ensuing ten minutes other than the large crowd of schoolchildren that gathered around us in a ring, just like in the movies. I emerged with a black eye. I had, however, managed to inflict a black eye and bleeding nose on Simon Horswell. On a split decision, I was adjudged to have won on points. My reputation went up a couple of notches and no-one stole my chair in French ever again. Simon Horswell became a bit of a friend. We used to play *Man From U.N.C.L.E.* games together, with me getting to be the customary first choice, Napoleon Solo, with him settling for Ilya Kuryakin, such was the shift in the balance of power in our relationship occasioned by my victory. My mother was aghast when I returned home with my black eye, but was clearly pleased when the truth was extracted from one of my friends under her ruthless interrogation.

The Green, Green, Grass of Home

The sixties as it is fondly remembered in popular memory did not really happen in our house. Whilst Beatlemania was raging unchecked in the streets outside and the Rolling Stones were urinating on petrol station forecourts[3], we were sitting in our living room with tea and cake, listening to the Seekers (a saccharin coated development of Pete Seeger folk for the BBC light programme market), Engelbert Humperdink and, the nearest we got to the cutting edge, Tom Jones. No Elvis, Beatles or the Rolling Stones in our house. We lived in a sixties that seemed to be curated by Val Doonican. That is not to say that I came to hate these artists – the operation of some form of sonic Stockholm syndrome has led me to fondly remember some of them - The Seekers' *The Carnival Is Over* is still a poignant classic in my mind and heavy rotation of Tom Jones' *Green, Green, Grass of Home* has forever lodged it in the positive centres of my cerebral cortex. It was a number one single with the sort of bleak conclusion that these days would be unlikely to make it through the focus groups into the final of the X Factor. I did once put the Seekers' *I'll Never Find Another You* unsupervised onto the record player but my mother came rushing in to remove it. Our grandmother was staying and Mum whispered to me that I shouldn't play it as it reminded her of my grandfather, who had just died. I remember being mystified that a record could conjure up such strong emotions. Like Proust's madeleines, music has the capability of invoking involuntary memory in a hugely evocative way.

Music insinuates itself into our consciousness from almost the day we are born. Even at only six months, my daughter Millie, although generally approving of Geri Halliwell's first album (it wasn't mine, officer), took against one track and voiced her objections loudly every time it was played, fortuitously liming its tenure on the car stereo. My younger son, Charlie, managed at the age of less than five to identify the snatch of harp at the beginning of Sneaker Pimps *6 Underground* as being a sample from the Goldfinger film (the bit where Shirley Eaton is found painted gold and dead), showing a finely tuned musical ear and impressive knowledge of the Bond films (although he had already by this time been through my intensive Bond boot camp academy). He also would sing the Cardigans' *Love Fool* on continuous loop for about six months. My equivalents were the Beatles' *She Loves You* and Millie Small's *My Boy Lollipop*. Each had a chorus with the phonetic simplicity to be easily reproduced by a three year old. I did so with a regularity which amply demonstrated the love of repetition characteristic

---

[3] *Bill Wyman's highly un-rock and roll explanation for this outrage was that he was suffering from a bladder complaint. There are no other known instances of his condition causing him issues during the Stones lengthy sets.*

of most toddlers. The fact that most adults of my generation seem to recall watching at least 200 fifteen minute episodes of *Andy Pandy*, when in fact there were only 26, is a testament to this. For the harassed parent wanting some peace, plonking the toddlers down in front of *The Lion King* or *Toy Story* for the fiftieth time without juvenile complaint is a welcome application of this trait. I suspect that my parents took a less benevolent view of my 24/7 renditions of the Beatles and Millie. Mersey or Blue beat were never again heard in our house in their natural state.

Unbelievably, the Beatles did come to our town. Romford ABC Cinema, a mere four miles away. Obviously, we didn't go. The idea of any name band daring to take their show to anywhere near Romford these days would be considered madness. They were on one of those insane package tours, which in today's terms would be like having Radiohead supported by One Direction, Public Enemy, Roy Chubby Brown and the cast of Jersey Boys. When I went to school a couple of years later, just about everybody there recounted the magic of that evening, as I shamefacedly admitted to not having been there. It was only later that I realised that my schoolmates were probably also amongst the several million people who, if their stories are to be believed, crammed themselves into the 250 capacity 100 Club to witness the Sex Pistols and Clash epochal "gig that broke punk" there in 1976.

The Beatles were only admitted through the doors of our house once mediated by the de-radicalising filter of Alan Haven. Alan Haven was a jazz organist who specialised in re-inventions of current popular favourites. I can still remember *Lennon & McCartney Styled by Alan Haven,* with a toe-curling cover with him as a tailor cutting suits for two mop-top dummies. The lack of imagination evinced by the cover was sadly replicated in its contents, awful versions of early Fab Four songs, but the nearest we would get to hearing the Beatles on a music on demand basis.

In my father's record collection pickings were slim. It was dominated by the sort of horrible easy listening that was prevalent in the sixties - Bert Kaempfert and the James Last Orchestra. You'd never have caught James Last or Bert Kaempfert urinating on a petrol station forecourt. Although Bert Kaempfert can at least claim to have added something to human existence by writing the music to *Strangers In The Night*, James Last had, so far as I can tell, no redeeming features. His albums had titles like *Non Stop Dancing vol 3* and *Trumpet A Go Go.* He bizarrely prefigured the trend for post-modern ironic easy listening versions of leftfield[4] material with his early seventies version of a Uriah Heep track. As the old joke goes, what's the difference between the James Last Orchestra and a bull? Well a bull has horns up front and an arsehole at the back....

---

[4] *The description, not the electronic band.*

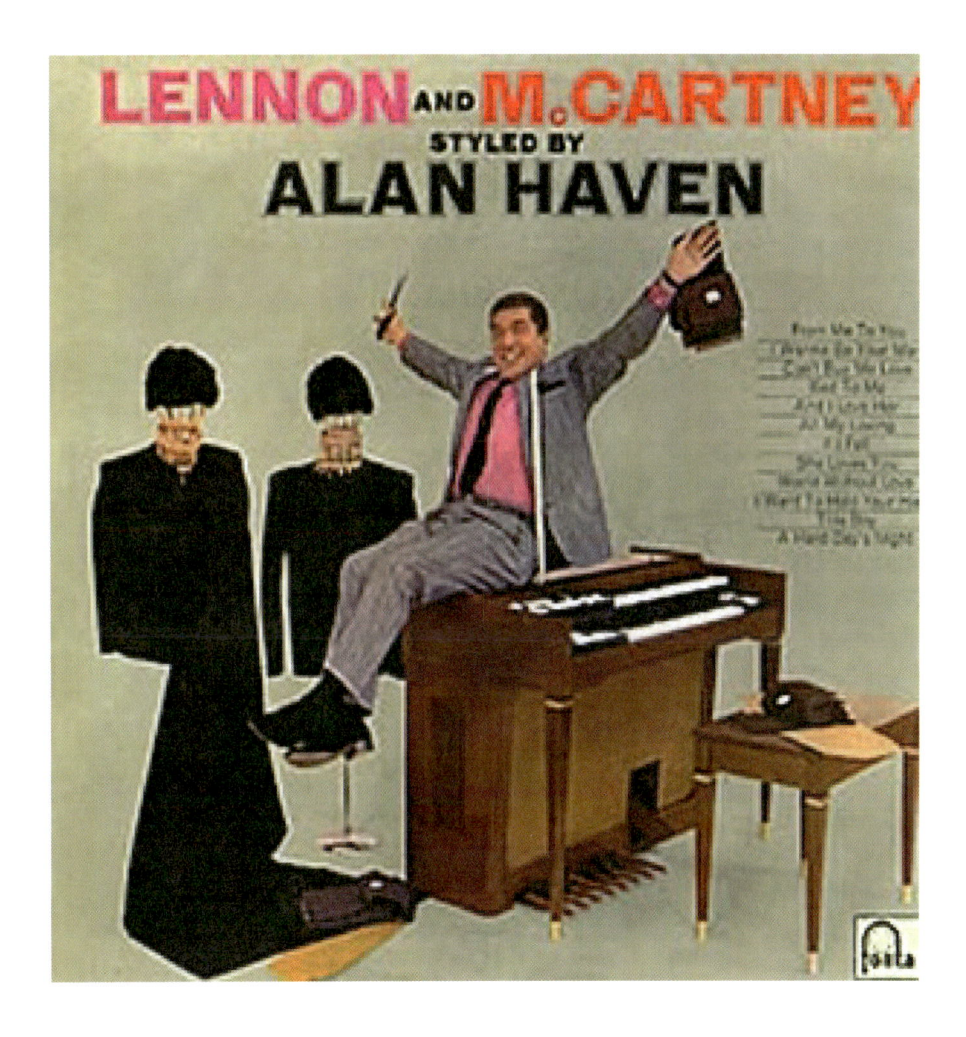

James Last died during the writing of this, denying the world *Non Stop Dancing vol 153*, *Theremin A Go Go*, *Last Plays Napalm Death* or *Hip Hop Polka*. Just to show that truth is stranger than fiction, whilst the first three of these were a joke, Last has in fact already recorded *Hip Hop Polka*. The Public Enemy tribute to James Last album beckons.

The rest of my father's record collection was pretty unapproachable. He played double bass in a swing band at some point and had quite a few jazz records but he was clearly one of those traditionalists for whom jazz ended at Benny Goodman. Bird, Miles and Coltrane didn't make into his collection. He quite liked Erroll Garner. When I started listening to jazz, when I played in a jazz band in my mid-twenties, I bought him a CD copy of *Concert By The Sea* but I don't know whether he ever played it. It still sits in my collection. Aside from these, there was a strange preponderance of stereo demonstration records, with BBC style announcers with polished vowels saying things like *"this is a journey into sound," "melody...and rhythm"* or *"sound on the left....and the right,"* with pointless recordings of trains travelling from one speaker to the other. I didn't hear the journey into sound again until about 25 years later when, all of a sudden, it started appearing sampled on Public Enemy and Bomb The Bass records and swiftly became a cliché as samplers' approximation of a daring but ironic culture clash. In fact, the lack of representation of the zeitgeist in our house was probably not an uncommon experience. The sixties revolution, as retrospectively frozen into our consciousness by most media depictions of the era, in reality left many households untouched. The record that was the best selling album in three separate years in the sixties was not *Sgt Pepper* or *With The Beatles,* but *The Sound of Music* soundtrack, with a total of 70 weeks at number one. We were not alone in our MOR cocoon.

    Alongside the television, the secondary altar of entertainment worship in our living room was, of course, the stereogram. For those unfamiliar with the device, it was borne out of the period when the makers of record players were fixed on the idea of integrating their equipment into the fabric of the room by the simple expedient of housing it in an attractive piece of furniture. Except that the concept of an attractive piece of furniture in the mind of a hi-fi manufacturing boffin was a bit adrift from the mainstream. Hence the stained wood monstrosity, like some singing sideboard, that dominated the living room of most houses during the sixties. The average stereogram had inbuilt capacity to house a decent record collection, or indeed a small family. It was, however, closely guarded by my father. The diamond stylus was treated as if it were the Koh Hi Nor itself and clearly could not be handled by anyone other than an experienced operator such as Dad or, in those rare moments of indulgence when he had been marginally relaxed by a can of Long Life beer, my mother. Once a record was playing, it was like being in the opera and movement around the room was strictly proscribed, lest an over-heavy footfall dislodge the precious stylus from its microgroove. The swinging Sixties was strictly a static armchair-bound experience in our house.

    A brief episode of piano lessons failed to provide any inspiring musical input. The dispiriting routine of having to play endlessly *There Is a Tavern In the Town* and *Bobby Shaftoe* sterilised any burgeoning interest in playing music. When my own children started their lessons thirty years later, it was indeed depressing that piano tuition seemed to have been preserved in aspic and they were still learning to play the same pieces, even more culturally irrelevant in the late nineties and early noughties than they were in the sixties, rather than something which they might have a chance of relating to and enjoying.

This was a hi-fi boffin's idea of an attractive piece of furniture.

For a five year old, the Tokyo Olympics in 1964 brought with it a series of images of people running, jumping and throwing things, but far more memorably a tune which is still lodged in my brain and I could still hum without having heard it for nearly 50 years. Researching this memoir, I now know it is *Tokyo Melody* by Helmut Zacharias and, wonderful thing that the internet is, I downloaded it and heard it again for the first time since 1964. If James Last had ever done a *Last Plays Sakamoto* album, this is what it would have sounded like.

If you looked out of my bedroom window you saw green. Fields and fields of green. Even the signpost for the footpath to Upminster Common was green. For the whole of my childhood, I lived in the same house, looking out on green. We were the frontline of green. The edge of the Green Belt. Behind us grey, before us green.

The fields opposite us were our playground. The adjacent countryside afforded us ample accessories for our adventures – a river with rope swing, an abandoned air raid shelter and numerous hollowed out trees were all present and correct. We inevitably established a hideaway where we could shelter free from the cares of the urban world that menaced us from the other side of Wingletye Lane. It was fully stocked with hidden supplies of

Ritz crackers, fig roll biscuits and dandelion and burdock, although I've never been sure in retrospect why we were so keen on the latter, as it seems to taste like liquid Germolene. It was our refuge from the coming apocalypse and the radioactive threats that were all around us - at least that was the way it felt to the mind of a reader of 60s Marvel Comics, where nary a week went by without someone being turned into a biological outcast by some careless isotope husbandry, radioactive insect or toxic plutonium spillage. We had enough supplies to see us through if not the nuclear winter, at least the nuclear weekend. Except that our hideout was a bush. So far as I'm aware, even allowing for the ludicrous improbability of some of the desperate measures by late 50s/early 60s civil defence guidelines, shrubbery has never formed a big part of protect and survive. Our den did, however, have direct line of sight onto our house and we dutifully recorded the movements of the various security threats who lived therein into our spy log.

It was also useful when we had to flee the house when one of our prank calls to the emergency services went wrong. Although it now seems to be common knowledge that the security services can trace your whereabouts instantly from a switched off mobile phone, many national security agencies depicted in films still seem to be working with equipment inherited from their sixties counterparts – with the chief investigator still trying to make small talk in a vain attempt to keep the international terrorist on the line as a big digital readout tells us for how much longer he needs to spin out the chat in order to establish that he's in the phone box on the corner of Westland Avenue and North Street, before inevitably the terrorist knowingly hangs up 2 micro-seconds before the 30 second deadline (taking a chance on the authorities not having received an App Store upgrade to 25 second tracing the week before). Confidently believing the 30 second safe zone that we had observed in endless episodes of *Z Cars*, *The Man From UNCLE* and *Mission Impossible*, it seemed a low risk piece of fun to call 999, croak a strangulated "He's trying to kill me" into the mouthpiece and then hang up a good 20 seconds clear of the trace threshold – there was no unnecessary international terrorist grandstanding in our operation. Our giggling and self-congratulatory celebrations were interrupted by the realization that the phone was now emitting a high whining noise. Frozen with horror, I hesitantly picked up the receiver and put it to my ear.

'The Police will be with you in a minute,' an officious female voice calmly stated.

Cue horrified panic as we fled the house, bolting for the sanctuary of our den in a convincing nuclear drill, and stayed there until satisfied that this was either a knowing telephone operator teaching us a lesson or the that the police clear-up rates in our area had reached a new low.

At the back and side of our house was Romney Chase, a rambling late Victorian pile straight out of a Tim Burton movie, with beautiful overgrown gardens and a pond. It was owned by a lovely old local solicitor by the name of Arthur Sackville-Hulkes. He was a widower and appeared to have stepped straight from the pages of a Dickens novel, where, having covertly watched over affairs from a distance for many years, he appears in the final chapter to announce the vesting of a generous endowment from his wealthy client benefactor in favour of a penniless but good-hearted youth. When I appeared on his doorstep during Cubs' Bob-A-Job week, my visit coinciding with the Apollo moon landing in 1969, he planted me down on his sofa to watch it with him, gave me the huge sum of ten shillings and marked the job down on my card as "holding down cushions".

His own children had grown up and he lived alone in Romney Chase and was happy for Laura and I to roam free in his grounds. Roam we did, as if in some estuary English version of *Swallows and Amazons*, collecting frog spawn from the pond and watching the tadpoles hatch in the round glass bowl in which we deposited it, sticking sticks into the beehives to see if we could harvest honey and picking apples in the orchard. We spent long, languorous days watching the two mallards who resided on the pond, whom we had named Harold and Gertrude, accompanied by Blackie, who kept his distance so as not to compromise his feline independence and maintain the possibility of successfully stalking Harold or Gertrude.

Laura was sworn in to a secondary but essential role in my action games. I never followed the Batman comics, but it was my favourite television programme at the time, and often formed the basis for our fantasy games. I remember crying when Catwoman plunged to her death in a bottomless cavern, eluding Batman's attempts to save her. Empathising with Batman's own emotional conflicts towards her and perhaps feeling the early stirrings of youthful desire, this was as hard a psychological blow as could be meted out to any child reared by the television. Although Catwoman later returned to use up her other eight lives, the replacement of Julie Newmar by a different, and clearly inferior, actress seemed to confirm her demise.

Marvel Comics provided a rich spread of possible subjects for role-playing games, but they seemed less attractive subjects for me to impersonate. Firstly, I wasn't sure I wanted to be a mutant freak with wings or a power beam coming out of my eyes (even if that did give me the power of flight or a useful tool for settling those bothersome playground disagreements) or the misbegotten result of some radioactive accident. Although there was the self-help school of super-herodom, people who'd just taken some special serum or had a bit of flash mechanical kit, this had mixed results – although Captain America and Iron Man were exciting derivatives of the appliance of science, all too often you ended up with Ant Man, whose sole skill was to pop a pill and end up the size of an ant, being menaced by giant spiders and mice. In 1967, there were people all over California who were managing the same thing daily. Second, it was not easy to achieve a passable impersonation of someone who could streak through the sky as a ball of flame or elongate his arms round an entire building. I spotted a wooden mallet in the garage, which could be a passable ringer for the enchanted uru hammer of the Mighty Thor, the legendary god of thunder, but soon tired of wandering around the garden looking as though I was preparing to put up a tent or peg out a croquet lawn. There were also difficult inconsistencies in the technicalities of some of the Marvel characters. Take Cyclops from the X Men, for example. In one early edition, Cyclops, whilst in civvies as his alter ego Scott Summers, has his blast ray inhibiting sunglasses removed by an interfering busy body and, without his specially designed eyewear, is unable to control his energy beam, which plays upon the surrounding buildings with destructive results. This was troubling to the mind of a detail obsessed seven year old. How then could he change from his official duty X Men protective visor to his sunglasses without scorching his dressing table or levelling his bedroom? Did he sleep in his sunglasses? Cool but a mite impractical. When a subsequent edition showed

Cyclops effortlessly negotiating the visor to sunglasses transition by simply keeping his eyes shut, I felt obliged to fire off a nerdish letter to the house of Marvel. It was never published. They simply weren't catering to fanboys as picky as me.

So, Batman seemed a safer bet – his secret identity as millionaire society charmer and all purpose ladies man, Bruce Wayne, tended upon by his butler Alfred, seemed more acceptable than the standard Marvel hero alter ego of eight stone weakling bookworm who was shunned by society or was the butt of playground jokes[5]. The fact that he couldn't fly or burst into flame, but had just spent a lot of time at the gym, made him a more approachable subject for role-playing impersonation by a mere mortal like me. A birthday present of a moulded black Batman mask, when combined with a length of old curtain doubling as a cape and the underground air-raid shelter in the grounds of Romney Chase as the Batcave, provided a more than credible backdrop for the continuing adventures of Hornchurch Batman and Robin. Laura, naturally, was Robin. We couldn't afford a butler.

The grounds of Romney Chase also played host to epic re-enactments of Gettysburg and other great American Civil War battles. Extant cine film footage shows Laura selflessly leading Pickett's Charge whilst I repulse the Confederate assault upon little roundtop (a wooded slightly raised area next to the pond doubling adequately) with my blue Union cap and plastic sword. It was difficult to portray the sheer weight of bodies with an acting cohort numbering two but I feel we captured the essence of those great battles. The American Civil War entered my life via bubble gum. Although satisfying and carrying the faint whiff of glamorous illegality which came with parental disapproval, it was the accompaniment to the gum that really counted. *Bazooka Joe* was my bubble gum of choice – as it came with cartoons that you could save to claim a prize – for example, a record player for only 4,500 Bazooka Joe cartoons - or 5 cartoons and £15. It would have taken only a short calculation and assessment break from gum-chewing to work out that the all cartoon route to the record player was a folly and that there was a saner alternative, but that was not the point. With chewing gum came collectible cards, first footballers – as I fruitlessly tried to offload my six surplus Andy Lockhead cards for a coveted George Best – and then the American Civil War. The "*Bloody Combat*" card, depicting troops being impaled on stakes, was the prize of my collection. They were apparently withdrawn in the US after being linked with delinquent behaviour. They were also linked with some alleged delinquent behaviour on my part. I say 'alleged' as I was the subject of a massive

---

[5] *With the honourable exception of Tony Stark, moustachioed millionaire charmer Marvel analogue of Bruce Wayne and the only acceptable Marvel secret identity in the whole of the canon, were it not for the fact that he had to plug himself into the mains every few hours to keep his life saving transistors charged up. The miners' strike could have been fatal.*

miscarriage of justice at the hands of the Langtons school authorities. I was charged with using a swearword as I stormed across the playground at the head of my Union posse, yelling 'bloody combat!' re-enacting the Confederate skewering depicted on the card. Appealing my sentence of detention, I patiently explained that one could only judge whether 'bloody' was being used as a swearword by examining the context in which it was used. The detention stood. It was a scandalous injustice, but war is hell. The chewing gum cards, combined with the US TV import of *Custer,* an airbrushed pre-*Bury My Heart at Wounded Knee* depiction of the butcher of countless Native Americans as a swashbuckling flaxen haired hero, led me to the fantasy role of Union general.

The scourge of Dixie, General Stephen J Cooke, prepares the Union Army of the Potomac (Laura) for the Battle of Gettysburg. Only the generals were provided with Union Army caps in this particular campaign.

My father was a tireless proponent of lost causes. Occasionally, he would be so tireless that the cause that everyone assumed was lost would be won. Witness his single-handed generation of opposition to the proposal to build a housing estate on the green fields and farm opposite our house. The supine acceptance by most of our neighbours of this incursion into the Green Belt seemed to indicate that this was truly a no hoper. Cue my father, mobilizing mass opposition. I was sworn in to conduct a traffic survey. Normal technological assistance, such as a pressure strip across the road, was beyond our means and therefore the data gathering method was for me to be perched by my bedroom window for an eight hour shift, noting down every time a car went past. Laura occasionally relieved me for comfort breaks and meals, but her data gathering discipline was viewed with suspicion by Dad so I bore the brunt of the burden of the exercise. Although nowadays this would be viewed as a monstrous intrusion into summer holiday leisure time, I didn't have four or five mobile devices or screens (apart from the one downstairs showing *Andy Pandy* for the twentieth time) to compete for my attentions, just Tony Blackburn and Johnnie Walker on Radio 1 for company and a temporary pardon from all shelf erection and other DIY activity. It seemed like a good deal.

Naturally, we couldn't afford a high-powered QC to represent us against the battalions of mass development, so Dad had to deputise for him. His only legal training was watching Raymond Burr go through his paces each week as Perry Mason. Perry would also take on cases rejected by others as lost causes so he was a good model, although I don't think he did much local planning work. I wasn't there but Dad was apparently brilliant. I don't know if, following razor sharp questioning from my father, the head evil property developer broke down and confessed his guilt in a dramatic denouement in the final reel, but *The Case of the Lilyputt's Farm Redevelopment* ended happily, with the virtue of the Emerson Park strip of the Green Belt remaining intact. There was a brief moment of pride from Mum, playing the Della Street role, before it reminded her of what my father could have achieved, when she returned to her customary irritated frustration at his abject lack of ambition.

This was, however, an exception and generally the lost causes remained so, from Coventry City F.C. to Betamax video. The Liberal Party was consequently the natural political home for my father. The then Liberal leader, Jo Grimmond, was viewed as deity in our house and seemed a very nice man. The fact that the Liberal Party only had six seats in the House of Commons did not seem to detract from his appeal. The Orpington by-election in 1962 promised a new dawn and, indeed, in the 1966 election they had doubled their parliamentary tally to twelve seats, but in 1970 they were back down to six again. My father was selected to be the Liberal candidate in a local council election in the early sixties. I say 'selected', but I suspect there may have been no other eligible party members apart from my mother in the relevant ward and she declined to stand. God knows why he wanted to be a local councillor, as most local councils are a ship of fools with an alarmingly long passenger manifest, with each of them generally aspiring to board the largest vessel of that type in the UK, the House of Commons. Maybe he felt the hand of history upon his shoulders. If so, it was quite a small hand, and a very local history.

Prospects for Liberal candidates were not generally that good but my father had managed to pick one of the least auspicious constituencies in the whole of the country. Hornchurch was not a place that was remotely liberal, with or without a capital 'l'. The standing Conservative MP for Hornchurch, had a central casting name for a bigoted baddy straight out of a Thomas Hardy novel. Godfrey Lagden. You couldn't make it up. In a late fifties debate on the Wolfenden recommendations, he described homosexuals as *"people with warped minds who have little self-control"* and opined that *"in the general run the homosexual is a dirty-minded danger to the virile manhood of this country"*[6]. Havering's 70 per cent vote in favour of Brexit showed little has changed.

Even by my father's standards, standing as a Liberal in a Hornchurch local council election was the mother of all lost causes. Maybe he'd been promised a safe seat in Orkney and Shetland or Montgomery or one of the other Liberal strongholds, as a reward for fighting a hopeless campaign in Hornchurch. I don't recall any impassioned speeches to the electorate of Emerson Park encouraging them to throw off the yoke of stultifying local council disempowerment, as the intellectually newly enfranchised crowd threw up their sweaty nightcaps and bayed for more Bevan-like oratory, or him atop a flat bed truck with a loud-hailer demanding greater frequency of trains on the Romford-Upminster single track line. I do, however, remember the rather fetching "Vote Cooke" posters. The budget didn't run to a photo of the candidate, just big black letters on standard Liberal yellow. They looked very stylish but the print run seemed to be well in excess of demand and copies remained strewn in various corners of our house years after the polls had closed and Dad inevitably lost his deposit. Maybe he thought he might be able to use them for the future Orkney and Shetland battle, but the call never came.

My parents remained Liberals but the relationship never quite recovered from Jo Grimmond's retirement as leader and his succession by Jeremy Thorpe, whom both my parents regarded with some suspicion, later proven to be well-founded. Harold Wilson was regarded as an untrustworthy twister, to all intents and purposes an accurate thumbnail sketch. Mum claimed that she could never vote Tory, which was an easy promise during the tenure of Ted Heath, whom she regarded as a pompous

---

[6] *Interestingly, in the subsequent unsuccessful attempt to decriminalize homosexuality, amongst the small number of 22 Tory MPs to vote in favour was Margaret Thatcher. Harold Macmillan, Harold Wilson, Jim Callaghan and Ted Heath did not vote.*

and unlikeable creep[7]. When Mrs Thatcher arrived, this came under more pressure, as my mother clearly admired her. I suspect she never abandoned her antipathy to actually voting Tory (which probably came from her father, a Labour supporter) but her heart had in truth moved on.

The green surroundings were for a time a truly idyllic existence – or at least as near to a pastoral idyll that any child living within 4 miles of Romford had any right to expect. I often think back to those times – lying on my back in the orchard looking at the sky is one of my own happy places, young and easy under the apple boughs and happy as the grass was green. Fifty years later, remembering my own child-life and the happy summer days, I channelled these memories into a song I wrote for a BBC documentary series about life in the country:

> *We lay beneath the sky*
> *The apple boughs were fluttering in the breeze.*
> *We watched the dragonflies*
> *Dancing on the lily pads and trees.*
> *The grass seemed so much greener then,*
> *The sun shone when it should*
> *And no one wondered why*
> *We spent our days out in the fields and woods.*
>
> *We walked through fields of rye*
> *And lay our heads wherever we might please.*
> *Our summer's lullaby*
> *The swallow song and droning of the bees.*
> *The stars seemed so much brighter then,*
> *It always felt so good*
> *And no one asked us why*
> *We spent our days out in the fields and woods.*
>
> *The builders came and razed the ground*
> *Where the cherry trees once stood.*
> *We said our last goodbyes*
> *And walked away from the fields and woods.*

Just as in the song, as the spirit of Woodstock turned to the hangover of Altamont and the clouds gathered at the end of the sixties, Sackville-Hulkes sold up and moved to a smaller house. Romney Chase was levelled

---

[7] *When, later in life, I sat next to him on a plane, this proved to be an accurate description and he heads the leader-board for the most unpleasant person I have had to sit near to on a plane. Paul McCartney (twice) heads the leader-board for the most delightful.*

and the grounds turned into a small housing development, presaging an asphalt future. Garages replaced the corner of the grounds where the orchard used to be. They paved paradise and put up a parking lot. The diggers moved in at pretty much the same time that Joni Mitchell first sang those words. The sedge had withered from the lake and no birds sang. The pond remained but Harold and Gertrude did not survive the transition.

Glory, Glory, Hallelujah

With so much football on daytime and peak time television today, we tend to forget how little televised football there was in the 60s and 70s. Football was more talked about than actually watched. There was not a single televised live league match between 1960 and 1983, when Spurs v Nottingham Forest ushered in the era of live television football. Although Saturday afternoon television was entirely dominated by the two main channels' sports programmes, these were largely soccer free.

The BBC's offering, *Grandstand,* started promisingly for the football fan with a soccer preview section but then generally lapsed into a frighteningly dull rugby league game between Wakefield Trinity and Hull Kingston Rovers, with Eddie Waring's comedy commentary offering the bleakest of light relief. This inculcated a deep hatred of rugby (league and union) in me for the rest of my life. Football returned at around 4.40pm when there was a nail-biting live action segment, featuring a camera focused on what appeared to be a typewriter transcribing the results as they came in. David Coleman gave expert commentary in case the on-screen action was too complex for the inexperienced viewer to follow. It was necessary to sit through the results of that fascinating clash between Stenhousemuir and Stranraer in the Scottish Second Division, knowing that, were you to leave the room for just ten seconds, that would be the time that the result of your team's game would appear.

With little or no real time access, this was as exciting as live television football got in the 1960s. The ITV Saturday afternoon sport programme, *World of Sport*, was similarly football free but, instead of rugby league, featured hours of wrestling and horse-racing. Not realising at this point in my life that wrestling was not real sport but a theatrical pantomime, it seemed dramatic and gripping. Veteran commentator Kent Walton seemed to have been imported from WWF as he proclaimed "greetings grapple fans!" with his exotic transatlantic accent; this turned out to be as much of a charade as the in-ring action, as it emerged that he grew up in Surrey and went to school at Charterhouse.

The villains often wore dark ski masks to remove any lingering doubt that they were really bad. The front row of the audience would be generously populated with handbag wielding old age pensioners anxious to demonstrate their dislike of the evil nemesis. Kendo Nagasaki was the leading exponent of this genre. An aura of oriental mystery surrounded him – with his pre-bout mystic rituals we obviously assumed him to be a samurai warrior who had become Ronin and turned to grapple in his fallen state. This obviously turned out to be as fictional as Kent Walton's accent and he was later revealed to be one Peter Thornley from Stoke-on-Trent. Mick McManus was the most reviled bad guy, enraging the handbag wielders with his blatant cheating. Naturally, the only person oblivious to his outrageous and continual infraction of the laws of wrestling was, of course, the referee, who was required to look away from the ring at all critical moments. So he would miss the evil Mick cunningly, but in full view of the crowd, pull up the padding on the corner post with the intention of slamming his opponent's body against the now unguarded wood. Natural justice would prevail, however, as generally there would be a turnaround and it would be McManus who was thumped against the post, much to the delight of the grandma group. Staggeringly, his bout against Jackie Pallo in 1963 was watched by over 20 million viewers. If ever anyone tells you that there are loads of channels but nothing on now and it was much better in the 60s, just quote that statistic back at them.

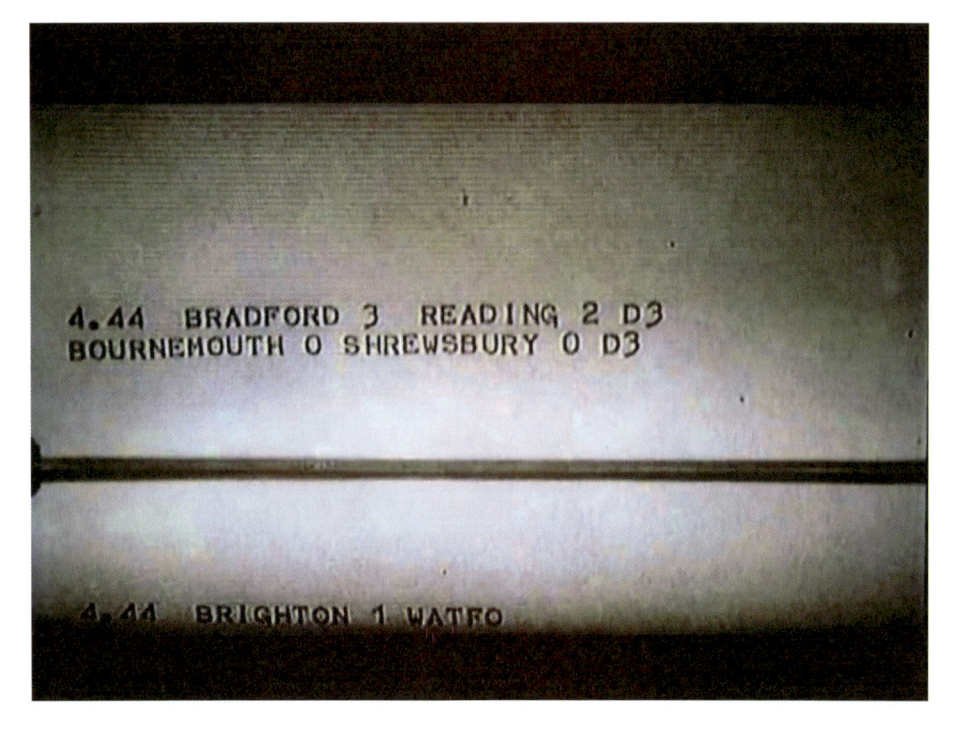

This was as exciting as live football got in the 1960s.

Big Daddy was the king of the good guys and usually wore a white leotard, entering the arena with a glitter cape and top hat, to emphasise that persona. Bizarrely, his real name was Shirley Crabtree. I went to Oxford Town Hall in 1980 to watch a grapple extravaganza featuring Big Daddy, who was by then 50 and around 25 stone, and it was a hysterical piece of theatre, although blindingly obvious in the flesh that Big Daddy's huge gut was not actually making any contact with his opponent during his trademark stomach body check. The OAP handbag brigade were well-represented and were not perturbed by this blatant fakery.

So football was a limited presence in our house in the mid-sixties. The only exceptions to the lack of live televised football were the F.A. Cup Final (shown on both main channels and – in the pre-Champions League era when it really meant something – a real male street clearer on the Saturday afternoon of the match) and the World Cup and other international matches.

The only other evidence of football's existence in our house was the weekly ritual of Mum and Dad doing the football pools. By Thursday night, when the football pools man would come to collect the coupons and payment, my father would have meticulously completed his coupon, based on in-depth research of the form and record of each of the teams. Mum would, however, be scrambling around to complete hers, whilst at the same time putting the finishing touches to her latest culinary abomination. She would always pick Grimsby Town for a draw, which was the only fixed element in an otherwise entirely random selection. There was a comedic inevitability to the fact that her methodology produced our only household pools win. There was celebration and triumph in the house at the news, but the jackpot of £18 only changed our lifestyle to the extent of the new toaster it funded. It was hardly *Spend Spend Spend*. My father continued his more cerebral analysis, unabashed by this rogue success.

The first football game I can recall watching was the World Cup Final in 1966. In the run up to the final I remember much talk about the theft of the Cup, and its retrieval by a plucky dog called Pickles,[8] and my father and, supportively, my mother echoing England manager Alf Ramsey's words that the Argentinians were "animals" and proclaiming the justice of the sending off of Argentinian captain Rattin. I had no idea who any of these people were. The final was clearly a major occasion – the fact that Mum and Dad were together in the same room marked it down in my mind as a flagship event. My father was berated by my mother for leaving the room in the last few minutes of normal time and apparently, therefore, giving rise to the late German equalizer. What he was doing leaving the room with only two minutes of the match to go, I really don't know. Perhaps it was habit, as I suspect he was probably one of those irritating people who leave football games ten minutes from the end to miss the crowds and traffic, even when the game is at 4-4, on a knife-edge, with the prospect of a penalty shoot out to decide the Champions League final. He did, in fact, have an even more irritating habit of being absent from a room in which his presence was essential to events, resulting in the commencement of proceedings being deferred. So, for example, on Christmas morning, the most exciting

---

[8] *As a reward, Pickles was invited to the celebration banquet when England won the cup. Sadly, he died the following year, when he choked on his lead while trying to chase a cat.*

morning of the year, present opening was on hold whilst my father had to be located and tied to a chair, whilst Laura and I chafed at the torment of such delay. After the German equalizer my mother had issued him with instructions to remain seated for the full half hour of extra time. The finale was, of course, an excellent early demonstration of the need for goal line technology, even if the truth of the correctness of the Russian linesman's decision is rarely spoken by English football fans. If the crowd on the pitch thought it was all over, for me it was only just beginning.

In fact, the biggest excitement for me of winning the World Cup was the "England Winners" reissued version of the Royal Mail World Cup stamp. I dutifully trooped off to the Post Office on the day of issue to buy a stamp and post it to myself on a first day cover, which my mother had assured me would become immensely valuable in the future, possibly even valuable enough to be spared from her next annual spring clean purge. Stamp collecting continued to be a hobby well into my teens, with regular trips to town to visit Strand Stamps. I soon sensibly rationalized my interest just down to British stamps and had a pretty creditable collection, with a suitably nerdish knowledge, able to survive in the highly specialized spodosphere that is stamp collecting, comfortably able to discuss the Guernsey stamp with the error on the longitude on the map of the island. I of course had both correct and incorrect versions.

West Ham would have been the obvious team for me to support. After all, they won the World Cup for England and were the local team. Geoff Hurst was my mother's favourite and lived locally, like many of the players. Their influence was all-pervasive. John Sissons, a minor local West Ham player, owned the mandatory trendy boutique, but no-one ever seemed to go into it. We knew where the players lived and any excuse was taken to knock on their doors. I hit paydirt during Cubs Bob A Job week in 1970. Martin Peters had already declined the opportunity to have his flash new Lotus Cortina (with an England rosette on the side – they didn't exactly keep a low profile, these footballers) washed for a shilling. However, a few days later a visit to the house of Brian Dear (West Ham striker 1962-70) hit the spot as it coincided with a small gathering of players including Peters and Hurst. Geoff Hurst's ensuing entry in my autograph book was my most valued, although the whole book subsequently fell prey to one of my mother's scorched earth attic campaigns in the mid-seventies.

The sister of Chelsea defender David Webb lived five doors down the road but this did not become of any interest until he attained instant celebrity by scoring the winning goal in the replayed 1970 cup final, after which I became a regular companion to my mother during school holiday coffee mornings at her house.

Notwithstanding the World Cup boost to West Ham, I was drawn to Spurs. I'm not sure why, but they just seemed to have that indefinable glamour that West Ham lacked. I think it might have been their kit – white shirts and navy blue shorts. White has always been a look I've liked. One of the only stylish facets of Sting's self-indulgent and tedious set at Live Aid in 1985 was his all white garb[9]. Spurs had white shirts. West Ham's maroon and light blue concoction simply did not meet with approval of my design conscious eyes. This was a great period for football shirts – in the era before they became besmirched with the vile logos of naff sponsors or cursed by the financial imperative to redesign them each season, the period when football kit had a clean simplicity, eschewing the concessions to fashion that produced skimpies in the 1980s or baggies in the 90s. Spurs' team song was *The Battle Hymn of the Republic - Glory, Glory, Hallelujah*, neatly fitting in with my American Civil War obsession. John Brown's body may have lain-a-mouldering in the grave but it was not John Brown but John White, the brilliant inside right 'ghost' who would suddenly appear unexpectedly where it most mattered on the pitch, who became my primary legend. His body also lay-a-mouldering in the grave, as he had been tragically killed at the age of 27 when struck by lightning,

Spurs were not a popular team in our household. Mum disliked Danny Blanchflower, the Northern Irish captain of the 1961 double winning team, with an intensity that I thought no footballer would be able to inspire in her. For one, he had walked away from Eamonn Andrews and refused to appear on *This Is Your Life* live on air, leaving the BBC with an empty half hour, an unforgiveable slight in her eyes. Worse still, she had read in the Daily Mail that he thought West Germany would win the World Cup Final. He was clearly the Sir Roger Casement of the footballing world. The fact that I can find no trace on the internet of this probably shows that the Daily Mail's reporting was as accurate then as it is today. Jimmy Greaves was also viewed with suspicion and his replacement by Geoff Hurst was applauded by Mum.

They were the only team at that point to have done the double in the 20th century and the first British team to have won a major European trophy. On the day I was born, they won 6-0 against Leicester City. This seemed a good augury. My choice appeared to be justified when, the very next season, Spurs won the F.A. Cup, wearing, better still, white shirts accompanied now by white shorts and socks. It was a footballing and style triumph. Little did I know that 50 years (and counting) of hurt were to follow, as football glory visited White Hart Lane all too rarely. Worse still, the clean simplicity of their shirts became besmirched in the 80s by Holsten Pils and Thomson Holidays.

---

[9] *Johnny Borrell, a keen student of rock iconography, tried to pull the same trick at Live 8, but merely came across as too eager to capture the zeitgeist crown and instead succeeding in capturing the nation's ridicule for the remainder of his career, enhanced by the leaking of his highly prescriptive laundry instructions. The nation knows a prat when they see one.*

I was soon obsessed by football. *Charles Buchan's Football Monthly* had the sort of information and data packed content that appealed to my detail hungry brain, refreshingly free of tedious interviews with players and managers. These were the days that football journalism naturally assumed (generally correctly) that nearly all professional footballers have little or nothing of interest to say. I soon had an encyclopaedic knowledge of Spurs. I knew that they had only used 17 players in their 1961 double-winning campaign, with three of them playing only once; that they were the only non-league team to have won the FA Cup; that they often seemed to do well in years ending in a '1', winning the FA Cup in 1901, 1921 and 1961 and the league in 1951 and 1961[10] and that they had the first mixed-race outfield player to play in the First Division[11]. Dad spoke fondly of Arthur Rowe's league winning 1951 'push and run' side, in particular Len Duquemin and Ted Ditchburn. Any Spurs artefact was eagerly assimilated. Sadly, audio recording was no exception.

By 1967, my nascent record collection consisted of three EPs – 7" vinyl which played at LP speed of 33 1/3 RPM. None of them contained music, or what could popularly be considered to be music. The first two EPs were extracts from a Dr Who episode featuring the Daleks and a Thunderbirds episode. The Daleks disk was endlessly played whenever my father was out and control of the stereogram was relaxed. Having no video recorders and only a weekly dose of Dr Who, with the Daleks appearing at even more irregular intervals, this was all I had of Dr Who and his greatest enemy. The sounds of the Daleks became as menacing as the visuals on the television - not just the predictable 'exterminate' before turning someone black and white negative and dead - oh how the Daleks could have truly conquered the universe had they not spent so much time chatting and announcing their intentions - but the sinister thrumming pulse of the Dalek ship and machinery. The same pulsing sound is still used in the new Dr Who and probably similarly sends a pavlovian shiver of fear through most TV watching adults of my generation.

The Thunderbirds record featured arch-baddie the Hood kidnapping Lady Penelope and, as was then standard evil villain practice, deciding to kill her not by simple shooting but strapping her to a bench and turning a laser beam onto her. His slightly suggestive interjections ("Are those straps too tight?" "Only three inches to go") later formed excellent raw material for a audio cut-up X-rated version of Thunderbirds perpetrated by my friend Russell and I during one of our many work downtime moments at university.

I also received a birthday present of *The Spurs Go Marching On*, an EP

---

[10] *This continued with Spurs winning the League Cup in 1971 and the FA Cup in 1981 and 1991.*

[11] *Walter Tull in 1909.*

of the Spurs team singing. Whilst it was undoubtedly rousing to hear them sing *Glory Glory Hallelujah*, my love for Spurs led me to overlook their vocal inadequacies and, not having heard it for half a century, I fear that, whilst Terry Venables' performance of *Bye Bye Blackbird* might just about pass muster, revisiting *When Irish Eyes Are Smiling* voiced by Pat Jennings and Joe Kinnear (bizarrely accompanied by Welshman Mike England) would not be a happy experience. Football players and recording studios really should never be allowed to come into conjunction. If you ever doubt this, take a listen to *Side by Side* by Ray Clemence and Peter Shilton or *Diamond Lights* by Glenn Hoddle and Chris Waddle[12]. There is only one good football record – *Three Lions* – and even that barely makes it over the line on account of

---

[12] *Unaccountably, they called themselves "Glenn and Chris", rather than the more obvious "Hoddle and Waddle".*

including the vocals-that-only-their-mothers-could-love of Baddiel and Skinner. *World In Motion* doesn't count as it's just a routine New Order song customized for football use – and no, it's not improved by John Barnes' rapping or the mass 'En-ger-land' vocals of the team. Back then it seemed very different and *The Spurs Go Marching On* was rarely off the stereogram.

A protracted period of nagging to be taken to watch Spurs play eventually paid dividends when it was announced that Dad would be taking me to the Spurs v Coventry City game at White Hart Lane. This was obviously a matter of great excitement. My father was a Coventry supporter, but in such a muted way that there were no difficult father/son conflict moments during the game. Strangely, although I remember my curiosity at the layout of Bethnal Green station as we passed through it, the overwhelming excitement on entering the inside of the ground and the fact that *Love Is Blue* and *The Good, the Bad and the Ugly* (Hugo Montenegro version) were played over the tannoy, I don't actually recall whether Spurs won and what the score was. Such are the vagaries of memory. Maybe it was because, as with most seasons since, Spurs results in the First Division and Premiership were of little import as they staggered to their normal placement between fifth and seventh.

The apogee of my pride in Spurs was around the 67th minute of the World Cup Quarter Final in Mexico between England and West Germany, when it appeared that, just like in 1966 when it was West Ham who won it for England, it would be Spurs who won it, with goals from Mullery and Peters putting England in a seemingly unassailable position. As a Spurs fan, I would soon get to learn that a two-nil lead with just over twenty minutes to go is far from an unassailable position. Like many people in this case, I blame Peter Bonetti. Gordon Banks had food poisoning. He should have avoided the enchiladas. Peter Bonetti was nicknamed 'the Cat', but on the basis of his performance that day, the only feline resemblance was that he was never anywhere to be found when you wanted to shut up shop for the night. If only Pat Jennings had been English.

The aspirations of most Spurs fans are probably the most perfect example of the triumph of hope over experience. Every season seems to be a transitional one on the road to the sunlit uplands of the glory, glory days. Failure in previous seasons never stops us believing that we are just about to turn the corner. Generally this was accompanied by the acquisition of a hot new player. In 1969, it was Roger Morgan, from QPR. He had a silly modish haircut and an air of laddish rebellion, like a proto-Marsh or Bowles, and always seemed to be injured. We came 11th the following season. In 1970, it was Martin Peters. That was followed by the crushing blow of Arsenal repeating our unique feat of winning the double. The following season, it was Ralph Coates, for a Spurs cash transfer record of £190k, satisfyingly signed in secret from under the nose of Arsenal, who were also interested. Ralph had an even more absurd haircut than Roger Morgan, a ludicrous comb-over. A comb-over is not a sensible haircut for anyone engaged in strenuous physical activity, like a footballer, unless recourse is had to extremely strong glue. Consequently, Ralph spent most of his time as he hared around the pitch being followed by some very long strands of hair which had formerly been attached to his head. It was a ridiculous sight, and one which seemed to put him off his game. He never seemed to click. Spurs fans wondered how that £190k might have otherwise been spent.

Ralph Coates' comb-over, in contrasting modes of operation in the team photo (L) and on the pitch (R)

Later, after the retirement of Bill Nicholson, it was a new manager who brought the new hope of a fresh start and revitalised leadership to restore us to our rightful place at the top, but they came and went with a regularity that became commonplace in the top division. The low came in 1977 when Spurs were relegated and shortly afterwards Pat Jennings was bizarrely sold to Arsenal. I've been saying that we need to get a decent centre back since Mike England retired. Eventually, my interest in Spurs waned. The last Spurs game of the 20th century that I can remember watching was the 1987 FA Cup Final against Coventry, ending as I had begun. I spoke to Dad on the phone after the match and he almost sounded excited by his team winning the cup for the first time.

Football mad children reconnected me with Spurs in the early noughties and it didn't take long for me to return to the obsessively tribal way that the sport demands. The excitement of an out-performing run in the Champions League in 2010-11 was capped by my almost certainly one and only visit to the Bernabau to watch Spurs play Real Madrid. It was a glorious occasion, the crowd awesomely loud and every Spurs fan's heart swelling with pride at his team. Then the match started. At least the hotel was nice.

Back in 1968 it seemed only natural that I would start my own football team. Not natural in the sense that I had extraordinary on-pitch skills that marked me down as a talismanic player around whom others would gather — although I was a fast runner and therefore always placed on the wing, my pace was not, however, accompanied by an ability to control the ball at speed and, aside from the potential for distracting the opposition by having a player randomly darting into the opposition half without the ball, was therefore only of limited utility to most teams. I did, however, have an OCD-like mania for organisation and activity around any subject that caught my imagination. So, for example, at the age of ten, I produced the first comprehensive map of all London's railways, Underground and British Rail, a good 20 years ahead of it being produced by London Transport. Admittedly, it was a long way from the topological masterpiece that was Harry Beck's original Underground map, and it was almost impossible to follow, but it was a plucky attempt. Sadly, my schoolwork never captured my imagination, and remained free of any such intensive application. This, reader, will be a theme throughout. What was natural, therefore, was that I would vigorously apply myself to the development of the infrastructure of a highly evolved football club, with, even more naturally, me at its head. Thus Wingletye Wanderers F.C. ('the Wings') was born. Proprietor: S. J Cooke. Manager: S. J. Cooke. Captain: S. J. Cooke. There were no doubt many other more lowly positions not worthy of inclusion in the club prospectus that I also filled, including chief talent scout as I tirelessly pressed a random collection of football misfits into service.

My earliest pair of football boots were purchased from the budget rack at Bata Shoes in Hornchurch High Street and looked as though they had come direct from a black and white film of the White Horse cup final. The boots went half way up my ankles and had bulbous toe-caps the like of which had not been seen on a football pitch this side of the retirement of Stanley Matthews. An upgrade was demanded from Santa Claus. Gratifyingly, he was listening and a pair of Puma boots with screw-in studs appeared on Christmas morning. In fact, rather fittingly, Santa had acted through the agency of his local proxy - legendary Spurs keeper Ted Ditchburn, who owned a sports shop in Romford. I was escorted to the shop by Mum and actually met Ted, a very exciting moment, but rather overshadowed by the acquisition of the Puma boots. I couldn't wait for Christmas. Sadly, on Christmas morning it was tipping with rain, so I had to content myself with walking around the house with my new boots. This

*Proprietor, manager, chief scout and captain of Wingletye
Wanderers F.C., S. J. Cooke.*

generated multiple complaints from Mum at the possible stud damage to her newly-laid Amtico tiles, so I had to default to checking the tightness of my screw-in studs (still then a dramatic new innovation which marked out the boots and their owner as one of quality).

As I recall, we only played a few games. There was a record gate of around six (despite attendances being hit by a car lift sharing scheme which reduced the number of supportive parents) at St Andrew's Park, the home of the Wings, as the players took the pitch for our debut. Almost all the players, that is, as a key defender and midfield stalwart had both failed to turn up. We later discovered that the midfielder's dad's car had broken down and he was giving a lift to the defender as well. In our world, this was a setback equivalent to the Munich Air Disaster. Again, I don't recall the score but I suspect we lost.

Dad told me that we played against a team including Spurs striker-to-be Clive Allen at the playing fields at the end of Hubbards Chase. I don't remember this, but fear that we would have shipped a considerable tally of goals, such was the gulf in footballing standards that would have been apparent even at the age of nine.

The official club colours, as recorded in the club prospectus, were green shirt with white collar, white shorts and yellow and white hooped socks. These colours had the merit of not being shared with any Football League team at that time (Hibernian was I think the closest) and, more importantly, also being the only kit owned by the club team apparel designer (S. J. Cooke). Onto my green jersey were sown a pair of over-lapping wings in the shape of a "W" (executed and probably conceived by my very game mother and pre-dating the McCartney Wings logo by five years or so). Sadly, this was not a colour of jersey owned by any other player in the team, all of whom were strangely reluctant to commit their hard-earned pocket money to acquiring one and therefore de facto team colours became whatever football jerseys the team happened to own. This made for a confusing mélange for players and spectators alike. The golden generation of '68 went their separate ways, scattered by the four winds to bring their magic to various local cub-scout teams and school 3rd elevens.

As for Spurs, it is only now, with Pochettino in charge and some excellent new signings, that we seem to have turned a corner and this season are finally on the road to the sunlit uplands of the glory, glory days of Premiership dominance and regular Champions League football[13].

---

[13] *This was originally written in the 2014-15 season with knowing, self-deprecating comic irony. On re-reading the manuscript at the end of the 2016-17, the joke has disappeared, as it seems surprisingly accurate. Mike England has finally been adequately replaced.*

Set The Controls For The Heart Of The Sun

The first holiday I can recall was probably around the age of two or three in Cleethorpes in Lincolnshire, where my gran and grandad lived. We went to the beach. It was called Suggit's Lane. The beach and the sea should have been very exciting but there was a superior attraction. There was a railway running alongside the beach. As we stood at the Suggit's Lane level crossing, a huge steam locomotive chuntered past. This was far more exciting. The rest of the day was spent walking along the side of the track to Cleethorpes Station, where more locomotives were on display. It was the beginning of a fascination with railways.

Summer holidays were invariably taken in Wales. There was promise of sunshine and sand. It was Wales, so there was quite a bit of rain as well. We had no Welsh connection but it was assumed to be the natural place to go. We started by lodging with a Mrs. Shears, who owned a boarding house in Narberth in Pembrokeshire. The journey was something that is impossible for most people born in the last thirty years to comprehend. The M25 did not exist and the M4 only existed as a brief stretch of motorway terminating well short of Reading. We would set the controls for the heart of Cambria and get there about 12 hours later. The family Humber would be packed up in the dead of night. On awaking the next morning, we were still just short of the Severn Bridge, with a good five or six hours still to go, along the choked A roads of Wales. I suspect that our 'Are we almost there?' count topped a hundred comfortably and we were stilled only by sparingly deployed distributions of Spangles and Opal Fruits and games of I-Spy and, when our interest in that was exhausted, "peep and snail", an obscure game unique to our family. The rules of "peep and snail" were simple. Laura and I would each be allocated one brand of petrol station - BP (peep) or Shell (snail) - to see who could amass the most spots during our journey. In fact, Mum (the referee of the game) was saying BP and Shell but I translated this into "peep" and "snail". Laura repeated this faithfully. The Shell sign does look a bit like a snail to a four year old. The advent of motorway travel would render this game somewhat tedious but, in the era of journeys without iPods, Game Boys, in-car DVDs or laptops, it was the best we could manage to eat up the miles to Haverfordwest.

Each day we would pack up our lunch and head to a beach or castle, or, on very good days, both. After a couple of years, Mrs. Shears moved to Laugharne, a nice small town on the Taf estuary. It was home to Dylan Thomas and is supposedly the inspiration for Llareggub, the fictional village in *Under Milk Wood*. Mum loved Dylan Thomas and we would regularly be taken on Thomas-themed tours of Laugharne, stopping first at his boathouse on the cliff walk and finishing by the wood overlooking the village, which she claimed was clearly the inspiration for the milk wood.

This bit was generally accompanied by Mum intoning *"It is spring, moonless night in the small town, starless and bible-black…."* This was prior to the King Crimson album of the same name but subsequently became useful knowledge with which to impress other Crimso fans who had not been under such tutelage. Thomas was buried there, once Evans the Death had come looking for him, after the years of Felinfoel with whisky chasers in Brown's Hotel had taken their toll.

We tried out North Wales one year but it took even longer to get to than Pembrokeshire and seemed to rain incessantly. And no, Laura and I weren't remotely interested that the road we seemed to have been on for several days was originally a Roman road, which accounted for its straightness. Roman road planners were like that. After taking into account all the contours, the geological parameters and the logistical requirements for linking up of communities and other communications arteries, they just got a ruler out and drew a straight line between the beginning and the end of the road.

So, we returned to the south, to Solva, a beautiful fishing village in Pembrokeshire. As the years wore on, my father's participation in our holidays would be limited to driving us there and then remaining in the car to listen to the test match on the car radio. Meanwhile Mum, Laura and I would strike out on our own. Blackie the cat had been left at home, together, in later years, with our expanded menagerie of my goldfish (Flipper) and Laura's budgie, improbably named Jimmy, after, even more improbably, one of our neighbours. In fact, Flipper was, unbeknown to me, four different goldfish who were covertly substituted into the Flipper role, when the previous incumbent shuffled off his mortal coil. My relationship with Flipper was not such that I detected any difference between his various incarnations. When we craved more active animal company, Laura and I would swear in Steph, an Alsatian from a couple of doors down the road. He was a lovely dog and clearly was keen for more regular human companionship than was available at home, joining in our adventures enthusiastically. His finest moment came when Martin Sharp, a rather mean spirited child whom Laura disliked intensely, was showing off his extensive stamp collection to me and my friends, spreading the entire accumulation out on my bed. We stared in wonderment at this philatelic cornucopia. Martin bore a smug and self-satisfied expression. That swiftly disappeared when Steph, accompanied by Laura, who had clearly whipped him up into a state of acute excitement, bound up the stairs, into my bedroom and onto the bed, scattering Martin's stamp collection throughout the room. Martin was petrified of dogs and so was caught in indecision between trying to stop this rogue mutt salivating all over his Penny Blacks and fleeing the scene. Steph was having the time of his life. He eventually bounded back down the stairs, with various valuable parts of Martin's collection stuck to his whiskers. Laura smiled conspiratorially at the resulting carnage, affecting a look of surprise that Martin's stamp collection had been so cruelly violated. In fact, when gathering the photos while writing this, I noticed that Mum had written "*Steph II*" on the back of his photo, clearly indicating that Steph too had been the subject of a Flipper-style re-incarnation. At Solva, we would invariably be accompanied by a posse of local dogs up for some tourist action. Our expeditions got more ambitious as time went on, with six mile coastal walks becoming the norm, eventually requiring Ordnance Survey maps and a compass. I loved these walks and still really enjoy a good long yomp across the countryside. Laura took a different view and would almost certainly have preferred to stay in the car, had the test match coverage not been on.

Cinema was only a limited influence in my life in the sixties and seventies. My mother dragged me to see *A Man For All Seasons* when I was around six or seven – hopelessly young to appreciate it but pulled along by her passion for the history and characters. She would curl her lip at any mention of Thomas Cromwell or Richard Rich in a way previously reserved for the likes of Danny Blanchflower. As far as she was concerned, Cromwell and Rich were right up there with Richard III in her pantheon of historical villains. Had she still been alive, she would have had no truck with the Cromwell rehabilitation of *Wolf Hall* or the post Leicester car park reassessment of Richard as just a product of his turbulent times and victim of Shakespearean propaganda. They were just bad, through and through.

My only regular exposure to the big screen was the regular Saturday morning children's cinema, where, for only sixpence, you would have a whole morning of entertainment – an episode of *Swallows and Amazons,* a few cartoons and then a main feature, all accompanied by a 'Jubbly' - a pyramid of fruit flavoured ice encased in waxed paper which could be sucked for hours on end and then deployed as a sticky missile onto the stalls below. The main features were generally the runts and rejects of the movie world and of such blandness that I cannot remember any of them, with one exception. In a moment of uncharacteristic rebellion, my whole group of friends decided that watching Elvis in *Clam Bake* was too out of tune with the new waves of experimentation that were sweeping the film and music worlds and departed the cinema early. We were, however, only eight at the time, so received a severe telling off from Mum. I think I detected a slight lightening of her disposition when I mentioned that the film was *Clam Bake*.

Aside from the ritual of *Those Magnificent Men In Their Flying Machines, Chitty Chitty Bang Bang, It's A Mad, Mad, Mad, Mad World, The Great Escape* or a Bond film at Christmas, films were rarely a feature on our television. I do, however, remember the memorable exception of *Barbarella* in the mid-seventies. As the BBC presenter announced details of the film at 9.25, straight after the news, I was unenthusiastic for what seemed to be a half-baked science fiction drama lacking the grit and tension of *Captain Scarlet* or *Dr Who*. My parents were more open-minded. It started unpromisingly with

Mum and I on a beach in Wales – predictably, I am reading and my father is absent. Laura is probably elsewhere trying to avoid our next long walk. Less predictably, the sun appears to be shining.

Laura with Steph II, fresh from feasting on Martin Sharp's penny blacks.

Milo O'Shea hamming it up as a character called Duran Duran. At this point in time that name was not scarred in my mind by association with ridiculous new romantic garb, horrible mullets and sub-Morrison song titles like *Union of the Snake,* so I merely tolerated what appeared to be a lightweight frippery. As the film unfolded, however, my interest was piqued. My parents' direction of travel was roughly opposite. Jane Fonda's increasing state of undress was overwhelming any qualms I had about the scripting or plot, but my parents were visibly regretting their earlier permissive posture. Just before Jane was about to shed her silver thigh length boots and couple with a winged birdman, my father announced that this was not suitable for me and I should go to bed. This was hugely memorable as one of the few decisive interventions he made in my upbringing. Such was my state of shock at this unexpected paternal oversight, I complied without dispute or complaint. I went to sleep to dreams of sharing a giant bird's nest with Jane Fonda.

Discipline was generally solely enforced in our house by my mother. She almost never resorted to physical punishment, preferring psychological means. Her twin threats were the cottage homes and "Bosul". The cottage homes were supposedly some form of workhouse to where naughty children were shipped off by their despairing parents, never to return. The threat of a one-way trip to the cottage homes was generally accompanied by her picking up the phone to call them, by which time Laura and I were normally pleading desperately for her forbearance. Although the cottage homes had some minor basis in reality, "Bosul" was entirely the product of my mother's fecund imagination, purporting to be some demon who would be summoned up to encourage submission in recalcitrant children and generally utilised when the threat of the cottage homes was not proving persuasive enough. Bosul remained only sketchily constructed and was a rather vague entity but there was enough detail to convince Laura and I that if he ever did hove into view, some seriously bad shit would be going down.

Programmes like *Ready Steady Go* and, later, *Top Of The Pops*, never seemed to be on in our house. *Juke Box Jury* seemed to be more acceptable, with a be-suited, neatly coiffured and well-spoken David Jacobs speaking to the values of my parents' generation. Brian Matthew was gradually being supplanted on BBC radio by younger DJs who had come aboard from Radio Caroline and other pirate stations. Brian tried to move with the times, but always sounded vaguely uncomfortable saying things like *"hey you tuned-in, turned on, way out fans, here's where things get good n groovy, a swingin' blues and they're fixin' to blow you mind"*[14] Radio did not betray the fact that, in all probability, he was still wearing a sensible suit and tie. *The Magical Mystery*

---

[14] *Brian Matthew actually said all these things. Check out "Cream – BBC Sessions" for proof.*

Tour premiere was viewed on Boxing Day 1967 and pronounced (in accord with popular opinion) unintelligible nonsense. It did seem quite hard to follow what was going on but I didn't have a strong view other than worrying about what Alan Haven's version of *I Am The Walrus* was going to sound like. But who needs a silly Beatles indulgence when we have the Eurovision Song Contest? We now forget that this was not always viewed with the ironic detachment that it now attracts in the UK and we did once take it as seriously as the rest of Europe. The 1967 contest, when Sandie Shaw won with *Puppet On A String*, was the biggest television event in our house since the World Cup Final. 1967 looks to be the year that the Eurovision Song Contest attempted to catch up with the pop zeitgeist. I've never heard the UK entry in the year of my birth but I'm doubting that *Sing Little Birdie* by Pearl Carr and Teddy Johnson was a rootsy rock n'roll homage to Elvis's Sun sessions. In 1966, months before *Paperback Writer* and *Revolver,* the UK entry was Kenneth Mckellar, the kilt wearing Scots tenor. He came ninth out of eighteen, sentencing him to a television life consisting solely of appearances on New Year's Eve Hogmanay programmes, until the equally tedious Jools Holland was invented and institutionalised. *Puppet On A String* reversed this national injustice the following year and, although intensely hummable, has remained hated by Sandie and most of her fans since. It was an early lesson in how Eurovision could blight a previously successful career, leading to it becoming a refuge for naff pop concoctions (viz Belle & the Devotions, Samantha Janus), desperate has-beens (the Shadows, Katrina and the Waves) and of course Cliff Richard, who straddles both these categories.

In 1968 it was widely assumed that Cliff's *Congratulations* was a sure-fire winner and set to continue our winning streak. Although leading for nearly the whole of the contest, the last vote fell to the German jury who favoured the Spanish entry, relegating Cliff to runner-up. The air (at least in our house) was thick with recrimination and accusations of petty German bias and revenge for our glorious World Cup win two years earlier. Even at the age of nine, I doubted the objective basis for such outlandish claims. It was only in 2008 that we discovered that there had been rigging of the vote by the Franco regime, as it dispersed vast wads of pesetas throughout the cable knit sweater wearing European easy listening opinion formers. The Spanish winner was titled *La La*, which established the winning blueprint for the future. Thus, the UK entry in 1969 was Lulu's *Boom Bang A Bang* (returning us to our winning ways after the coffers of Franco's treasury had been emptied) and later winners with titles like *Ding-A-Dong* and *Diggi-Loo Diggi-Ley* established the new Esperanto of Europap.

I had always assumed that Engelbert Humperdinck had been a UK entry in the 60s, prior to his more recent post-modern ironic appearance, but that must be due to deeply embedded latent memories of my mother's constant moaning that he had not been selected to be the UK entry. The preposterous Engelbert was her big musical hero in the post-Seekers void. *Release Me* was a rare record purchase[15] and for a period James Last was forced to cede his pole position on the stereogram. I think it was shortly after the second big hit *The Last Waltz* that my mother discovered that Engelbert's real name was Arnold Dorsey, and he came from Leicester, that the relationship began to sour.

Things had taken a darker turn on the television. Alien invasion paranoia was writ large in *The Invaders*. "How does a nightmare begin?" intoned the pre-credits announcer. "It began with a closed deserted diner, and a man too long without sleep to continue his journey," continued the ominous voice before concluding "The Invaders – a Quinn Martin Production. This week's guests stars are ….." which rather dissipated the atmosphere of paranoid foreboding that had been painstakingly established. The man too long without sleep was our hero, David Vincent, architect (for the ominous voice told us that was his profession), who had inadvertently become the only person on Earth to be aware of a covert alien invasion. It is unclear why it was necessary to let us know that our hero is an architect, as we never see him designing anything. I suppose that, when you're single-handedly preventing an alien invasion, there isn't much time to fit in loft extensions. The aliens assume human form, generally after killing the original person. The Invaders are working off the same technology as the Mysterons and cannot imbue their duplicates with a voice other than a dull monotone, no sense of humour and near-homicidal antipathy to anyone not like them, but, since most episodes are set in middle America, they blend in well. Each week, Vincent would manage to make contact with a lone fellow witness to the covert invasion and persuade his new comrade to accompany him to the authorities in order that they may finally expose the conspiracy. It is at this point clear to all but the most dim-witted viewer that Vincent's unfortunate accomplice for the week is a doomed man, as the Invaders catch up with him and he meets a grisly end, seconds before he is about to spill the beans to the waiting authorities. Vincent of course remains viewed as a crazy crank, until the next episode when he manages to make contact with a lone fellow witness….

Obviously no-one can understand *The Prisoner* from the moment *Danger Man* Patrick McGoohan takes a tab of acid, drives into the underground car park opposite the Houses of Parliament and emerges in the Village, a refuge home for former spies who cannot be trusted with contact with the outside world. Albeit with some fashionable Italianate styling, the Village is a bleak community, far from civilization, and all those who enter truly do abandon hope. It is only later, when we establish that the

---

[15] *In 45 RPM single format – mercifully love of Engelbert did not extend to outlay on 'Engelbert Sings Release Me and Other Hits for Young Lovers' or whatever his predictably titled cash-in LP was called.*

Village is not in Italy but in Wales, do we begin to empathise with the plight of the inmates. Some spies did, however, remain operational in the late sixties but the glamorous world of Bond and U.N.C.L.E. had been abandoned in favour of a Harry Palmer gritty reality in *Callan,* as evidenced by the downbeat opening theme with a dour shot of a swinging bare light bulb and the fact that we see Callan buying his own groceries. You never saw Napoleon Solo buying brussels sprouts and tea bags. Glamorous crime fighting was still available in *The Avengers,* where all light bulbs were safely behind groovy lampshades and the crime fighters had helpers who did their shopping, including the champagne they would inevitably uncork at the end of each episode. *The Baron* was a shameless copycat of *The Saint* – like the Saint, the Baron appears to be a do-gooding busy body with too much time on his hands. In this case, he is, rather improbably, an antiques dealer who just happens to help out British Intelligence on an informal basis. His deep cover does not however prevent him, like the Saint, from having a flashy car with a personalized number plate (BAR 1 to the Saint's ST 1) just in case the bad guys don't know who he is.

Gerry Anderson carried on with his puppets in *Joe 90*. Eschewing action and the sinister menace of *Captain Scarlet,* Anderson instead put the emphasis on characterization, a risky strategy when you are relying on wooden puppets to convey the mood and complex emotions of your characters. Joe was not in fact just a nerdy looking 9 year old school kid but the "Most Special Agent" (apparently an official designation) of the World Intelligence Network. It being the future, the Cold War is over and petty inter-service rivalries have been set aside and there is now just one intelligence organization. Who the baddies are working for is, however, unclear. Each week Joe would get inside what looked to be a giant salad spinner, but was in fact the "BIG RAT", an acronym which stood for something involving brain stuff, and would have the brain waves of some expert implanted in his head so he can insinuate himself into some fiendish enemy plot under the cover of a nerdy looking 9 year old school kid. The series was not a success and was discontinued. Maybe Joe was shipped off to the kindergarten district of the Village. Maybe he was just implanted with the brain waves of a nerdy looking 9 year old school kid and allowed to get on with his life.

1970 was a momentous year. Jimi Hendrix, the Who and the Doors played the Isle of Wight Festival. In Wingletye Lane, however, the stereogram was playing *Look What They've Done to My Song, Ma,* a song title which would surely deter the faint hearted from attempting a cover version but not the New Seekers, whose incremental blandness made the original Seekers appear authentic and edgy. The Beatles split was announced but had little impact on our household other than some subconscious relief that it spelt the end of the Alan Haven restyling series. The Tories returned to government with a 30 seat majority and Apollo 13 returned home on a wing and a prayer after some inspired technological improvisation. More importantly, Spurs sold Jimmy Greaves to West Ham and I cried when I heard the news. Admittedly, Spurs did acquire Martin Peters, who became the UK's first £200,000 footballer and no doubt the owner of yet another ostentatious sponsored car. Objectively, this was a good deal, but it was emotional trauma to which I was unused. In a break with tradition, I was allowed to watch Top of the Pops for the performance of the England 1970 World Cup squad singing *Back Home,* which is where they returned sooner than I expected, with no silverware to show for their trip other than the bracelet that the devious Mexicans had claimed our great captain Bobby Moore had liberated from a Mexico City jewellery shop. For someone who had grown up accustomed to England winning the World Cup, this was a major re-arrangement of the natural order of things. After all this, moving school was a doddle.

Journeys Without Maps

Brentwood School in Essex was a direct grant grammar school, which then seemed an unremarkable place, but was the holy grail for all parents ambitious for their children in the local area and who couldn't afford school fees. At the time I arrived, their alumni included Jack Straw (the Labour minister, not medieval radical), Hardy Amies (the fashion designer), Keith Allen and Noel Edmonds. Hardy Amies addressed speech day in my first year there. I don't recall Keith Allen being invited back to address speech day. Current pupils when I got there included Griff Rhys-Jones and Douglas Adams. Frank Lampard and Jodie Marsh would go there years after I had left. I had been thoroughly prepped for my 11 plus and Brentwood entrance exam by my ever diligent and dedicated mother and, by the time I sat both, my knowledge of the seven wonders of the ancient world and the number of sheets in a ream was second to none. She was understandably elated when the letter came from Brentwood announcing I had been awarded a free place.

It all seemed much more grown up and forbidding than Langtons. It had a school song, which we were required to learn. The nearest thing that Langtons had to a school song was a chorus of *The Good Ship Venus* (unexpurgated version) in the playground. No-one was sucking anything, and everyone was fully clothed, in the Brentwood school song. Each pupil was given a school term-book which we were required to carry round at all times and produce on request, like identity papers in Nazi Germany. The term-book had all the names of the masters on the inside front page and we dutifully wrote their nicknames against each of them. Some of them were blindingly predictable but others were confusing. The junior gym teacher was called *Spiv* but the senior gym master had a pencil moustache, strutted around in a pair of white mocassins with a gasper hanging out of the corner of his mouth, looking like an older version of Private Walker in *Dad's Army* and seemed much more deserving of that nickname than his rather bland deputy. When he arranged for a select group of 12 year old boys to smuggle multiple packs of cigarettes back from a school skiing trip, this seemed to confirm the aberration in nomenclature. We were tested on the school song and important school facts in a test organized by the head of junior school and on the masters' nicknames in one organized by the school bully. It was all very alien. How strange the change from minor to major. The school house system came as a bit of a shock. Coming from Langtons, where we just had classes, I found the idea of being placed in a 'house' a bit strange, as that had hitherto been the place where I lived with my family. I had a momentary panic when I feared that I had been wrongly enrolled as a boarder and sentenced to the rest of my secondary education away from home. My house was called West, possibly after the former headmaster, Dr

West. One of the other houses was called Hough, after former headmaster James Fisher Hough. However, the other day houses were called North, South and East. I wondered whether the school had a policy of positive discrimination towards heads whose names were points of the compass. Each boy was defined by his house, which became an indelible part of his identity, usually at the expense of his forename, which, aping the tradition of minor public schools, was rarely used and discarded. For example, I think of the former Brentwood pupil who was leader of the House of Commons in the 2010-15 Coalition government as Lansley (South). It was only when he joined the government that I became aware that his name was Andrew.

Wearing my newly acquired school uniform. The ensemble never again appeared in such composed order.

    During the summer holidays after my first year at Brentwood, all pupils were required to complete a project about a subject of their choice. There was to be a competition with prizes for the best three projects. I was a bit unenthused about the idea of spending large chunks of my summer holiday writing a boring project but Mum predictably approached the challenge with gusto. A copy of the Penguin classics version of *The Kon Tiki Expedition* by Thor Heyerdahl was thrust into my hand. I have no idea how this was selected, but I didn't have any better ideas. Thor was not a common name at my school, even amongst the boarding complement. The only Thor

I had come across was the Marvel Norse god of thunder and he was pretty cool. My instructions were clear – read the book, inwardly digest and produce my own account with my own perspectives on the expedition and the fearsome challenges Thor and co faced. I preferred to adopt the simpler approach of shamelessly copying the Penguin text into my project. There was, to be fair, a pretty neat fold out scale map of the expedition, with dates and commentary, but otherwise the project was a lazy uninspired effort. Lazy and uninspired, that is, other than the true centrepiece of the offering. Yet again, this was my mother's conception. She had determined that we would win gold medal by a hand constructed scale model of the Kon Tiki raft.

This seemed rather daunting and sounded as if it would take up quite a lot of time but my mother brushed aside such concerns. Thor H constructed his famous wooden raft to make the journey from South America to Polynesia. I reflected that his namesake wouldn't piss about with wooden rafts but simply point his hammer in the direction of Tahiti and, hey presto, journey over in a matter in minutes. Thor H set out to prove that migration from South America to Australasia was possible by constructing the raft by using only materials available locally. My mother had no such adherence to authenticity and set out to prove that a scale model of the raft could be produced satisfactorily by her usual substitution of key ingredients. So out went the critical balsa wood logs which became dangerously waterlogged during the latter parts of the original journey and in came great chunks of hardwood dowelling, which were more easily obtainable from the local hardware shop. For me, this was a tiresome substitution, as balsa wood was a modelling staple, being soft and easily shaped with a craft knife in a matter of seconds, whereas the hardwood needed to be painstakingly sawed at the precise angle, ideally whilst gripped in a vice. Sadly, Dad was not the sort of father who owned a vice, although my mother would have no doubt dearly have loved to present him with a Black and Decker Workbench one Christmas morning just to see the expression of horror on his face as to what this might presage. Wedging the recalcitrant logs between the fridge and the kitchen worktop had to suffice. This seemed to take weeks. At least I was absolved from my usual sentence of summer D.I.Y. tasks but the replacement project offered little succour. Thor probably ruled out a bit of nylon curtain as material for his sail, eventually plumping for hemp, but my mother did not feel constrained by such conventional thinking. Under my Mum's tireless project management, the raft was eventually complete in about the time it took to undertake the original journey. It looked great. I was merely glad that the tedious interruption to my summer holidays was over. Mum, however, bore the warm glow of pride at her creation.

The day of the awards ceremony came. Parents were invited and I could tell that Mum had an expectation of a podium position for Kon Tiki, with good odds on the top slot. Tensions were running high when we entered the hall where all the projects were displayed. It soon became clear that Kon Tiki had merely received a commendation. Worse still, although the shamelessly derivative text was displayed, there was no sign of the model. I suggested a gentle inquiry the following week, being relatively relaxed about its non-appearance. My mother was having none of that. Marching up to the junior school headmaster, she demanded an explanation. He was a rather remote type, who never really got the hang of interfacing with parents. To use Alec Cairncross's words, it was rather like an encounter between a whale and an elephant [16]. Sadly for him, he gave what Mum clearly viewed as a rather flip answer, compounded by him then asking if it was an Airfix model. This roused her to a fury worthy of the god of thunder himself. The clouds darkened and a storm the like of which had not been seen in the Brentwood junior school hall broke around us as she gave the hapless head a short but pithy description of the construction of the raft and what would happen to him if he did not locate it in the very near future. He visibly paled before us and went off to make urgent enquiries. The raft was located a few weeks later and a mealy mouthed apology from the school followed, unconvincingly assuring us that the model had been taken into account in the marking and awards, notwithstanding the complete absence of any reference to it in the school's appraisal of the project. My mother fumed but eventually decided against having a second snap at the hindquarters of the useless junior head. A brooding sense of injustice lingered in Wingletye Lane. The great Brentwood junior school project debacle was not easily forgotten.

Next to a journey across the Pacific on a balsa wood raft, a weekend trip down the Thames aboard a creaky old cruiser called *Roma II* might seem rather tame but, as ever with my family, it took some unexpected turns and was no less dramatic. It was announced that we would be taking a trip with one of Dad's friends, Gene Traynor, aboard his newly acquired boat. We had met Gene a few times before. He was a likeable American and we assumed he was an experienced sailor. We were meant to be joining Gene and his mother on the trip but it transpired that she had declined the invitation, because she didn't feel safe out of sight of land. As it turned out, we never were out of sight of land but this was scant guarantee of safety with Captain Gene at the helm.

The first four hours of our adventure were relatively uneventful. This was because we were still in dock at Teddington, as Gene couldn't get the boat started. The whole thing started to take on a deeply comic aspect as Gene charged around the ship with a can of "Easy Start" which I think was

---

[16] *He was describing a meeting between Selwyn Lloyd and some trade union leaders.*

designed for lawnmowers, rather than a 60 foot cruiser. It was a familiar experience, as Dad used to spend most Saturday mornings trying to start our recalcitrant lawnmower. Mum, Laura and I started to get the giggles while Dad attempted an impersonation of a helpful first officer. Given that he couldn't even change a light bulb, it wasn't a very realistic one and we weren't fooled. We did however seem to be appearing in a remake of *Carry On Cruising,* except that Sid James and Kenneth Williams would have been marginally more competent crew than we seemed to have available.

The crew (Laura and I) prepare the Roma II for sea as the skipper and first officer try to start it like a lawnmower.

Eventually the engine spluttered into life and we got under way. It was not long before our first incident. Gene had an impressive pile of charts, which he regularly consulted but, as with all maps, they are only of any use if you actually know where you are on the map. Whilst the middle reaches of the Thames was only a limited navigational challenge, with features like the Houses of Parliament and Tower Bridge to give the skipper a clue to his whereabouts, once we hit the relatively anonymous expanses of the river east of Greenwich, we bumped up against the limits of his navigational abilities. We soon ran aground, hitting a sand bank with a horrible thud. Fruitless revving of the engine in reverse ensued. It reminded me of when our car had got stuck in the mud on Upminster Common and we'd been there for hours, until it was dark and the RAC arrived to tow us out. I wondered whether the RAC had a maritime remit. Otherwise, this was going to be a very dull weekend. Fortunately, the tide was coming in and eventually released us from the grip of the Gravesend gunge. Gene seemed completely unabashed by this incident and cheerfully continued the journey.

I think it was beginning to dawn on my mother that we were in the hands of a jovial lunatic and that things could end very badly. The sense of alarm increased when Gene announced that we would be heading down the Medway and that this would necessitate us going a fair way out of the Thames estuary to make the turn back. We weren't out of sight of land but when we got beyond Southend pier, the elements hit us big time. It felt as if we were in the middle of the North Sea in an inflatable raft. We were being tossed around like a toy. Suddenly, *Carry On Cruising* had morphed into *The Cruel Sea* but without the reassuring presence of Jack Hawkins aboard. I could see that my mother was worried and she maintained a vice-like grip on Laura's and my hands. I remember her saying something vaguely comforting and jovial but there was an uncertainty in the delivery that betrayed her true concern. We joined her in worry.

By the time we had successfully made the turn into the Medway, I think at least two of us were violently seasick but that seemed a small price to pay for escaping with our lives. By now, it was starting to get dark and it was time for dinner. Gene had spotted a pub on the river. We were all very hungry and had visions of hot pub food. We would, however, have to take the dinghy to get there. The dinghy, however, would only take three people and there were five of us. The planning of the two trips to convey us to the hostelry resembled a cross between that schools intelligence test, where you have to deliver a wolf, a goat and a cabbage across a river without any of your charges being eaten by one of the others, and the preparations for Operation Overlord. Eventually, Laura and I were given our orders for Omaha beach, ferried by my father rowing. We set off, my father setting a brisk pace worthy of the first third of the boat race. We seemed to be making good distance. We were, compared with the water. My mother reappeared on deck after five minutes to check on our progress and was slightly surprised to find us in exactly the same spot as she had left us five minutes previously. My father's vigorous rowing was not enough to counter the considerable effects of the tide. Our rerun of Overlord was abandoned and no-one ate any goat or cabbage.

By the time we arrived at what Gene informed us was Sheerness Harbour, it was very late and dark. After a few minor collisions with other vessels, we successfully tied up for the night and retired to our bunks. The night passed without major incident. By this time, the un-drained and overflowing bilges seeping up through the floor of the boat and soaking all our bed linen, and the boat almost being left hanging on its ropes as the tide went out, seemed minor events when set against the dramas of the journey so far.

The next morning we emerged and took a look around. Sheerness

Harbour seemed a rather anonymous, utilitarian and unwelcoming place, with a faintly militaristic feeling. Mum, Laura and I set off to try and find provisions. We walked for about five minutes and found a checkpoint with a dozing uniformed sentry. He was the only person around so we sought directions. The sentry, clearly faintly embarrassed at literally being caught napping, immediately moved into pompous functionary mode. In a rather peremptory manner that had Mum bristling instantly, the sentry ordered us to stay where we were. Rigorous interrogation followed. We crumpled quickly, dazed with hunger.

'What are you doing here? This is a restricted high security area.'

I decided not to point out that if it was such a high security area they might want to find a sentry who could stay awake.

'Which boat are you from?' he continued.

'The Roma II,' Mum responded.

He was soon raising the alarm and on the radio:

'Have you got the Roma II down there? I've just caught three members of the crew wandering around'.

This flagrant distortion of events by the self-important lackey was immediately pounced on by Mum.

'Actually we're just a woman and two small children and we gave ourselves up,' she snarled.

Her version was scarcely more accurate as we hadn't actually given ourselves up, not realizing at this point that we could be suspected of being in the centre of a terrorist conspiracy to infiltrate and cripple one of south-east England's most critical maritime military industrial facilities. We were just trying to buy a tin of baked beans and a loaf of bread.

The Roma II left the dock under heavy escort.

The journey back up the Thames passed without incident. Life on the water was beginning to pall and it was getting dark, so I retired below decks to listen to Fab 208 Radio Luxembourg. Radio 1 seemed to disappear during the evenings in the early seventies – I have the feeling that it merged with Radio 2 so you were sentenced to having to spend the night with Jimmy Young – so Radio Luxembourg was the only viable choice until the forbiddingly late John Peel *Top Gear* programme. They played things that you had never heard before (and many that you would never hear again), with DJs following in the Emperor Rosko tradition of having fabulously transatlantic accents. It had long been a training ground for DJs who would later find fame on Radio 1 and in the early 70s the class was full of the vacuous Radio1 school of the later seventies. They even had their own magazine – Fabulous 208 – which was a bewildering mixture of profiles of their DJs, pin-ups of Peter Wyngarde (generally fully clad in his Jason King finery) and their fab fancies feature – a picture of their hunk of the month, accompanied by important data about him, including height, weight, eye colour and favourite food. I like to think my sister bought Fab 208 and I read her copy, but I can't be sure.

I don't recall whether it was Paul Burnett or Tony Prince spinning the disks that evening but I do distinctly remember that the Hollies' *Long Cool Woman In A Black Dress* was playing. I was thinking that it was quite good, even if it was a shameless rip-off of Credence Clearwater Revival (whom I loved). Just as Allan Clarke's best slapback echo Fogerty impression hit the final chorus, there was an almighty bang and the radio fell into my groin, with eye watering consequences. It was only time that the Hollies have moved me to tears. Simultaneously, all the crockery fell off the shelves, smashing on the floor. There was complete disarray in the cabin. Up top there was similar mayhem. It transpired that Gene had encountered another inexperienced helmsman coming in the opposite direction. Both were either unclear what the various coloured lights on the other craft connoted, or didn't know who had right of way. The result was that the skipper of the other craft, a smaller 20 footer, changed his mind at the last minute and cut across our path, presenting its full length to the oncoming bows of the Roma II, which scored a crunching direct hit, leaving a gaping hole in the other vessel. It limped in the direction of the banks. They were only 15 yards away and just made it to shallow water before being inundated. Whenever I hear *Long Cool Woman In A Black Dress,* I think of the Roma II's greatest hit.

It was around this time that my parents decided to build an extension onto our house. Dad was appointed project manager. I have the recollection that he drew up the plans for the extension himself, despite having no architectural or construction background. If so, it was entirely characteristic of him to master a new subject and go straight in at the deep end. He also did the planning application himself and ended up writing a layman's guide to planning law, which was put out by a small publisher. Project management was another thing. From the perspective of the builders, my father was an excellent choice, never imposing constricting deadlines or requiring compliance with tiresome work schedules. My mother unsurprisingly didn't share this viewpoint. I suspect that the rabble he engaged to do the work were in fact not builders but a demolition gang with no previous construction experience. They laid waste to our garage with an impressive despatch and efficiency. There then followed a lengthy gap without any noticeable activity, almost as if they were scratching their collective head and saying "What next?". What next, indeed. Three months into the schedule, the project manager professed them three months behind schedule.

'What are they actually doing?' raged my mother to him.

The project manager was unable to provide a convincing explanation, so busied himself with providing refreshments for his charges. The fact that Dad was making tea for the builders enraged my mother even more. Mr

Hunter, the chief builder, would occasionally visit site to inspect the pile of rubble residing next to our house, as if this were an unexpected new development in construction planning, and then retire to the garden to chat to his men, who were usually taking afternoon tea under the apple tree. Mum would be simmering in the kitchen. Eventually, she exploded. Mr Hunter was obviously unused to being addressed by a woman in such terms and attempted to patronise her and deflect the discussion, in order to continue the debate with the obviously more compliant project manager. This was a huge error. It should have become apparent to him that the tenure of the project manager had ended. Meet the new boss, who wasn't remotely the same as the old boss. From then on, the builders brought their own hot drinks, but found that the amount of time they had to drink them was considerably constrained. The project proceeded according to schedule.

I remember the day, once the extension was finished, that our new washing machine arrived. This was the cause of considerable excitement as it was a top of the range Hoover, with the latest programming advances. It was, however, straight from the *Thunderbirds* school of pointless technology. The USP of the Hoover Keymatic was that, rather than having a simple rotary dial, it was equipped with a pair of key plates which had a series of grooves cut into them, which would determine the wash sequence. It was an entirely pointless refinement. Characteristically, my father embraced it enthusiastically. My mother welcomed any upgrade from her previous mangle monster but when, entirely predictably, the most important key plate disappeared, rendering the machine largely useless, her enthusiasm waned. We switched to a more prosaic but less vulnerable rotary control model soon afterwards. The only problem was that the project manager had omitted to place an electrical socket in the space reserved for the new washing machine. Mr Hunter and his feckless crew had departed the premises long before this oversight was uncovered. Mum gave my father a look of resignation and proceeded to lay out the plans for the remedial action. Somewhat alarmingly, she seemed to be addressing her remarks to me. Now, I had served a useful apprenticeship in the house construction department - my wallpaper stripping skills were second to none and my airing cupboard shelves were the toast of the household - but I felt a little ill-equipped to be installing an electrical socket. My mother had always instilled into me that electricity was dangerous and playing with electricity was exceedingly dangerous. Wouldn't this escapade be playing with electricity big time? I can scarcely believe that 90% of this job was in fact completed by the two of us with no professional supervision, from chiselling out a trench in the brickwork, laying the conduit (as I now knew to call the white tubing which holds the cable), to mounting the new socket. Health and Safety wasn't such a big thing then. A real electrician was enlisted to examine our work.

The other missing element from the building of our extension was a garage. In his wisdom my father had decided not to engage the useless builders to replace the garage that they had levelled in the uniquely productive first week of the building works. Rather, he had decided to buy a garage in kit form and attempt to put it up himself. For someone who had never even put a picture up, this was a monstrous folly. Being a veteran of shelf erection, I was naturally suborned to the construction gang, together with one of his friends, Bill Faulkner. We were never formally introduced but somebody told me that his name was Bill. I don't think it was the same person who wrote *The Sound and the Fury*.

The first morning was spent staring at the assembly instructions.

'It'll be just like putting an Airfix kit together,' claimed my mother.

Up to a point, Lord Copper.

I had a long pedigree of making Airfix kits. My Lancaster bomber ('G George', which flew over a hundred missions) was the prize of my collection, it being one of the rare occasions when I had had the patience to paint the craft and let it dry before applying the transfers. A garage was a completely different thing altogether. For one, Airfix Lancaster bombers and Spitfires have many distinct parts and are made of very light plastic. Garage kits consist of many seemingly similar – but in fact subtly different – blocks of extremely heavy concrete. It was not a case of simply removing the right engine nacelle, and replacing it with the left one, when you discovered too late that you had in fact placed block H3 where block C8 should have gone, particularly when you had already placed blocks H6 and J9 on top of it. In theory, Blocks A1-20 should fit snugly under blocks B1-20 but as Einstein said "in theory, theory and practice are the same. In practice, they are not". He had probably attempted to put together some MFI flat pack furniture shortly before making that pronouncement. Our garage was the same on a much larger and heavier scale. By some miracle, we finished it by the end of the weekend and it didn't fall down, even after years of me relentlessly kicking a football against the side of it. I was knackered. Although a good lick of camouflage paint might have helped the concrete monstrosity blend in a bit better, I was relieved to hear that there was no plan for painting or the application of any transfers.

Hearing Secret Harmonies

Official music activity at Brentwood was as stifling and uninspiring as the rest of the official school offering. There were individual music rooms ostensibly for use of pupils during free periods but I soon discovered that free-form tinkling at the piano keyboard was discouraged. Fearing seven years' incarceration under the yoke of *Bobby Shaftoe* and *There Is a Tavern In The Town* I fled the building, never to return. The press gang for the school choir competition was savage and undiscerning and just about everyone who could walk upright had to do a six month tour of duty of mind-numbingly tedious lunchtime choir practice singing *Heraclitus*. I don't recall whose musical setting it was, but the tune was elusive and still could not be located at the end of the six months. It did however take well under three minutes to locate the tune to *Chirpy Chirpy Cheep Cheep*. Once heard on the transistor radio secreted in our classroom by one of my enterprising classmates, it was not easily eradicated from the brain. The lyrics – *"Where's your mama gone? – little Baby Don – Where's your mama gone? – far far away"* - made scarcely more sense to me at the age of eleven than words about Carian guests in *Heraclitus,* but this was classic bubblegum and bubblegum is what I craved. The class contraband radio was brought out of its hiding place every Tuesday lunchtime to hear the secret harmonies of Mungo Jerry, Norman Greenbaum and Christie and follow the chart rundown on the Johnnie Walker show. We would write down the chart positions in school exercise books, faithfully recording the ebbs and flows of hit parade fortune. This comfortably exceeded my use of school exercise books for legitimate purposes for some time.

The band responsible for *Chirpy Chirpy Cheep Cheep*, Middle of the Road, went on to record further searing examinations of the human condition such as *Tweedle Dee Tweedle Dum* and *Soley Soley*. They were fantastically uncool, with three blokes with moustaches, wearing matching burgundy jackets and bowties – reflective, I assume, of the Glasgow chicken-in-a-basket circuit from which they had just graduated and to which they were shortly and inevitably to return - but were fronted by a blonde wearing hot pants. I was twelve and my heart was there for the taking. Had we but world enough and time – but the romance was brief and Suzi Quatro and Agnetha from Abba beckoned from around the corner. Middle of the Road were dropped as soon as I heard *Get It On* by T. Rex. History records that John Peel, Marc Bolan's cheerleader and most ardent supporter, turned away from Bolan with the release of Get It On. I enthusiastically took his place. T. Rex released a peerless run of nine classic singles from *Ride A White Swan* to *20th Century Boy* in just under two and a half years. *Electric Warrior* was the must have album of 1971. Its self-consciously heavy cover, with a silhouetted Bolan ripping out a riff on his Les Paul, shadowed by his

100 watt stack (as we had learned to call impressively large guitar amplifier/speaker cabinet combinations), was the perfect summation of the end of Bolan's journey from his hippy imp acoustic noodlings to his approximation of full wattage boogie. This was entry level rock for those raised on *Chirpy Chirpy Cheep Cheep*. The contents were no less enthralling, with titles like *Cosmic Dancer* and *Mambo Sun*. The news that Marc danced himself right out of the womb came as no surprise and his mystique was only marginally dissipated by a bizarre appearance on Cilla Black's TV show to duet with Cilla on *Life's A Gas*. I don't recall whether she called him 'chuck' but I preferred the original version.

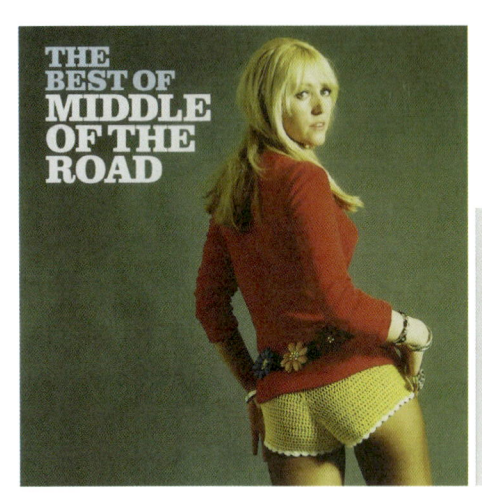

The teenage boy-friendly cover of a Middle of the Road album (L). Sensibly, the rest of the band (R) weren't pictured.

Novelty records were a major feature of the charts during these years. The Christmas No 1 in 1971 was Benny Hill's *Ernie (The Fastest Milkman In The West)* and No 1 records in 1972 included *Mouldy Old Dough* by Lieutenant Pigeon, Clive Dunn's *Grandad* and the Royal Scots Dragoon Guards bagpipe version of *Amazing Grace*. It was no surprise to find records like *Grandad* at the top of the charts, but it certainly was to find that its writer, Herbie Flowers, was heard the following year playing bass on Lou Reed's *Walk On The Wild Side*. Grandad might have been lovely, but he never shaved his legs en route to becoming a she and certainly didn't know what giving head was, although it is conceivable he might have sneaked a bit of Grandma's valium into his end of day Horlicks to help that insomnia bash.

Clive Dunn was a household favourite from his role in *Dad's Army*, which was required viewing every Saturday evening in our house. It was a consistently funny programme – the relationship between Arthur Lowe's middle class bank manager captain and John Le Mesurier's effete upper class sergeant, subordinate in Home Guard rank but not in the social pecking order – was a fantastic device and expertly executed by the writers, Jimmy Perry and David Croft, and the actors. Fortunately, Clive Dunn was not such a cross-over favourite that we purchased a copy of his album *Permission To Sing, Sir*. Perry and Croft were never funny again, following it with laugh-free fare such as *It Ain't Half Hot Mum* and *Hi-De-Hi*. *It Ain't Half Hot Mum* was unfunny despite some good comedy acting performances and mercifully remains clear of the television repeat circuit on account of some outrageous blackface casting of the white (albeit Anglo-Indian) Michael Bates as an Indian bearer and some ghastly racial stereotyping of a lazy punkah wallah. Sadly, it also spawned a novelty spin-off record, Don Estelle and Windsor Davies' risible *Whispering Grass*. Although we always watched Croft's *Are You Being Served?* it rarely raised a smile. The laboured repeat jokes about Mrs Slocombe's pussy failed even to excite the prurient interest of a hormonal 12 year old boy.

Navigating musical choices at Brentwood was a hazardous voyage. I observed the long-haired cool sixth-formers strutting around with albums by bands like the Groundhogs under their arms. The LP under your arm was the ultimate personal signifier in those years and *Split* by the Groundhogs signified that you were a cauldron of restless disenchantment who was not having any truck with tired establishment values or the bread-head adults who embodied them, except when they gave you your pocket money or a lift to school. It was better to have records on progressive and slightly alternative imprints like Harvest, Virgin and Vertigo. It was right out of the question to own anything on RAK or Bell, regarded as being refuges for teeny-bop trash. Decca and Pye were viewed with extreme suspicion. Although Decca had been home to the Rolling Stones, the Small Faces and Thin Lizzy, each of those bands had absconded to more credible accommodation, and the label also housed the likes of Val Doonican and Engelbert. I felt hideously ill equipped to find my way through this jungle. After all, I owned only one proper record at this point – Slade's *Mama Weer All Crazee Now* – and that simply was not a plausible option for parading under my arm. Fortunately, salvation was at hand in the form of my friend Julian Lewis. Julian had been at Langtons with me, but had gone to the Royal Liberty School in Romford, rather than Brentwood. Royal Liberty was well known locally for being the only school in the area which had a computer. No-one knew what they used it for, but it was reputed to take up an entire classroom and generated enough veneration about the forward thinking of the school, for the governors to be happy with their investment.

    Julian and I had stayed friends. He was the sort of child who strutted around on a Chopper bike, sucking on a *FAB* ice lolly, giving the impression that this was merely a temporary stepping stone to the motorized version and a more adult form of sustenance. Like a true nature's child, *Born To Be Wild* and Class B drugs beckoned irresistibly to Julian. By contrast, Laura and I had to make do with the much more sober *Raleigh Sun*, a truly ugly creation, which resembled an early exercise bike which had escaped from the gym. It is described on the web as 'a pleasant ride, if a tad ponderous'. It was more sensible than a Chopper, but sensible is not what we wanted. Julian seemed to hit puberty a good two years in advance of me and consequently was a foot taller and sprouting hair in areas that seemed unthinkable. Consistent with this greater physical maturity, he was also much cooler and had an insolent air of delinquency about him. Julian also had an impossibly large record collection. Either he got much more pocket money than me, or the delinquency was not just an air.

While our friends got to head out on the highway looking for adventure on their Choppers (L), Laura and I got to pootle around sedately on the truly hideous Raleigh Sun (R).

    The protocols surrounding use of the stereogram in our household were complex and raised high barriers to entry. The record for which permission to play was sought had first to be presented for inspection by my father, for any sign of scratching or wear which might damage the rare gem attached to the playing arm. Much tut-tutting from my father would generally follow. This was followed by a cursory review of the artistic merits of the disk. More tut-tutting. Eyebrows were raised at the misspelling of *Mama Weer All Crazee Now,* but it was a virgin copy, fresh from the record store, so no physical fault could be found. Eventually signed permission in triplicate was granted.
    In contrast to our repressive regime, Julian had unfettered access to his house stereo and seemed to have colonized the snug room in which it was situated. I never saw any other members of his household in this room. We would spend hours in the snug, exploring Julian's latest acquisitions.

When I expressed a liking for Mott The Hoople's *All the Young Dudes*, Julian would naturally produce a copy of their earlier Island album *Wildlife* and explain to me that they got their name from a cool sixties book. I listened with rapt attention, although the ten minute live version of *Keep A Knockin* strained my patience a little. Mott became a great love of mine. They did embrace many of the more ridiculous aspects of glam but produced some great records and were a huge influence on the new wave generation. Their 2009 reunion concert was one of those rare events when the audience was more star-studded than the personalities on stage.

It seemed only natural to Julian and me that we should form our own band.

The fact that my piano lessons were long forgotten, and neither of us could play an instrument, did not seem to present an insuperable obstacle. In the punk years to come, that would not have seemed an outlandish attitude, but we were in the years of prog rock when a classical training and ability to play fifteen minute virtuoso solos was a pre-requisite to even discussing forming a band. In the Cooke household, however, we were never deterred by the absence of seemingly essential components of any activity, no doubt subliminally influenced by our mother's approach to recipe ingredients. My sister did not feel constrained by her lack of a horse in order to sate her equestrian desires. Who needed a horse when there was a perfectly good farm gate opposite which she could saddle up and rein in with a rug and a piece of rope? Similarly, notwithstanding the absence of any musical instruments in our house, I had already mastered many of the essential techniques of lead guitar playing by the simple and very common combination of tennis racket and bedroom mirror.

Less common was the concept of men's doubles being extended to fantasy guitar playing, but Julian embraced the idea enthusiastically. The awesome force of the twin guitar attack of Dunlop Maxply and Slazenger Victory, the Les Paul and Strat of the tennis world, was something to behold. Our favourite piece to mime to was *Do Ya* by the Move, the excellent b side of *California Man*. It had satisfyingly heavy opening chords and we thrashed the catgut in unison. At the end of the lengthy set we eschewed the tie-break in favour of the encore - our thunderous version of Yes's *Yours Is No Disgrace*. We also brought technological innovation to the world of the fantasy rock group - an old-fashioned racket press with a sprung lever was brought into service as a tremelo arm. A refitted school desk subbed for my keyboard rig (complete with ruler and button ribbon controller, for those essential wailing noises that Donny produced on the Osmonds' *Crazy Horses*), when our fan base demanded a wider sonic palette from the band. Attempts to lash together two rackets, to emulate a Jimmy Page/John McLaughlin double-necked Gibson SG, however failed at the development stage, as the rubber bands struggled to maintain the structural integrity of the bastard axe during particularly harrowing renditions of

Stairway To Heaven or *Birds of Fire*.

There was a considerable period of time that I believed Rod Stewart to be singing into a hammer on the cover of *Every Picture Tells A Story,* never having ever seen a singer grasp a whole mike stand as a prop before. I thought this was a commendable D-I-Y ethic, well in advance of punk. Hammer was seriously considered as an addition to our armoury, whenever the mood demanded we step out from behind our instruments to front a lead vocal, but it brought back too many scarring memories of chiselling out a cable trench in our kitchen.

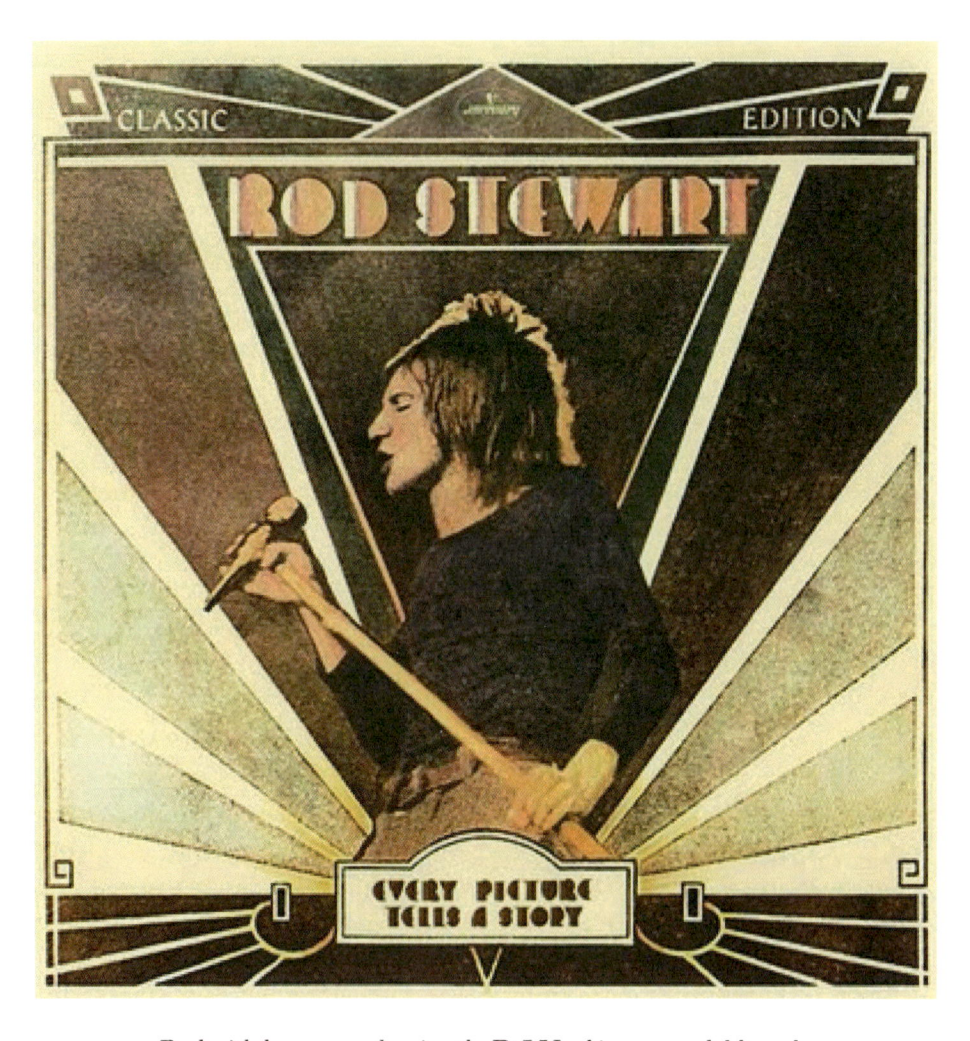

Rod with hammer embracing the D-I-Y ethic commendably early.

Whilst coveting most of Julian's record collection, my limited means dictated a strictly constrained buying policy. I didn't actually own a copy of *Electric Warrior (*until a few years later when I came across a copy in the bargain bins in the short period when T. Rex had fallen from favour but had yet to be adopted by punk and each generation of musicians that followed it) but managed to borrow a copy from one of my friends. This was sufficient for my purposes – which were, firstly, obviously to parade around the school with a copy of it under my arm and, secondly, to record it onto my reel to reel tape recorder. The reel to reel, together with my valve radio, complete with dial indicating exotic stations like Hilversum, were both recent releases from my father's collection of obsolete 1950s technology, having both served their statutory period of quarantined storage in the attic without attracting my mother's hawk-like attention for potential disposal in one of the many clearouts which will have occurred in the intervening years. They quickly became the hub of my nascent home entertainment system. The seven or eight vintage tapes, which accompanied the donation of the recorder, were sparingly filled with recordings of key early 70s records but mainly with songs grabbed off the radio. The recording process was hardly 96mhz digital to analogue conversion. *Electric Warrior* was committed to tape in a guerrilla operation utilizing my father's stereogram when he had left the house one afternoon. With no obvious line out socket to hand, I was forced to sit for the full length of each side of vinyl with one hand holding an ancient microphone positioned against one of the speakers, with my other hand trying to ward off Blackie's playful incursions into the recording area. The resulting feline intervention mix of *Cosmic Dancer* became a staple of my tape collection.

The choice any impecunious record buyer faced was whether to save up three or four weeks' pocket money to buy a full price album or whether to get more immediate satisfaction by investing in a lower priced item. I'm afraid I was seduced all too often by the siren call of Music For Pleasure (otherwise known as *mfp)*, the low priced imprint of EMI. Why would I buy *Electric Warrior* when I could acquire T.Rex compilation album *Ride A White Swan* on *mfp* for a third of the price? Sadly I only discovered the answer when I got the album home. Expecting the electric warrior, I found instead (the wonderful title track apart) that the contents had fallen prey to the power cuts of the three day week and were filled with selections from the elfin acoustic noodling years, when Bolan made albums with titles like *Prophets Seers and Sages, the Angels of the Ages* and *My People Were Fair and Had Sky in Their Hair, but Now They're Content to Wear Stars on Their Brows*. This was not what I wanted. Sadly, I made the same mistake many times. Repeated plays of a rather turgid Procol Harum compilation (predictably not including *A Whiter Shade of Pale*) did not lead to increased fondness.

Jimi Hendrix was a minefield for the unwary budget album purchaser. Eschewing the full price delights of *Hendrix In The West,* my parsimonious investment policy led me instead to *Birth of Success* and *The Eternal Fire of Jimi Hendrix,* both masquerading as Hendrix albums, complete with cover depictions of late sixties Hendrix. I wanted Band of Gypsys Jimi, but instead got Band of Brothers Hendrix, fresh out of 101st Airborne division and serving his apprenticeship as a sideman with mid sixties journeyman Curtis Knight, as they choogled their way lamely through some then current soul hits. The recording quality of the former album made my remastered tape version of *Electric Warrior* sound like a 2.8Mhz SACD.

Julian had recommended an album by Atomic Rooster, principally because the line-up included Carl Palmer, who had since moved on to major rock super-group ELP. It also met with favour in the accountancy department of my brain as it was selling locally for the price of a single. It had a suitably modish cover of a rooster with tits in a glass cube, serving well the display-under-arm-whilst-walking-to-and-from-the-school-bus requirement. Its service of the audio requirements was, however, less satisfactory. I tried to like the miserable tuneless dirge that lurked within its grooves, but it was an unlistenable dog. This was all part of the learning process that there is no such thing as a free lunch. Eventually I found more listenable material, which fitted within the Stalinist strictures of the cool kids' listening policies. Cream were likely candidates. They had good songs and album covers that looked hip. Somebody sold me a second hand copy of *Live Cream Volume 2* for less than the price of an *mfp* album. I had never even heard *Live Cream Volume 1* but it seemed a sensible investment. It had some of their good songs, albeit elongated by some interminable jamming. The verdict of Robert Wyatt's wife Alfie on her husband's former band Soft Machine – "too much going on all at once for too long" – was equally applicable to Cream in their worst moments.

Early 70s glam rock was not enthusiastically embraced at my school. Everyone pretended not to like the Sweet or Suzi Quatro but the reality was that they were irresistible. It is not a truth universally acknowledged that *"Hiawatha didn't bother too much/ 'Bout Minnie Ha-Ha and her tender touch"* is one of the great first lines of pop music, but it bloody well should be. *Wigwam Bam* was one of the finest pieces of nonsense pop to grace the charts. The fact that it had practically the same tune and chords as their previous single *Little Willy* troubled few listeners. Even by the ludicrous standards of 70s glam, the Sweet looked ridiculous, big beefy blokes done up in heavy make up, platform boots and satin, resembling hod carriers who'd collided with a children's face-painting party. They did, however, release a string of hugely catchy and fun records. The trouble was, the Sweet didn't want to be catchy and fun. They hankered after the rock credibility of the NME and wanted to be a serious band. That was always going to be a bit of a stretch. So, on the A side of *Co Co,* you found an infectious Archies-like bubblegum calypso, perfect for the pre-teen market. Flip it over and you might be forgiven for assuming there had been a pressing plant error as you played *Done Me Wrong Alright,* a lumbering rock monster, with the Sweet trying to be Deep Purple (complete with *Speed King-Little Richard* referencing derivative lyrics about the "house of blue light"), but without the melodic touch that brought Purple hit singles like *Strange Kind of Woman, Black Night* and *Fireball*. Worse was to come, including a tedious live album complete with long drum solos. Drum solos had become a mandatory fixture of serious rock since the mid-sixties, when jazzers like Ginger Baker journeyed to rock and brought with them their improvisatory moves and the genre of tedious twenty minute jams was born. Why is a drum solo like a sneeze? You know it's coming but you can't do anything about it. Cream defined the model. The drum solo would (live at least) be of a duration of at least 15 minutes, have a short, probably one word name, and be bookended by a brief burst of heavy rock guitar at the beginning and end. So Cream's *Toad* from 1966, although a moderate five minutes in the studio, was extended to a 16 minute live behemoth on 1968's live *Wheels of Fire*. It was a blessed relief that, when I went to see the reformed Cream at the Royal Albert Hall in 2005, Ginger Baker's health only permitted a modest eight minute *Toad*. In its wake followed Led Zeppelin's *Moby Dick* (which often extended to 25 minutes plus live, replacing the normal intermission as a convenient time to the audience to head to the bar for a refill and the rest of the band to head to their on-site pharmacist), Deep Purple's *The Mule,* ELP's *Tank* and the absolute nadir of the genre, *Hobbit,* by those clod-hopping Cream copyists Ten Years After. The Sweet's offering was a relatively modest eight-minute version of *The Man With The Golden Arm,* but was only less tedious than its peers in quantitative terms.

To be fair, the Sweet released a couple of good metal pop singles, *Fox On The Run* and *Action,* but their direction of travel was unfortunately timed – for most of their chart career they were scorned by the rock cognoscenti, but just as they arrived at their desired destination of being a serious band with long guitar solos, the era of punk had dawned and the tide had turned, with a generation of bands influenced by the classic period Sweet and everyone was hankering for the Sweet of old who made brilliant three minute singles, which by then everyone said they loved. The band never recovered from this betrayal by their fickle audience and splintered after a few more turgid flops.

It was 1973. Glam rock came and went. Mick Ralphs left Mott and was replaced by a guitarist who was renamed Ariel Bender for no apparent reason. His real name was Luther Grosvenor, which already sounded like a rock star pseudonym, so God knows why he felt the urge to change it. Right at the other end of the name changing spectrum is Fat Boy Slim, who in his earlier incarnation as bass player of the Housemartins was the only known example of a pop star changing his name to Norman - his birth name of Quentin being deemed not rock n roll enough. Norman certainly had the edge there. Ariel Bender left and was replaced by Mick Ronson, which sounded like a match made in heaven, so much so that he wasn't required to change his name, but spelt the death knell for Mott, going out with a glorious valedictory single, *Saturday Gigs*. Mott didn't reform, at least not until they were all old age pensioners. The same is not true of most of the other farewells from the glam arena. David Bowie famously announced his retirement from live performance from the stage of the Hammersmith Odeon, melodramatically finishing with *Rock n' Roll Suicide*, but his departure was less permanent than this would indicate and he was reincarnated onstage within a year. Gary Glitter announced various farewells but none stuck until incarceration prevented his return. One wonders whether legal redress should be available to hapless fans who have attended so called 'farewell' tours, only to find their hero treading the boards again shortly afterwards. Surely the plaintiffs' bar in the US could mount a class action to injunct REO Speedwagon from ever again entering a recording studio? Indeed, it is in the US that the jurisprudence of band reformation has been taken forward most impressively. Mötley Crüe appeared on television in 2014 to announce their final tour and signed a legally binding 'cessation agreement' in the presence of their attorney, supposedly assuring the world that we are at last free of their lame cock-rock. It is not known whether the text of the cessation agreement also features unnecessary umlauts over every other vowel. The band do, however, assure us that a breach of the agreement will have legal consequences and that they can be sued. The lawyer in me just wonders about that. If, like the substantial majority of the population, you really wanted cast iron assurance that there would be no sequel to *Theater of Pain* or *Generation Swine*, you would have advised a deed specifically enforceable by any single person on the planet, not just the band, or alternatively a more permanent solution to the dreadful risk of a Mötley reünion. Slade lumbered on for years. They starting spelling their song titles correctly and writing sensitive ballads, a couple of which were brilliant, leaving behind their stomping noise and, with it, their audience. Marc Bolan got fat and made increasingly dull records, having a brief run of acceptance by the punk generation before his collision with a tree on Barnes Common precluded the possibility of a T. Rex farewell tour or indeed any reunions.

When my friend Julian handed me a copy of *Free Live!* with the look of a knowing connoisseur, I was a bit sceptical. Its slightly tacky envelope cover bore all the hallmarks of a post-band split cash-in. Then I played it. It is surely one of the most underrated live albums of all time. On extended loan from Julian, I listened to it again and again. Most people's knowledge of Free didn't extend beyond *All Right Now*, which I have always found to be one of their least inspired songs. A brace of catchy hit singles, *Little Bit of Love* and *Wishing Well* confirmed them as my new favourite band and it was time to put my money where Paul Rodgers' mouth was and make an investment.

Fortunately there was no mfp budget album featuring tracks recorded when they were sidemen to the Geordie equivalent of Curtis Knight to entice me away from the main event and a trip to Downtown Records in Romford yielded my very own (numbered, as per the Beatles' White Album) copy of *The Free Story*. The omission of *Wishing Well* from this supposedly comprehensive overview of the band's career was only a minor disappointment. It was mandatory in compilations of this period for a major hit to be excluded, supposedly demonstrating that the band in question were not in thrall to the singles charts and were a serious album act – thus *The History of Eric Clapton* eschewed the inclusion of chart fodder like *For Your Love* or *Strange Brew* in favour of his less well-known work as a sideman with King Curtis and Delaney and Bonnie. Best of all, *Weird Scenes Inside The Goldmine,* the Doors' compilation, did not include their most famous song, *Light My Fire*. Seasoned fans nodded approvingly at these wilfully obscure acts of apparent discernment. Deep Purple hedged their bets and whilst *24 Carat Purple* did include *Black Night* and *Strange Kind of Woman*, they were both in elongated live versions rather than the hit single takes, to ward off any greatcoat brigade concerns that they had sold out to Top of the Pops. I played *The Free Story* to death, even though for the most part I preferred – and still do – the live versions on *Free Live!* True gratification came when, after only a couple of days of walking to and from the school bus with it under my arm, I was approached by a sixth former who told me knowingly that many people in his year "who really knew about music" thought that Free were "the real deal". My heart swelled with pride. It was a rare moment of positive musical enjoyment and street cred coming into conjunction. Let's face it, I never really liked any of those Atomic Rooster albums I had been persuaded to buy, but loved Free and still do.

A turning point in my relationship with Julian came on an organised trip to France. My mother thought it would be a good idea if we all went on a day trip to Le Touquet. Mum, Laura and I and Julian, Mrs Lewis, his mother, and his younger brother Geoffrey. Geoffrey was a bit of a menace. Mum used to seethe at the lack of parental control imposed by Mrs Lewis, as he ran amok. His father was even more invisible than mine and, even though I spent days round at Julian's house, I can only recall seeing Mr Lewis once or twice. Perhaps he was sitting in a car somewhere, listening to the test match.

    Geoffrey was tiresome even to other children and, even then, we would smile at the mismatch between the slightly faux-aristocratic name and the feral little beast who bore it. We once got so fed up with him trying to disrupt one of our games that we tied a length of washing line around his waist, first attaching him to our go-cart as he trailed helplessly in its wake and then lashing him to a post at the far end of the garden, whilst we moved back to the opposite end to continue our play undisturbed, his furious screams only enhancing our enjoyment of the little brute's discomfort.

The ungodly racket he made did, however, attract the attention of Mrs L, who came rushing out to rescue Geoffrey, as though he had been in mortal danger. Pausing briefly to indulge Geoffrey and mop his fevered brow, she then proceeded to berate Julian, Laura and me for endangering her angel's life by almost suffocating him by cable round his waist. Even at our tender age, it was obvious to all of us that Mrs L's grasp of the human physiognomy was sketchy to say the least. Mum looked on admiringly at our handiwork with a twinkle in her eye.

The day trip was organised by the Romford Women's Institute or some similar organization and consisted of a coach full of mothers and children. My French was poor and, due to the strange priorities of the French syllabus, I knew that the French for "potholing" was "la speleologie" but could not sustain even the most basic of conversations. Julian's grasp of the language was no better, although he had amassed an impressive collection of French swear words and, courtesy of the recently released *Lady Marmalade*, some conversance with the francophone language of love, which he was anxious to utilise. Thus we left fully linguistically equipped for cave exploration, which in a sea level coastal town seemed rather unlikely, and sexual congress with the girls of Le Touquet, which seemed even more unlikely. Hopefully someone would deserve to be called a wanker or arsehole in French.

The coach journey to Folkestone took a couple of hours, pushing right up against the limits of Geoffrey's tolerance of having to sit in one place without a break for charging around making a lot of noise. By the time we hit the cross-channel ferry, he was liked a caged beast being released into the wild. Geoffrey was momentarily appeased by the attractions of the on-board amusement arcade, having first extracted a Danegeld-like tribute from his mother of a huge pile of sixpences, which he proceeded to disburse at an impressive rate. Laura and I had never seen such largesse deployed so casually, but I think we both knew that thinly veiled threats of bad behaviour would not cut much ice with our mother. His coffers emptied and with his entreaties for replenishment being rebuffed by his pay-mistress (not of course out of any sense of responsibility or proportion, but because she'd run out of change), Geoffrey sought amusement outside of the arcade. The resulting spectacle was one to behold, as he careered madly around the boat, screeching like a crazed banshee, completely oblivious to other passengers, into whom he would regularly crash. Mrs L looked on with a horribly complaisant expression. Mum looked on as if she wished she'd brought a length of washing line with her. At one point, Geoffrey attempted to climb up the deck guardrail, the only thing separating him from the foaming waters below. Julian and I looked at each other knowingly. Responsibility prevailed and he was brutally yanked down from his perch. It was the sort of mayhem not seen again on a cross-channel ferry until Oasis bizarrely chose it as their mode of transport to Ostend, the definitive booze-cruise. Geoffrey was eventually apprehended and restrained by a member of the crew and taken to Mrs L, who looked pained that her reading of *Woman's Realm* had been interrupted.

Le Touquet seemed very glamorous, even if its twenties casino grandeur had faded a bit. It was reputedly the model for Royale-Les-Eaux, the fictional setting for *Casino Royale*. We were only allowed an hour and a half in the town, which seemed a rather paltry allowance of time for such a long journey, no doubt betraying the true purpose of the trip as the chance to stock up on gin and duty free fags. Geoffrey was under close personal guard after the mayhem on the ferry and Julian and I were considered old enough to look around the town free of parental supervision. Mum of course first delivered detailed instructions on making sure we could find our way back to the coach and to be there on the dot, 90 minutes later. Yes, yes, yes, we thought impatiently, can we get on with it? Released from the preparatory lecture, we bounded off, ready for *les caveaux et les mademoiselles,* although 90 minutes seemed scarcely enough time to do justice to either.

What could possibly go wrong? We had of course taken in every word of my mother's pre-flight demonstration so we couldn't possibly get lost. Sensing the potential for disaster, I did in fact listen hard and whilst Julian probably didn't have a clue which way he was going, I was carefully noting where we were. I generally have a very good sense of direction, albeit a rather linear one (so Amsterdam, where every canal-bordering street looks like the others and they are all subtly curved, so you are soon walking in a direction 90 degrees away from the way you think you're going, is just about the only place where I've ever got lost). I returned us safely at the appointed hour to the car park and the coach.

Mum, however, had not taken in her own lecture and she, Mrs L, Laura and Geoffrey had got horribly lost. By their own account, they then attempted to seek directions. My French was U.N. interpreter standard compared to Mum's, so that approach was always going to be fraught with difficulty. The end result was them heading to completely the wrong end of town. The coach driver fretted that he couldn't wait much longer and Julian's mask of cool insolence melted away with the realization that we were just about to leave France without his guardian. Other parents expressed sympathy. I mentioned that our mothers had our passports, which clearly caused some consternation, although they tried to hide it, for fear of alarming us further. It did occur to me that events at Calais immigration could be even more stressful. Reluctantly, the coach driver announced he could wait no longer and pulled out of the car park to return to Boulogne. We seemed destined to be international detritus, strays without a country to call our own. As the coach passed the last turning out of Le Touquet, we all looked down the side road. It seemed a forlorn hope. In the distance you could just see two figures, clearly identifiable as our mothers, running up the road dragging their offspring behind them. Everyone on the coach saw them and a collective yell went up, commanding the driver to stop. The coach screeched to a halt. The crisis was over. My mother and Mrs L looked quite red and flustered and were very out of breath. Even Geoffrey had had enough exercise and drama to keep him subdued for the rest of the day. I could see that Mum's biggest relief was that I was on the coach. How could she have doubted it? I always listened to her advice, even if she didn't. Julian quickly tried to compose himself and resume his aura of knowing detachment.

'Are you alright?' said my mother tenderly.

By now, although obviously relieved that they had made it back and that we were not all going to be stranded separately in France, I was feeling just a little smug and revelling in the novel experience of feeling more mature than Julian.

'Yes, fine. I kept my head, but Julian went to pieces,' I announced pompously. It would be quoted back at me by Mum and Laura for many years to come. My response would generally be to enquire if anyone could remember what the French for "completely lost" is.

Sherlock and Verloc

    Cooke awoke abruptly and looked at his watch. 6.45. Mondays were hell. Seven hours of Maths, Chemistry and French to plough through. He was disgusted to find he was thoroughly bored with the prospect of the day ahead. He kicked the single sheet off his naked body and swung himself onto the floor. Flicking away the black comma of hair over his right eye, he went down on his hands and did twenty slow press ups, lingering over each one until his arms could stand the pain no longer. Panting but exhilarated with the exertion, he entered the avocado tinted shower cubicle and doused himself with the hottest shower he could bear. Slipping on a white poplin cotton shirt and grey school suit, made for him by Hornes of Romford, and knotting his dark blue nylon house tie, he headed downstairs. Breakfast was Cooke's favourite meal of the day, other than when his father was in charge. It was generally the same, consisting of two very hot cups of strong tea, a special PG blend made for him by Brooke Bond of Ashton-under-Lyne, brewed in a pre-warmed bone china pot, two thick slices of lightly browned white toast with a large pat of deep yellow butter from the Anchor creamery in Auckland, New Zealand, which had a saltiness missing from most continental and Scandinavian blends, topped with a egg, sourced by his mother from local Essex hens, poached for exactly three and a third minutes, sparingly sprinkled with salt and freshly ground black pepper. With all this under his belt, he began to feel more sanguine.

If Ian Fleming had been describing my start to the day at the age of fourteen, this is what it might have sounded like. James Bond would have approved of my school day routine, apart from the tea, which he considered to be responsible for the downfall of the British Empire. I was around that age when I read my first Bond book. Before that, my reading had been largely confined to children's classics like *The Lion, The Witch and the Wardrobe* and (best of all – a brilliant prequel) *The Magician's Nephew*. I remember visiting C.S.Lewis' house just off the Headington roundabout when I was at Oxford and being entranced by the garden, in particular the series of pools on the hillside in his wilderness garden – which to me were clearly the inspiration for the time pools in *The Magician's Nephew*, but strangely no-one on the internet has commented on this.

    My mother had taken me to see *Diamonds Are Forever* a couple of years earlier when it came out in the cinema and, despite a distinctly portly and rug wearing Sean Connery, I was smitten. A year later, Roger Moore arrived as his replacement, having abandoned his aversion to weaponry, but without having broadened his range of facial expressions. Such a shock could have killed off my nascent attachment to Bond, but the recent arrival of Jon Pertwee as Doctor Who had prepared me for the nasty turns that franchises can take. I had taken Patrick Troughton's substitution for William Hartnell in my stride and, in due course, he became my favourite Doctor, but the downgrade to the buffoon dandy that Pertwee seemed to be portraying was too much to bear. I was ready to give up on Doctor Who, but the scriptwriters came to the rescue with the best run of stories in the whole of the classic Who canon, from the opening *Spearhead From Space,* with its nightmare-like rampaging showroom dummies (so effective that it was reprised for the opening of the new generation Who), to the giant maggots, all without recourse to classic Who baddies the Daleks and Cybermen. When the Daleks eventually did return to Earth, following their longest absence from the series, it was not in force. Cutbacks on the Planet Skaro meant that an invasion force of just three Daleks could make the journey, which made for a distinctly underwhelming visual experience. Fortunately the scriptwriters again saved the day and, budgetary constraints notwithstanding, the episode, *Day of the Daleks,* was brilliant, utilising the classic temporal paradox premise that was not new but would later form the basis for *Terminator* and a slew of other movies.

"The scent and smoke and sweat of a casino are nauseating at three in the morning. Then the soul erosion produced by high gambling — a compost of greed and fear and nervous tension — becomes unbearable and the senses awake and revolt from it" are the classic first lines from *Casino Royale*. I had never been to a casino or experienced soul erosion at the age of fourteen, but it seemed a wholly persuasive and evocative description. I had also never heard the word 'compost' used other than as a product of my father's Saturday morning toils with the lawnmower, once he had gone through the regular ritual of coaxing the useless piece of kit into life. I can't remember if *Casino Royale* was my first Bond book, but my organized mind soon appreciated and embraced the importance of reading the books in the correct order.

Wednesdays, Fridays and Saturdays were market days in Romford and during school holidays I was unwillingly press-ganged into service by Mum to help her carry the shopping. We seemed to spend an inordinate amount of time standing at the fabrics stall. This was run by a fez-wearing showman (who was therefore predictably known as "Fez"), brandishing exotic cloths, who contrived to appear as if he had come direct from the souk at Casablanca, but probably hailed from Chadwell Heath. One day, tiring of prolonged exposure to this charlatan's act, I wandered off and discovered a nearby second hand book stall[17], chock full of 1960s Pan editions of the Bond books at prices that even my meagre pocket money could bear. Within six months I had read the lot. I was addicted. I have never smoked cigarettes but if anything was going to entice me into doing

---

[17] *I am told by my friend Jeff Randall that it was called "Bob's Books".*

so, it would not have been peer pressure from my friends, but the idea of extracting a Macedonian blend Morland with three gold bands from my gunmetal cigarette case, tapping the end on the case, Connery fashion, laconically putting it in my mouth and lighting it with my battered black oxidized Ronson lighter, came close.

For a mind appreciative of detail, they are a fantastic read. The first ninety pages of *Moonraker*, with the description of Bond's daily routine, dinner at M's club (with lamb cutlets you could cut with a fork and Bond's idiosyncratic habit of sprinkling the surface of his vodka with black pepper), followed by the game of bridge with Drax, are to my mind the most gripping and enthralling in the whole thriller genre and certainly Fleming's finest moment. I also made a mental note never to mix a dry martini, vodka shot and a couple of bottles of champagne, particularly when gambling for huge amounts of money, unless my secretary was able to dispatch me a pouch of Benzedrine to mitigate the overall effect. Sadly, unlike Miss Moneypenny, she has never had access to a ready supply of the latter and therefore the primary rule has never been departed from.

The sense of disappointment when Bond had despatched Scaramanga at the end of *The Man With The Golden Gun,* and there were no more Bonds to read, was intense. There were other Bond books but none could match the Fleming suite. 007 first fell into the hands of Fleming admirer Kingsley Amis, writing under the pseudonym of Robert Markham, and the resulting work *Colonel Sun* was dressed up like the Pan Flemings to give a reassuring feel of official canon, but the contents were disappointing, sorely lacking the Fleming sweep. Greater desecration of the Fleming legacy was to follow with a series of aberrations penned by John Gardner and others, until some dignity was restored to the franchise by the admirable offerings by Sebastian Faulks, William Boyd and Anthony Horowitz.

The comedy low point in the Gardner dark ages must be the novelisation of the *Licence To Kill* film. In the Bond films, scenes taken from unrelated books were often included – for example the harrowing keelhauling sequence from the *Live and Let Die* book (unused in the film) was used in the *For Your Eyes Only* film, and the *Property of a Lady* short story featured in the *Octopussy* film. *Licence To Kill* was designed as a darker film than Bond film fans were used to and the sequence where Felix Leiter is fed to and half-eaten by a tank of sharks was appropriated from *Live and Let Die* (again unused in that film, as presumably viewed as too dark for that safari-suited light confection). The only problem, once you decide to do a novelisation, is that all the Gardner books are designed to be faithful to canon, so that Felix Leiter had already been dismembered by a shark in the book of *Live And Let Die* and hence had a prosthetic leg and hook instead of right hand. How to deal with this conundrum? Leave it out all together? Hmm – it was quite central to the revenge plot of the film. Oh well – just biff on and have 007 exclaim *"Oh no – it's happened again! Leiter fed to sharks!*

Lightning does sometimes strike twice!" Remarkably Leiter did not seem to suffer any incremental injuries, as it was a faithful carbon copy of the first shark attack, but with this time the underwater predators feasting on the bakelite and stainless steel of the leg and hook and shunning the tasty flesh of Leiter's remaining limbs.

For someone in thrall to the books, the Bond films are, to say the least, a mixed bag. The Connery years peaked with the *From Russia With Love/Goldfinger/Thunderball* trio and thereafter slid into implausible technological plots and equally implausible wigs mounted on Sean's pate. His return after the Moore years in *Never Say Never Again* was a plucky attempt, with the only gadgetry deployed presumably being the corsetry required in order to persuade us that Connery could still resemble an active SIS agent, even after a trip to Shrublands to detox and rid himself of all free radicals. Temporary tonsorial technology had visibly not moved on and the wig was as poor as ever. *On Her Majesty's Secret Service* had the potential to be one of the best Bonds, were it not for the decision of Broccolli and Saltzman to hire a male model, rather than an actor, for the lead role, with predictable results. At least he looked the part, which is more than can be said for the 70s fashion aberration spy portrayed by Roger Moore. A better Bond than popular caricature allows, Moore was not, as almost all males other than ludicrous contrarians will tell you, an adequate substitute for Connery, even with the latter's paunch and toupee. He was forced to substitute levity for the implied menace that Connery brought to the part. Moore was an enjoyable and charming actor and brought a sunny vigour to his roles in *The Saint* and *The Persuaders*. Also check out late sixties classic *The Man Who Haunted Himself*. On the negative side, his performance as a German POW camp commandant in *Escape To Athena,* acting against type (but shored up by more familiar central casting baddies as Anthony Valentine), is a comedic car crash. Moore at least had the good sense to withdraw from the ghastly Lloyd Webber late 80s musical *Aspects of Love,* It is a shame that his successor Pierce Brosnan did not have the sense to follow his example before he thrashed *SOS* to within an inch of its life, in the *Mamma Mia* film. Fortunately, the song is made of stronger stuff and survived the onslaught. Moore also joins the massed ranks of celebrities with autobiographies with truly awful punning titles. His offering in this crowded field, *My Word Is My Bond,* is merely an entry level contender when set alongside such masterworks as Shane Richie's *Rags To Richie,* Davy Jones' *They Made A Monkee Out of Me,* Alan Wark's *Wark On* and that 1966 England world cup winning duo Gordon Banks' *Banks of England* and Alan Ball's *It's About A Ball*. With footballers so well represented in the autopunography charts, it is deeply disappointing that Ledley King merely titled his memoir *King* when obvious possibilities like *Playing The King, King For a Day* or *A King Amongst Men* were available.

The Moore films are only enjoyable if you banish all memory of the books. The nadir was the deathly dull *Man With The Golden Gun*, despite the suave menace of Christopher Lee. The end credits of the risible *The Spy Who Loved Me* (which didn't even have John Barry doing the music, replaced by a cheesy Marvin Hamlisch cod-disco soundtrack) told us that James Bond would return in *For Your Eyes Only,* but tricky as ever, and avoiding the predictable routines that can mean death for an agent, he in fact returned in *Moonraker*. This was a shameless attempt to cash in on the space movie craze generated by the success of *Star Wars* and is often castigated as the worst Bond ever. Granted, the last hour or so is dreadful and is essentially a space re-run of the underwater battle from *Thunderball,* but the first 45 minutes are saved by a delicious performance by Michael Lonsdale as Drax,[18] with some excellent scripting to give Drax lines like *"Afternoon tea – the one indisputable contribution of the British Empire to civilization. May I press a cucumber sandwich upon you, Mr Bond?"* and *"Ah Mr Bond, you have the habit of appearing with the tedious regularity of an unloved season"*. No-one other than Roger's agent was sad to see him hang up his shoulder holster and a generally more consistent and well-balanced era of Bond films, continuing to this day, was ushered in.

    My Bond book binge was conveniently combined with spending more time in bed. Most teenagers are constantly negotiating to get their bedtime extended and stay up as late as possible. Around the age of 14 or 15, I suddenly realised I liked sleep and would head up to bed at around 8 or 8.30 to enjoy a luxurious session of a Bond book and slowly drifting into the embrace of the soft embalmer of the still midnight and get a good 10 hours or so of high quality z's. I also reasoned that you couldn't enjoy a bit of a lie-in in the morning unless you knew you were having it, so would set my alarm for a good half an hour earlier than I needed, so I could hit the snooze button a few times and luxuriate in some additional sleep before the get up for school deadline. The only problem with this is that you need to keep a mental note of how much additional snooze time you've had. This is made more difficult by the fact that nearly all alarm clocks have a snooze period of eight minutes. Why not ten minutes to make that calculation a bit easier? Did someone do some research that showed that eight minutes is the optimum light snooze time? Perhaps, like the chairman of Sony, who reputedly decreed that the compact disk should be 74 minutes long so it could fit Beethoven's 9th, his favourite symphony, on one disk, the CEO of Westclox had a preference for an eight minute lie-in, finding ten minutes too indulgent for his hectic schedule. Eight minutes it was, however, and so after a couple of presses you find yourself mentally rehearsing your eight times table, adding the product of the snooze pushes equation to the original time set and hey presto you're wide awake. In the summer holidays there were no such disciplines required, but I can scarcely believe that, in

---

[18] *Coincidentally, Drax is described in the book as a "sort of Lonsdale figure".*

stark contrast to my own children when they were teenagers, I would get up at 7am and really relish the sunny early mornings. What a freak. Then again, if you only had *On The Buses* to tempt you to tarry downstairs after nightfall, rather than FIFA 18 and the world's entire television library on Netflix, it might seem less weird. Now it seems inconceivable that I took huge pleasure in going out to the fields opposite our house with Mum first thing in the morning to pick mushrooms and then come back to cook them, but I did and it remains a hugely pleasurable memory.

There were only a limited number of watchable TV programmes on in the early-mid seventies and indeed many of these appeared to be exactly the same. Take, for example, *The Persuaders!* and *The Protectors*. The absence of a gratuitous exclamation mark in the title of the latter was one of their few differences. The former starred former Saint and soon-to-be Bond Roger Moore and the latter former Man From U.N.C.L.E. Robert Vaughan. Both concerned the exploits of an affluent bunch of playboys with no apparent employment or other tedious commitments, sticking their noses into the affairs of bad guys and thwarting international conspiracies, following which they would crack open a bottle of Bollinger and return to their glamorous lifestyles, until the following week when another ne'er do well would catch their attention. Roger Moore was partnered by Tony Curtis, playing respectively Lord Brett Sinclair, rich aristocrat, and Danny Wilde, hard nosed American. Robert Vaughan was partnered by Nyree Dawn Porter, playing respectively Harry Rule, hard nosed American, and Contessa di Contini, rich aristocrat. They all seemed to spend their time swanning around the South of France, on television budgets that *Z Cars* could only dream of. Both series were blessed with great theme tunes, John Barry's brilliant and catchy synth instrumental for *The Persuaders!* and Tony Christie's *Avenues and Alleyways* for *The Protectors*. There was a more parochial and low budget version of this concept in *Hadleigh,* a story centred around a suave affluent local squire who corrected community injustices and brought local ruffians to book. They couldn't afford Roger Moore and John Barry, so instead got Gerald Harper and Tony Hatch. Harper looked and sounded suitably suave and affluent, and they put him in an Aston Martin, just like Roger Moore in *The Persuaders*. Hatch, veteran of low budget television themes like *Crossroads,* bashed out a routine tune[19]. The tales of rustic derring-do soon palled. It was just a bit boring. However, this was nothing compared with daytime television, which was our first refuge on rainy days during the school holidays.

---

[19] *On the plus side, he did write 'Downtown', which not only had a brilliant tune but the outrageous rhyme of 'listen to the rhythm of a gentle bossa nova / You'll be dancing with 'em too before the night is over' and later went on to be a wonderfully dismissive proto-Cowell in mid-70s Britain's Got Talent precursor 'New Faces'.*

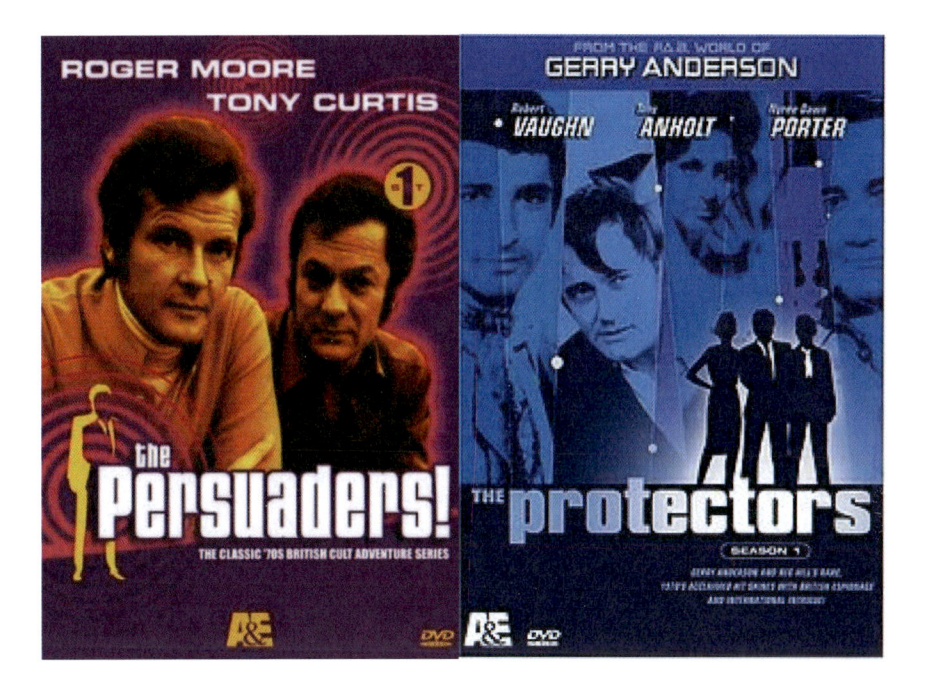

Many 1970's television series were completely indistinguishable.

It was a bit of an entertainment desert. *Marked Personal* was set in the personnel department of a large company. No-one has ever attempted to repeat this setting for a TV series. It was as dull as one would expect. It did, however, star Stephanie Beacham, who a year before had got her kit off in a film with Marlon Brando, and I was hoping she might repeat this. Sadly, she dealt with all HR issues fully clothed, which made for very tedious viewing. *Emmerdale Farm* was effectively *The Archers* (which I have always hated) on television. It was like *Hadleigh* without the Aston Martin or girls, with a load of blokes sitting around gossiping in the Woolpack, the local pub, presided over by the landlord, who went by the name of Amos Brearly. You had to be pretty desperate to watch it.

With daytime television so bad, and doing schoolwork being completely out of the question, I had to find something to read to fill the void left by Bond. But what? It was quite a three-pipe problem. I went to the last and highest court of appeal in detection. The verdict was, of course, Sherlock Holmes. Given the organised way I went about reading Bond in strict order, I unaccountably started with *A Scandal In Bohemia*, omitting *A Study In Scarlet* and *The Sign Of The Four*. The game was, however, afoot. Maybe I should have allowed a great hiatus – a three year gap after *The Final*

Problem to replicate Holmes' fictional absence[20] – but youthful compulsion dictated that I should rip through the lot in a matter of months. All else fell before my binge reading of Holmes. If there is any point to which I should wish to draw your attention, it was the curious incident of the homework in the night-time. But, say all my teachers, there was no homework done in the night-time. That was the curious incident. Even more curious was that schools didn't encourage us to read Sherlock Holmes, preferring to just adopt the piano teacher uncompromising approach of a deep dive straight into the hard stuff. The Holmes stories are the perfect bridge between children's books and serious literature but a route that was rarely encouraged by schools in my day.

It was, however, through a forbidding school diktat that I made my next literary leap. Conrad's *The Secret Agent* appeared on an absurdly aspirational pleasure reading list circulated by our English teacher, a wildly Panglossian view of the likely appetite for serious literature in fourteen year-old boys. *The Wreck of the Deutschland* might be a rousing masterpiece but it's just not going to cut it next to the words of *In The Court Of the Crimson King* in the teenage hive mind. Although set in the late nineteenth century period of paranoia and international subterfuge that was the backdrop for many of Holmes' best stories (and set around the time that Holmes was investigating *A Study In* Scarlet), *The Secret Agent* is scarcely a mystery worthy of the talents of the master detective. A denouement where Holmes discovers the identity of the victim because his address is sewn into his collar is not a regular feature of the Holmes stories and one would have thought well within the normal capabilities of Lestrade and more commonplace detection methods. Elementary in the extreme, Watson, but I divine that complex detection was not Conrad's purpose. *The Secret Agent* was also the title of the first chapter of *Casino Royale* and I therefore naturally assumed it contained sophisticated espionage intrigue and thrills on a scale with Bond at his best[21]. The low-key Penguin classics cover of a misty London tableau should have alerted me to the likely absence of dry martinis, card games and plentiful sex and gunplay. Although having a Bond-like plot of a sinister conspiracy to subvert the world order by a faked terrorist outrage, with a *From Russia With Love* style exposition at the outset of the details and motivation of the conspiracy by the evil mastermind, Verloc is, notwithstanding his mixed British and continental European parentage, as far from Bond as it is possible for a secret agent to be – an indolent, fat laggard who was caught by the

---

[20] *Or even the longer eight years that was the actual gap between the publication of 'The Final Problem' and 'The Hound of the Baskervilles', to replicate the frustrated yearning of Conan Doyle's original readership.*

[21] *I have been similarly misled on many occasions by book titles, but, as with 'The Secret Agent', it has led to new pleasures. For example, I read Hermann Hesse's 'Steppenwolf' expecting either a werewolf adventure or a Born To Be Wild stoner tale, but I loved it anyway and it led me to the brilliant 'Narziss and Goldmund', one of my favourite books.*

opposition on his very first mission. It was not the book I thought it was.

It was, however, a true voyage of discovery. The unexpected leaps forward and backward in time were at first confusing, but then enthralling, to a child used to strict linear narratives. The sinister chance meeting between Inspector Heat and the bomb-making professor in a narrow alleyway might have come out of Bond, but had a degree of craft in the finely constructed tension to which Fleming could only aspire. I was not at this stage aware of Chekov's dramatic principle that if a gun is hung on a wall in the first act, it must be fired in the second or third, but I naturally assumed that the detailed description of the Professor's proto-suicide bomber apparatus was a piece of technology that must play a role in a necessarily explosive denouement. That the Professor simply remained a foreboding presence, surviving beyond the end of the book, was the biggest surprise. The density of the writing and depth of characterization came was a revelation. Conrad is not a fashionable author these days and, indeed, I fell out of love with him for a while when I had to study *Nostromo* for A level, which although is generally regarded as his masterpiece, I found turgid and long. Maybe it was the enforced rigour of study that did for it. I became a willing participant in my mother's shopping trips to Romford market, diving into Downtown Records and Bob's Books as my mother stood entranced by Fez as he weaved his Barking Berber magic with his silks.

One of these two books promises car chases, dry martinis, card games and plentiful sex and gunplay. It should not have been difficult to work out which.

It is not known whether John Masefield had ever visited Canvey Island, but I can still remember Mum reciting *Cargoes* by then poet laureate, as we stood on the sea wall there, waiting for the biggest oil tanker in the world, the Manhattan, to pass by. The local newspapers had told us it would be loading or unloading or doing something important at Canvey Island that day. We didn't see a quinquireme of Nineveh from distant Ophir, or even a dirty British coaster, but there were plenty of anonymous looking oil tankers. Although being the setting of the end of *Great Expectations* and the opening of *Heart of Darkness*, Canvey Island has only been famous twice in the last 100 years – in 1953 when the North Sea broke into the island, flooding huge areas and causing over 50 deaths, and 1976 when, rather improbably, Canvey Island's finest band, Dr Feelgood, broke out of the island and to the top of the album charts. Pub rock had never before, and has never since, achieved such mass acceptance.

It is a bleak and soulless place, which feels like the edge of the world. Check out the cover photo of *Down By The Jetty*, the Feelgoods' first album. In keeping with the burgeoning DIY ethic, it's in mono and the cover photo in black and white. The cover photo could have been in colour and it would have still looked the same, with the monochrome clothing and pallor of the band and the grey backdrop of Canvey. It was never sunny when we went to Canvey Island. I remember sunny days at Thorpe Bay, our beach of choice, less than five miles away, but Canvey was where the slate grey sky met the concrete grey sea wall, season after season. Grey, grey, grey but when you lived in Hornchurch in the mid-sixties a trip to Canvey Island was what passed for a good time. Add the world's largest oil tanker and excitement levels were pretty high.

We always used to park in the car park of the Lobster Smack pub (reputedly the inn at the end of *Great Expectations*) and climb up onto the huge sea wall that had been built following the '53 floods. We would walk along it to gaze at the Hole Haven oil refinery. It was an anonymous, then rather futuristic, construction, strangely devoid of any manifest human activity, as if aliens had set it up and were operating it by remote control from some distant planet. If it wasn't the setting for one of the *Quatermass* films, it should have been. I don't think we ever saw the Manhattan or, if we did, were unable to distinguish it from the many other slightly less large, but still pretty enormous, oil tankers which passed by, but I can still remember the recitation of *Cargoes*. Although her taste in novels tended to the trashy, Mum loved her poetry and was often reciting something or another. Keats was her favourite, closely followed by Rupert Brooke. She obviously had something for those wan young men who died early. Keats' *Give Me Women, Wine and Snuff* was the *Sex and Drugs and Rock and Roll* or *Cigarettes and Alcohol* of its day. The opening lines of *To Autumn* and *The Soldier* are consequently firmly imprinted in my memory.

Hole Haven (top) and Dr Feelgood's 'Down By The Jetty' album cover (bottom), both on Canvey Island. One of these photographs is colour.

At school, we were required to memorise poetry by rote. It is a method of schooling which has long since fallen from favour, and which I predictably found to be a hugely tedious task, but on reflection has many merits. For one, I still remember great chunks of most of those poems. I also understood and appreciated them in a way that I wouldn't have if I had simply read through them as quickly as possible. Christina Rosetti's *Remember* was later to become Mum's favourite poem. Rosetti is of course best known as half of the smash hit writing team Rosetti/Holst that produced *In The Bleak Midwinter* (or at least its first and most famous setting), the Lennon/McCartney of Christmas carol composition. Christina and Gustav of course never met, but the idea of them sitting down together to pen the new Justin Bieber single is a lovely thought. *Remember* is one of the few poems I can still recite from beginning to end. I read it at my mother's funeral. I didn't have the nerve to fly solo without the book open in front of me and just made my way through it before the tears came. *Remember* is a poem I cannot forget.

Jonathan Franzen records the research that the habit of reading is either "*heavily modelled*" because, for example, one or both parents are serious readers or because the reader is a "*social isolate*" - "*the first lesson reading teaches is how to be alone*". The only serious book I can remember in our house was a library copy of William Goldman's *The Inheritors,* which became marooned there after it missed the library deadline and several amnesties on late return of books, so that my mother could not face the shame of such a significant infraction of the library rules. Apart from that, there were some Readers' Digest Condensed Books and the odd Neville Shute in our house, but no significant literature. Looks like the social isolate theory, then. The reading habit endures to this day. Although I temporarily lost it at Oxford, where there were too many other exciting things to do, it soon re-asserted its grip on my life in my mid-twenties. I now have a fear of being on a plane or train without a book to read and am almost never without one, wherever I go. As Groucho Marx once said, "*Outside of a dog, a book is man's best friend. Inside of a dog, it's too dark to read.*"

The Dean and I

1974 was a strange old year. Inflation was at 17%. Brian Clough unaccountably went to manage Leeds United. Lord Lucan disappeared from Belgravia. Manchester United disappeared from the first division. Enoch Powell made his "rivers of blood" speech, even though he never used the phrase "rivers of blood". Gary Glitter released a live album, *Remember Me This Way*. Sadly, we didn't. The darkness imposed by the three-day week provided a valuable new addition to my armoury of excuses for not doing my homework. The return of a Labour government in the February general election put the lights back on and I was forced to fall back on the cat eating my homework. It was also the year that I was caned by the headmaster.

Not actually a cane, in fact an old fashioned six of the best with a good sturdy cricket bat. I noticed that it was from a different generation of cricketing equipment. We all used the new coated Grey Nicholls bats with the scoop out of the back, but his was of a prior vintage, the type that still required regular treatment with linseed oil to keep it in peak condition. He didn't seem to have oiled it for a while. I guess he wasn't worried about getting the occasional edge, damaging the bat. In the event, he played a solid over, without any snicks to the slips. The target was such that he had no trouble middling each shot. There were no rivers of blood but it was eye-wateringly painful and it was indeed a relief when over was called. I never resented him for this, as he delivered the sanction without relish or prurience. It seemed a fair punishment, particularly as I had previously escaped detection for numerous other misdemeanours.

In fact, Richard Sale, the headmaster, had been a first-class cricketer, playing for Derbyshire and Warwickshire as well as opening the batting for Oxford in the Varsity Match. He was a left-hander, although this was not noticeable during corporal punishment. He had a considerable girth and 'Gut' was one of the easier nicknames to remember in the school bully's test. I actually liked him. He certainly wasn't right at the Mr Chips end of the headmaster likeability index, but although appearing pompous, he had a wry and slightly irreverent sense of humour, unlike most of the mediocrities who taught there. He also seemed to have a genuine interest in, and interaction with, the pupils and was involved in their lives in a way that many head teachers neglect these days at the expense of profile raising speeches or fund raising. I eventually established a good relationship with him, joining his small evening literature group. It was a bizarre affair called 'Candlesticks', just ten pupils from the school reading and discussing poetry and drinking sherry. It was the only time you were likely to share an alcoholic drink with the headmaster.

He was one of the few masters I liked or respected at Brentwood. My housemaster, Mr Tarrant, taught Geography, which just about summed him up. He was a tedious time serving bore, without a hint of empathy or humour. He probably saw each day as a chore, relishing the final bell, when he could rush home to inspect his antique garden gnome collection. He was in charge of what laughably passed for careers advice at Brentwood. After the most superficial of aptitude tests, he then asked me to help him fix his pull-down white screen, which seemed to be broken. I did so with some ease and assumed it was a marginally more sophisticated attempt to assess my mechanical abilities. It was only when I compared notes with my peers, who had not been put through this, that I realised that he just couldn't mend his screen himself. I can't remember what his recommendations for my future were but I certainly can recall my recommendations for his. Fortunately, my mother had already identified my skillsets and was gently inculcating the idea in my mind that I was perfectly suited to law. Mr Tarrant was perfectly suited to teaching geography. There were quite a few others like him.

My maths teacher, Mr Williams, described me in my report as "generally bone idle", which was a pretty fair description and corroborated extensively by other teachers. My housemaster added his own acerbic commentary on this evaluation, whilst the headmaster simply stamped the litany of charges with his signature chop, not wearying himself with any more detailed assessment of my performance, which seemed fair and appropriate.

Television reached new lows. *On The Buses* had never been held in particularly high regard, but it seemed like comedy gold compared with its successors, the spin-off *Don't Drink The Water* and a light entertainment variety programme featuring the star of *Buses*, called something like *Reg Varney Entertains*. A more implausible title is difficult to imagine. It was almost light relief to reach the drama of the adverts, where a mysterious man clad in black would undergo a perilous journey by parachute, abseiling and scuba diving to deliver a box of chocolates to the object of his devotions – and all inside thirty seconds. After all that, I hope she didn't leave the hard centres.

The arrival of *Bouquet of Barbed Wire* was a bit of an eye opener. It was neatly positioned in the Sunday night slot previously inhabited by the likes of *The Forsythe Saga*, *The Onedin Line* and *Poldark*, all worthy historical dramas but with little to excite the adolescent teenager. *Bouquet* was cut from a different cloth. It was on a bit later and had lashings of sex. Excitingly, I was also deemed old enough to watch it. I suspect my father disapproved of the content and the permissive regime which had invaded his house and absented himself.

It was a simple story – moody father (Frank Finlay, hamming it up) is in love with daughter and smoulders with jealousy at her recent marriage to oafish American. Father adopts simple and well-road tested expedient of

A typical school report - amongst the tributes are 'generally bone idle' (Maths) and 'he makes few efforts during the term' (Spanish). Richard Sale, the headmaster, abjured further commentary and just disdainfully stamped his chop on the litany of charges. Fair enough.

hiring attractive secretary and then shagging her. Oafish American then shags his mother-in-law. Life is quite complicated by the end of the series and daughter of Finlay/wife of Oafish American dies. There was, however, no actual nudity, just post-coital smoking scenes. This was remedied in the second series, *Another Bouquet*. In the first episode, three breasts are seen (on two different people, not the same person). I couldn't believe my eyes. The oafish American/mother-in-law affair is over, but then father hooks up with oafish American's new girlfriend and oafish American slips one to father's secretary. By the end of the series, all connubial combinations have been exhausted, together with most of the audience. Not the eternal triangle, this was the horny hexagon. At the same time, a similar *La Ronde* was being played out in the world of rock and roll, with Fleetwood Mac at its epicentre. Stevie Nicks (singer) is going out with Lindsey Buckingham (guitarist), but they split and she hooks up with Mick Fleetwood (drummer), whose wife Jenny Boyd[22] had been bonked by Bob Weston (previous guitarist), precipitating his departure from the band. Nicks and Fleetwood split when Fleetwood has an affair with Nicks' best friend, Sara, marrying and divorcing her and then remarrying his ex-wife Jenny and in turn divorcing her again. Stevie Nicks moves on to dalliances with most of the Eagles. Meanwhile, John McVie (bass) and his wife Christine (keyboards, singer) split when she runs off with the band's lighting director and then Dennis Wilson of the Beach Boys, who himself has twice married and divorced the ex-wife of Chicago's keyboard player, Robert Lamm. Dennis dies. This psychodrama was accompanied by industrial quantities of cocaine (Mick Fleetwood estimating his own lifetime intake to be a line seven miles long), brandy and other stimulants.

I have never much liked prog rock. The one exception is King Crimson. *In the Court of the Crimson King*, with its distinctive red face cover, was essential musical arm candy in the years 1970-3. The lyrics were overblown nonsense, but accompanied by good tunes, from the folksy *I Talk To The Wind* to never heard anything like it before or since and truly scary *21st Century Schizoid Man*. I have no less than seven different versions of *Schizoid Man* on my iPod, which is probably at the light end for serious Crimso fans. Their 1972-4 incarnation was the high point, with some truly breath-taking music. If you think you don't like that sort of thing, check out the first four minutes of *Starless* from their final studio album *Red*. It's beautiful. Admittedly, it does then turn into a bit of a prog widdle-fest. Robert Fripp is my favourite guitarist. Totally unique. His guitar playing on Bowie's *Heroes* makes the song. Ditto *Fashion*. Crimson split in 1974, leaving behind a great live album *USA*, concluding as they came in with a version of *Schizoid Man*.

---

[22] *Sister of Patti Boyd, herself the subject of an eternal triangle with George Harrison and Eric Clapton.*

For me, Crimson were pretty much the single shining light of prog. Yes had released no less than ten sides of 12" vinyl in 1973 - the three disk bloated live indulgence *Yessongs* and the preposterous double album *Tales From Topographic Oceans,* which contained exactly what their customer base seemed to demand: four twenty minute songs, each taking up the whole of a side, with titles like *The Revealing Science of God (Dance of the Dawn)* and lyrics like *nous sommes du soleil.* Even with my limited interest in my French studies, I knew this was nonsense. Keyboard player Rick Wakeman expressed himself dissatisfied with the length and pomp of *Tales* and left the band. Fans were left expecting taut three minute songs and a stripped down sound from Rick, but he then released the single long track concept album *Journey To The Centre of the Earth* and continued wearing a cape on stage. He later staged *King Arthur and the Knights of the Round Table* on ice at Wembley Arena. Yes' 1974 offering, the three-track single album *Relayer,* seemed like a model of concision by comparison.

Then there was Emerson Lake & Palmer. Sigh. They are, in my view, a band entirely without merit. At least Yes had some melodic sensibilities which enabled them to produce half-way decent songs like *Your Move* and *And You and I.* One of my mates used to work for Warners and once sent me some factory seconds, one of which was an ELP retrospective box set. Open minded, I decided that it was time to re-assess the work of ELP. It was a sorry old listen, with not a single decent track and capped with each member of the band performing a new version of a piece by his previous band. Greg Lake was in the original line up of King Crimson, but the world really did not need yet another (and crap) version of *Schizoid Man.* It is not one of the seven on my iPod. I could find no signs of damage to the packaging of the box set, so concluded that it must have been the quality of the music contained therein which led to it being classed as a factory second. Following the theory that monkeys hitting typewriter keys randomly will eventually write the complete works of Shakespeare, even the most useless bands generally contrive to write one half way decent track. ELP, however, have produced excrement without exception and in 1974, no doubt observing Yes's grandiose gesture, their latest release of effluent was another six side live album, *Welcome Back My Friends To The Show That Never Ends,* and, boy, did it stink. Fortunately, this preceded a period of musical constipation and was the last we heard of ELP for another three years, although Alan 'Fluff' Freeman (having abandoned his chart rundown intro of "hi there pop pickers" for his new prog president hail of "greetings music lovers") was still playing *Karn Evil 9* when the rest of the world was listening to the Pistols and the Clash. Not 'arf, Fluff.

In the early seventies, if you were a teenage girl, you liked either Donny Osmond or David Cassidy, but not both. Boys generally hated both without discrimination. Donny had a red corduroy cap and a voice yet to break. David had a dreamy look, a girl's haircut and some predictable hankerings to be a serious musician. Laura had previously tormented me with her recorder playing, her repertoire consisting of only one tune, *Cader Idris,* an isolated mountain in Wales, which suggested itself strongly as a possible future venue for her practices. This was replaced in 1973 by David Cassidy's *Dreams Are Nuthin' More Than Wishes.* At the time, having heard Donny's *Puppy Love,* I was thankful she was in the David, and not Donny, camp (although, proving the monkeys and typewriters theory, the Osmonds made two great singles[23]), but my mood soon turned as David was on 24/7 saturation rotation. *Daydreamer* was a pleasant enough song (without which Wham's *Last Christmas* would probably not exist) but I dreaded the arrival of his versions of *Bali Hai* and *Fever,* which still produced a reflexive gagging reaction in my throat when I listened to them when writing this.

By 1974, Cassidy was on the wane and the latest teen sensation were the Bay City Rollers. There were hordes of Rollers fans, all wearing ridiculous tartan scarves and half-mast trousers. The arrival of *Rollin'* in Laura's bedroom was not a welcome development and, within weeks, I found myself hankering after David Cassidy's long awaited six album set of the complete works of Rodgers and Hammerstein. The insipid, soulless noise that emanated from her room drove me to depths of despair previously only encountered by Leonard Cohen fans. The relentless repetition of *Shang-A-Lang* and *Summerlove Sensation* should be seriously considered by the men who stare at goats as the ultimate psychological torture weapon. Laura was unyielding, pointing out that two members of the band, Eric Faulkner and Stuart 'Woody' Wood (no relation to Ronnie 'Woody' Wood, although both had long black feather cuts and a gormless expression), had written some of the songs on the album themselves, as though this were conclusive evidence of talent. The Rollers came and went, dissolving into a morass of fiscal chicanery, bankruptcy suits and road accidents. They remain largely unloved to this day and you are more likely to hear Rolf Harris' *Two Little Boys* on the radio.

Music seemed a bleak landscape. Look at the UK chart toppers for 1974 and it will give you some measure of the gravity of the situation – the New Seekers, Alvin Stardust (if you're not familiar with his work, the name tells you all you need to know), the Rubettes (ditto), Mud, the Osmonds, Carl Douglas' one off hit *Kung Fu Fighting* and so on. Even Suzi Quatro's leather clad charms were beginning to wear off. T. Rex were a spent force. Mott The Hoople had split and Free had splintered the previous year, bowing out with the glorious *Wishing Well.* New band Bad Company was assembled from promising ingredients, with the remnants of Free teaming up with former members of Mott and King Crimson, but proved to be a poor

---

[23] *'Crazy Horses' – featuring Donny's standout ribbon controller work to make that wailing noise – and 'Goin' Home'.*

substitute for any of them, quickly descending into lame cock-rock bluster. Bowie was commencing one of those periods that everyone subsequently professed to love *(Diamond Dogs/Young Americans)* but few did at the time, particularly after they had heard *David Live*.

It seemed ridiculous to hope that the Eurovision Song Contest would provide any respite from the continuum of musical tedium, but old habits die hard, and we all sat down to watch it as usual. The UK's entry was Olivia Newton-John singing *Long Live Love,* which seemed to confirm this. Luxembourg had won it two years on the trot and their economy could not bear the expense of hosting the contest for a second year, so Britain agreed to stage it in Brighton. It looked like being another routine contest with the usual roster of mawkish balladry and boom bang a bang trash, until about half way through, when an actual band came on, accompanied by an orchestra conducted by Napoleon (Bonaparte not Solo). The two blokes looked like garden gnomes but the girls were one of the most exciting things that I had seen on Eurovision. They were all wearing the most absurd clothes, with the blonde being clad in blue satin that was satisfyingly tight in all the right places. The temperature rose considerably in our living room. Even more surprising was the noise they were making. *Waterloo* blasted out, sounding like the nearest thing to a proper rock band that Eurovision was likely to achieve in the 70s and was catchy as hell. They were clear winners. Abba had entered our lives. I got out my tennis racket to master the moves and wondered how I could replicate the exploding star-shaped guitar that one of the gnomes was playing.

I was a bit disappointed at the levels of enthusiasm on the school bus on Monday morning. Yes, the consensus concluded, it was catchy, but it was just Eurovision pop. Besides, Robin Trower had a new album out and he is the natural heir to Hendrix, David Coverdale is far better than Ian Gillan in Purple etc etc. Abba hung around for a few weeks and everyone then naturally assumed they would go the usual way of Eurovision and be quickly filed under 'where are they now?'

This looked to be the way it would go as successive singles failed to follow the success of *Waterloo* in the UK charts. Then one morning I heard a glorious song, direct from the gods, on the Radio 1 breakfast show. Noel Edmonds probably talked over the beautiful opening flanged piano part, but then a wonderful mournful, slightly teutonic and pure vocal entered : *'Where are those happy days, they seem so hard to find'*. Even Noel wouldn't dare chat over that. It was *SOS* by Abba[24]. I had not bought a single since my one and only purchase of *Mama We're All Crazee Now*, preferring to deploy my limited resources on my *mfp* budget collection, but I had to buy this. I can still remember the yellow and black Epic label. I played it to death. The

---

[24] *The only hit single where both the artist and title are palindromes. In case you're worried for my sanity, no, I haven't done an exhaustive check of the charts since records began, but I do believe this to be the case.*

intricacies of the production gradually unfolded and my love for it increased. It is a perfect pop record, a combination of brilliant song, fantastic production and beautiful vocal performance, with that rather precise diction, probably borne out of singing in a foreign language. Anyone attempting a cover version of *SOS* should be sectioned. Stand up, Pierce Brosnan. Abba's subsequent appearance on Top of the Pops revealed the vocalist to be the blonde one, Agnetha. It was love. It is still my favourite Abba single and in my own personal top five songs of all time. I have never attempted to write down my top five songs of all time, but am confident that *SOS* would be in there. *SOS* heralded the beginning of Abba's world domination and they returned with a string of great pop songs, peppered with the odd turkey like *Fernando, I Have A Dream* and *Chiquitita*. Their dress sense hadn't improved from their Eurovision appearance – a gobsmacking collection of leotards, capes, dungarees and thigh length boots, all made from satin and silver foil – and that was just Benny and Bjorn, the gnomes. We now know that their ridiculous clothing was a product of their manager Stig Anderson's far-sighted fiscal planning. The Swedish tax laws provided that only if an item of clothing purchased for show business use was so ridiculous that it wouldn't be worn in a public setting, could it be deducted as an allowable business expense. Even by the sartorial standards of the mid-70s, where huge flares and hang gliding capable lapels adorned with sequins were the norm, Abba's stage clothes cleared this bar with some ease. If only the Bay City Rollers had been this financially astute. Their tartan trews would have also passed the test and it might have saved them from bankruptcy.

 I continued to love Abba. There were many highlights. *The Winner Takes It All* is one of them and is often voted the public's favourite Abba song. Agnetha was in charge of the sad lyric (apparently a late change from Bjorn as lead vocalist – thank god). The video shows that by then Abba were financially secure enough to dispense with fiscal planning and the ridiculous clothes have gone. It is unclear whether the perm from hell that Agnetha is sporting was part of one of the new generation of Stig Anderson tax schemes. None of this detracts from a beautiful performance reflecting the emotional tremors of their personal lives. By the end, their popularity was waning, but even then they were making great records. Their penultimate single, *The Day Before You Came*, from 1982, didn't even make the Top 30, but it was a superlative record and my favourite Abba single after *SOS*, with another plaintive Agnetha vocal and beautiful melody.

 Even the misbegotten cinema offering *Abba: The Movie* could not dampen my enthusiasm. I was surprised that it got the popular vote amongst my friends for our Friday night film trip, but Agnetha's recent receipt of the UK "rear of the year" award might have influenced them more than the musical content. Previous democratically selected films had included *Confessions of a Window Cleaner* and Anouska Hempel cracking a whip as the dominatrix owner of an early 19th century black slave plantation

An early prototype of Abba's tax avoidance program. The Malmo tax inspector simply had to accept that these clothes could not be worn in normal life.

in Russ Meyer's *Slaves*. It seemed churlish for us to complain about the anachronism of Anouska's black zip boots. The Abba movie was pretty much par for the course for rock films of that era - patch together some concert footage with the odd fantasy sequence and a threadbare plot and hey presto you've got yourself a rock movie. To be honest, the laughable storyline involving a journalist's frustrated attempts to get an interview with the band really didn't matter. We got to see Abba playing all their best songs (and quite a few of their dodgy ones where one of the two gnomes sang, like *Rock Me* – you just know from the title that it's going to be awful). I might not have managed to see the Beatles at the Romford ABC but Abba was a good second best. My friends were satisfied with the extensive coverage of Agnetha's rear and concurred with the award jury.

Funfairs were regular visitors to Hornchurch but Mum viewed them with suspicion as places where unsavoury individuals would hang out, particularly in the evening. We were never allowed to go to them unaccompanied. There was muttering about gypsies and other slurs on ethnic groups that was most uncharacteristic of my mother. In the summer of 1974, I managed to persuade her that, at the age of 15, I should be allowed to fly solo at a fun fair which had come to Harrow Lodge Park. It was not literally on the other side of the tracks, but I knew that Mum only acceded to the relentless teenage pressure with considerable misgivings. When Julian and I arrived there, we could understand my mother's hesitancy. There was an atmosphere of menace, with lots of groups of threatening looking youths roaming ferally and on the hunt for some softies to duff up. We may as well have had "softies" tattooed on our foreheads in large letters. We were in enemy territory and it was only a matter of time before our position was discovered and shelling would commence. Even Julian, who usually affected a posture of rakish confidence, looked concerned. I was even more concerned when I noticed that Julian was looking concerned. Our dignity demanded, however, that we should go on a few hairy rides and then, our honour satisfied, withdraw under cover of darkness to the comfort of our leafy enclave.

After doing the mandatory big wheel, which was satisfyingly fast and the sort of thing that would make me seriously sick now, we decided to finish off with the centrifuge tube. I had only ever seen a centrifuge inside the school chemistry lab and wondered how it would translate into a fairground ride. Were there any emulsions in my body which might be separated by inserting myself into a centrifuge?

My scientific concerns set aside, we both climbed aboard. One feature of this centrifuge, as distinct from the laboratory version, is that its motion was accompanied by fearsomely loud music. As our ride commenced, a fantastically in your face guitar riff blasted out, followed by a huge and catchy song. By the end of the song I was exhilarated, mainly because of the breath-taking volume of the music, which combined rock components with a tuneful pop sensibility, but also because I was now upside down and most of the contents of my pockets were in free float around me. As we staggered from the human chemistry experiment, the necessity of finding a pipeline back to the free world was temporarily forgotten as I yelled at Julian "What was that record?" He didn't know but further enquiry exposed it as *The Wall Street Shuffle* by 10cc. I didn't see any tattooed ladies, but from the caravan I'd heard the fairground band. I have never since listened to it at such volume, or indeed inverted, but it never ceases to give me a little bit of the thrill I first experienced. We exited Harrow Lodge Park with our ears ringing just as the enemy search dogs were set loose.

I had first seen 10cc on Top of the Pops singing *Donna* and dismissed it as a weedy novelty single, but when they returned in the spring of 1973 with *Rubber Bullets* I liked the sound of them. It was eventually banned, not because of the line *"we all got balls and brains but some's got balls and chains"*, which the BBC missed, but because they thought it must be about the troubles in Northern Ireland, which it is clearly not. One wonders whether the BBC ever listened to the records it was playing. The follow up, *The Dean And I*, was a great favourite in the front row of the top deck of the school bus, where we would sing along with the tuneful guitar riff. The school bus was a central part of our lives. It was a decommissioned old style double decker which would take us the eight miles to school, with a conductor who wore a grubby mac and we all thought was about sixty but was probably only around thirty, such is the inability of children to distinguish between ages of anyone over 21. I got on at the first stop and dutifully went up to the front seats of the top deck, with my transistor radio. By the time that the bus pulled away from the Upminster Bridge Station stop, the party was in full swing, with Tony Blackburn, and in later years Noel Edmonds, in charge. The school bus party often got out of control as the prefects struggled to contain the merriment, ultimately leading to my appointment with the headmaster's willow. Tony Blackburn was well past his sell by date by the time he retired from the breakfast show – he had not yet reached the ignominy of pleading on air for his separated wife Tessa (who had also had enough of him by then) to return, accompanied by a play of Chicago's popular stinker *If You Leave Me Now*, but he was well on the way. It may seem strange now to those raised hating his smug countenance, but Noel Edmonds was, by comparison with Blackburn, a breath of fresh air. The fact that he was an alumnus of our school didn't even enter into the equation. His show had some funny segments, he played better music than Blackburn (admittedly a low bar then) and although it inevitably became stale, he never plumbed the depths of that arch-bore Dave Lee Travis.

DLT (as he styled himself) was never remotely entertaining. Contrived and tedious segments like snooker on the radio, coupled with mind-numbingly dull waffling, impossibly irritating and witless ideas like Chip the Robot and shocking music (apparently borne out of a complete musical disinterest), rendered him a no-go area for any remotely discerning listener. The case of *R v The Hairy Cornflake* is now concluded with a suspended sentence, but if I had been his lawyer, I would have advised him to ask for 10,000 other oral offences to be taken into consideration. The prosecution should have brought damning evidence of endless wittering about his Swedish wife and his farm, a cut and dried case of being dull with malice aforethought. His comedy record *Convoy GB*, created with fellow witless bore Radio 1 DJ Paul Burnett, under the amusing name of *Laurie Lingo and the Dipsticks* (they were both certainly the latter), was the apogee of DLT's folie de grandeur. Never mind Operation Yewtree, that was his first criminal record.

When the 10cc follow-up to *The Dean and I,* the too complicated and hookless for radio (and an insane choice for a single) *Worst Band In The World,* bombed, it looked as though 10cc were destined for the bargain bins. *Wall Street Shuffle* was a brilliant return and when the next single *Silly Love* sounded like heavy rock and there was talk at school about 10cc's new album being really good, I knew it was time to splash out on a proper full-price album. *Sheet Music,* the resulting purchase, did not disappoint and is still one of my favourite records. 10cc were never again as consistently good. Its successor, *The Original Soundtrack,* was hugely uneven despite containing their flagship hit. Like *SOS, I'm Not In Love* is not a song that anyone should ever attempt to cover. If you doubt this, check out Petula Clark blasting her way through it on YouTube. 10cc can themselves confirm this, as they fruitlessly attempted a stripped-down cover version of their own masterpiece in their years of decline. The song itself is not, on paper, a classic – try playing it on the piano – but the ground-breaking production, utilising massed overdubbed vocals, looped on tape and mixed through the desk to form chords, years before the advent of samplers, combined with a beautifully restrained lead vocal – make it a truly brilliant single. Over-exposure as the slow song at the end of teenage discos in the 70s dulled its appeal and, once it had been heard accompanying Joan Collins' bottom moving underneath Oliver Tobias on the soundtrack of uber-cheese movie *The Stud,* the song was indelibly tarnished. It was also the first of a series of six-minute singles which became de rigeur in the mid-seventies. Whilst we might smile with post-modern ironic indulgence at *Bohemian Rhapsody,* there are no such fond thoughts for John Miles' *Music,* the reductio ad absurdum of the genre, a record designed to be a classic but just ending up as a self-important oversized turkey[25].

One of the more enlightened members of the school music cognoscenti (the majority had a self-denying ordinance of confinement to Uriah Heep, The Groundhogs, Cream, Led Zep and their kin), Andy Gill (not the Gang of Four guitarist or the NME journalist, but a thoroughly good bloke), spoke enthusiastically of having seen 10cc at the Chancellor Hall in Chelmsford and that they had started with a ten minute version of *Silly Love* and encored with a fifteen minute *Rubber Bullets* and were very loud. This was good. Andy wasn't so enlightened that he had completely

---

[25] *The other paradigm example of a record contrived to be a classic, but ending up at the other end of the spectrum, is of course 'Classic' by Adrian Gurvitz, possibly the worst record ever made. 'Gotta write a classic/ Gotta write it in an attic/ Baby I'm an addict now' bleats Adrian. Well, first thing, if you've gotta write a classic, try and find better rhymes than 'attic' and 'addict'. 'Jurassic' (possibly a sly reference to his rock dinosaur background – check out the Baker Gurvitz Army) and 'thoracic' would have been no more contrived to fit into the narrative of the lyric than 'attic', and at least rhyme properly. Better still, just don't call your song 'Classic' in the first place. The follow-up was called 'Clown', which far better describes Adrian and his oeuvre than its predecessor.*

thrown of the shackles of heavy rock orthodoxy. It was time, I concluded, for me to see 10cc live.

It was not my first gig. At the age of 16 I was deemed old enough to go to a concert. I never called it a "gig" lest I risk dispelling my parents' illusion that the band would come on and sit behind music stands and receive polite applause from the audience between each movement of their masterworks. This was probably what happened at Yes and ELP performances, but it was not what I had in mind. So in October 1975 I went to see the Who at Wembley Arena. They were awesome but our seats right at the back rather gave the impression of watching people watching a rock concert. These were the days before big screens and Pete Townshend was just a small object in the distance. I could make out some flurry of activity, which I took to be his trademark wind-milling guitar playing. No amps or instruments were destroyed so far as I could tell from squinting towards the distant stage. It was however an exciting introduction to the world of live rock, but I made a mental note of caution about large venues. I still rarely go to enormodomes, unless the band is really special.

The Who's Wembley performance was surpassed the following year when they played at the Valley, the home of Charlton Athletic F.C. It was an all day gig and we wanted to get our full money's worth, so arrived promptly. We hit our first setback early on. There was a booze ban and we were given the choice of drinking all our supply or surrendering it at the gate. We predictably went for the first option. Our drinking chores complete, we entered during the first act, Widowmaker. My conscientious pre-gig research told me that they featured ex-Mott guitarist Ariel Bender and former Love Affair lead singer Steve Ellis. They came bearing unremarkable standard issue rock and I found myself hankering for *Everlasting Love*. Chapman-Whitney Streetwalkers were reasonable, as the electric goat Roger Chapman growled his way through the set. They played the old Family song *My Friend The Sun* but sadly their friend didn't turn up all day as the drizzle continued. I don't recollect anything about the Outlaws as the alcohol had kicked in by this stage and I had entered a comatose slumber. I awoke in time for Little Feat, who were much fancied at this point, but were too laid back even for my recumbent state. I don't think they played their then current single, *Long Distance Love*, which I liked, although I might have lapsed back into my stupor and missed it. The only excitement of their set was generated by a spaced loon illegally climbing the floodlights.

The Sensational Alex Harvey Band at least brought a bit of showmanship and vim to the proceedings, by which time, learning the lesson of Wembley, my group had made their thrust for the front of the stage and were pretty close to what would later be called the mosh pit. The Who were simply extraordinary – very loud and very exciting. It was in fact recorded in the Guinness Book of Records for many years as the loudest gig of all time – over 120 decibels - pain threshold - at 50 yards. We were closer than 50 yards. We didn't notice any pain, other than severe dehydration and throbbing in our temples that were the aftermath of our cider binge. The finale was stupendous – *Won't Get Fooled Again* with a multitude of laser beams bounced off dishes on the four floodlights. I looked upwards to check whether the spaced loon was still there and, if so, whether he had fallen prey to a Goldfinger-like sticky end. Still one of my top five gigs of all time. Again, I haven't done the list but I'm sure it could accommodate the Who at Charlton.

My first opportunity to see 10cc came in early 1976 when they were touring their last album by the original line-up, *How Dare You!* My school was a single sex boys school, but in 1975 there was a revolution. Two girls were admitted to the sixth form, just as I was joining it. One of them, Lucy, I quite liked. I had never been on a date with a girl and I could tell my mother was beginning to get a bit concerned about my development. There had been a pre-adolescent kiss with Judith, a girl from down the road and in my early teens I had been pretty keen on Sally, a girl from the housing development built at the back of our house, who had a Suzi Quatro style feather cut, a tight tie-dye top and some jeans flared by adding a piece of material to widen the bottom. She was great and, in retrospect, I recognize from the regularity of her visits to our house that she was pretty keen on me. She was, however, added to then nascent, but later extraordinarily long, list of girls I have failed to make a move on when the circumstances demanded it.

I planned my assault on Lucy meticulously, luring her into a date to go and see the film *Earthquake,* which was still showing in Romford, despite having been released the previous year. I had already seen it with my mother and my description of the Sensurround vibration effects accompanying the film was enticing enough to get Lucy's interest. By the end of the date, it was clear that it was the Sensurround she was interested in, not me, and the simulation of an earthquake under my lower half was the only action I was going to see that evening. The earth was not going to move any further.

I did, however, persevere and, adopting similar methodology as for the first date, dangled the lure of going to see 10cc at Hammersmith Odeon. The fish bit instantly and was hooked. 10cc were supported by Chas and Dave, whom I have never liked. The only other time I saw Chas and Dave was at White Hart Lane, when they came on at half time to mime to *Ain't No Pleasing You*, a really grisly noise. When it was announced immediately after the final whistle that they would return to "do a few more numbers", the stadium cleared quicker than I have ever seen.

Maybe it was that my concentration was on reducing the physical distance between Lucy and me in as covert manner as possible, but 10cc were a little disappointing. They started well but once it became clear they were going to play the whole of their new album, rarely a sound strategy, the audience's attention was being strained. By the end of *I'm Mandy Fly Me*, it had become obvious that Lucy had refused clearance for take-off and I was taxiing back to the terminal building. We had a repeat *Earthquake* scenario here. 10cc closed with *I'm Not In Love*, my lip trembling with the shared sentiments of the song. It doesn't mean you mean that much to me, even if I have invited you to both *Earthquake* and 10cc. I certainly hoped she wouldn't tell her friends about the two of us. A final *Wall Street Shuffle* and *Rubber Bullets* lifted my spirits slightly and I slunk into the night.

Fortunately, that was not my last experience of 10cc live. It was announced some months later that the Rolling Stones would be playing Knebworth. More importantly, they would be supported by 10cc. My mates and I decided we had to go. The drizzle of Charlton in May was the last we would see for some time, as the summer of 1976 was the driest, warmest and sunniest of the 20th century, with a period of 25 consecutive days when the temperature was in the 80s fahrenheit. I remember I was reading *The Death of Grass* by John Christopher and the sci-fi fantasy of the book seemed to be being acted out. On August 21 at Knebworth, it was still hot and dry and what seemed like perfect festival weather. We had arrived at the Knebworth site in the early hours of the morning, anxious to stake out our pitch near the front. With the excitement levels well into the red, we didn't get much sleep but bound into the festival grounds as soon as the gates opened. We spread our groundsheets and other territory-marking ephemera over a wildly optimistic area. It should have been clear that this was a salient that could not be held against even marginal pressure against our unguarded flanks, but all our energies went into holding our patch of land. It was the Rorke's Drift of Knebworth Park.

The day started promisingly with the Don Harrison Band, but only in the sense that no successful hostile incursion had been attempted onto our patch. The band was awful. They boasted the former rhythm section of Credence Clearwater Revival. Apart from Steely Dan, Credence were one of the few American bands that I liked, a short list comprising just them and the Band. Both seemed to me to be the only US bands which spoke with an authentic American voice. Little did I know that both were slightly fake; Credence's swampy grooves were borne not of the bayou but the bay – San Francisco rather than Louisiana; all bar one of the Band were Canadian, not American, true Acadian driftwood. This did not make them any less enjoyable. Authenticity is a much overrated concept. Who after all, would have known that the sun drenched vibe of the first two Eagles albums was captured in rainy London - in Olympic Studios in Barnes - because producer Glyn Johns refused to go to California? Sleeping in the desert tonight was not an option. They'd just have to hitch a tent on Barnes Common. The Credence representation in the Don Harrison Band was an illusory benefit and a demonstration of why John Fogerty was very sensible to monopolise the songwriting in Credence.

Hot Tuna produced some long jamming and guitar and bass virtuosity, which would normally have been tedious in the extreme but a fifteen-minute version of *Rock Me Baby* seemed to be just what the mood demanded, as we sprawled in the hot sun. More ominously, our increased relaxation had allowed the first incursion into our space and we reluctantly ceded a corner of our empire to the newcomers. I quite liked Todd Rundgren, who had made some good records like *I Saw The Light* and the *Love Of The Common Man* single released earlier that year. Sadly, in the short space of time after the release of that record, Todd had morphed into a wannabee prog rock god, with his set peppered with songs with titles that sounded as if they had come from a comedy psychedelic parody, like *Communion With The Sun*. Todd had his Spinal Tap moment when *Hiroshima* ended with a pathetic minor explosion, which rather understated the enormity of the subject matter, in much the same way as a miniature Stonehenge which could be crushed by dwarves. I don't want to make a big thing of it, but maybe he should have done. Todd at least played *Love Of The Common Man* and then unexpectedly ended with a cover of the Move's *Do Ya*. I reflexively reached for my Dunlop Maxply, but had left it at home.

It really didn't matter whether you liked Lynyrd Skynyrd. They were great. Exactly what the afternoon required. We were on our feet, dancing wildly during *T For Texas*, but in all the excitement a great chunk of our lebensraum was gone, fallen without us doing justice to the song with an Alamo-like stand. "Don't let that flag touch the floor," warned Skynyrd singer Ronnie Von Zandt to a group in front of us waving the ensign of the confederacy, whilst the yankee carpetbaggers who had invaded our space sat contentedly on their newly acquired homestead. An epic *Freebird* sweetened the pill.

There was an interminable wait for 10cc as they attempted to sort sound problems. To relieve the boredom, someone invaded the stage naked and played with his willy. Perhaps it was the chap who climbed the floodlights at Charlton. A local newspaper later artfully reported that "during a technical delay at Knebworth, a young man had entertained the crowd single-handedly". Mick Jagger later rode a giant inflatable phallus, but this was far more entertaining. When they eventually came on, 10cc started with *One Night In Paris,* a lengthy multi part piece not ideal for dancing. It was a suicidal choice. The crowd were restless. 10cc just managed to pull the plane up before it hit the cliff, as they apprehended the demands of the situation and delivered a guitar-heavy rocking set, well stocked with hits. I thought they were magnificent. The closing *I'm Not In Love* was magical, the perfect accompaniment to a warm summer night. I sang along and thought briefly of Lucy, now a distant memory and just a silly phase I was going through. By the time that 10cc encored with *Rubber Bullets,* strangers were trampling on our possessions and the last remaining fragments of our territory had fallen. We were idiot dancing and didn't care. The Rolling

Stones came on at around 11.30. We were knackered and the Stones failed to rouse us. They were sloppy and lacked edge. The Stones were best when they had two complementary guitarists. Ronnie Wood was just a more slapdash copy of Keef and the resulting sound was a muddy mess. I saw them again in 1982 and they were even worse.

Within months, 10cc had split. Gouldman and Stewart would continue with diminishing returns under the name 10cc. Godley and Crème went off to make a triple album featuring their newly invented instrument, the Gizmo, which was attached to the guitar, bowing its strings and sounding vaguely like an electronic string machine. The separate elements of 10cc never added up to, at best, more than about 7.5cc. They were the classic band where the whole was greater than the sum of the parts. Four members who could sing (each one of them had at some point sung lead on a top ten single, three of them singing number ones), write and play a variety of instruments, and all brought something different to the party. Once they had established a 10cc formula and fell into a groove, the party was over. Most people would describe 10cc as a guilty pleasure. I've never accepted the concept of musical guilty pleasures, except for a brief period in the year zero of punk, when the Stalinist regime required you to disavow any counter-revolutionary disks. It goes hand in hand with the half-baked notion of authenticity. "It's got to come from the heart, man," you can hear some tedious hipster intoning, whilst fingering through his collection consisting entirely of Ornette Coleman, Mississippi John Hurt, Roedelius and Augustus Pablo[26]. It doesn't matter where it comes from, it's where it goes to that counts. If it hits the spot, it just doesn't matter who sang it. Some of the greatest records have come from some of the most unlikely and least street credible sources.

There were a couple of small postscripts to my 10cc story.

I bought the Godley and Creme triple album, a brave thing to do in 1977, though not as brave as releasing it in the first place. It was a bizarre package, and hopelessly indulgent, but contained a few wonderful songs. Check out *Five O'Clock In The Morning* or *Lost Weekend,* the latter a beautiful duet between Godley and Sarah Vaughan. Against my better judgment, I continued with the Gouldman/Stewart 10cc. I tried to like the next album *Deceptive Bends,* but it was just two guys desperately trying to be 10cc. After having seen them live at Hammersmith (another disappointment, playing nearly all of the new album again), I wrote a truly nerdy fan letter to Gouldman and Stewart, suggesting, amongst other things, a title for the live album that I had read they were considering. I thought no more of this and had moved on, when in the summer of 1977 my mother shouted up the

---

[26] *To be fair, I own recordings by each of these artists, but a record collection consisting solely of them would be a truly soul destroying experience.*

stairs to me that there was someone on the phone for me.

'Who is it?' I shouted back down, showing no inclination to come down until I had the answer.

'Graham Gouldman,' she shouted back.

'Graham who?' I yelled. I didn't know any Grahams.

'GRAHAM GOULDMAN,' came the increasingly irritated reply.

A moment's hesitation, as I processed the information just communicated to me. I couldn't have got down those stairs quicker if a tiger had been loosed in my bedroom. Yes, it was the real Graham Gouldman and we had a fifteen-minute conversation, me being the nerd supreme who knows more about the band than its members. He was hugely optimistic about 10cc's future and, yes, they were going to use my title for their live album. What a nice man. He secured my support for 10cc for another couple of years, where otherwise I would have given up. They had another number one the following year with *Dreadlock Holiday*. I don't like reggae, I love it but I hated this and, yes, I would like something harder, by now preferring the Clash's account of a scary encounter in Jamaica, *Safe European Home*, to 10cc's version, but I was pleased that Graham had got to sing a number one. Graham Gouldman still gets my personal prize for nicest rock star – this is the man who wrote hits for the Yardbirds, the Hollies, Jeff Beck and others, as well as writing three number one singles for 10cc, and he can still be bothered personally to phone a fan. The live album eventually came out. To my dismay, it was a double, totally unnecessarily including all tracks bar one from the last album. It was pretty awful. My title *Live And Let Live* was, in retrospect, scarcely more inspired. In the unlikely event that you ever come into the presence of this record, check out the credits. I'm there. Only on the original vinyl – I bought the CD when writing this and I've been excised from history for the digital era. It may be one of the least auspicious albums of all time to have your name on, but thank you, Graham.

In the summer of 2006 I went to see the Producers (Trevor Horn, former 10cc member Lol Creme and others) play a gig in Camden. It was almost exactly 30 years after Knebworth. They played *Rubber Bullets* as an encore. The band hung out at the bar afterwards. Ever the fanboy, I went up to Lol Creme to tell him that the last time I had heard him sing *Rubber Bullets* was almost thirty years ago to the day at Knebworth.

'Funny that – that's the last time I sang it,' he replied.

A bit like Woodstock, Knebworth felt to me like the peak, and at the same time the end, of an era. Three days after Knebworth, Dennis Howell was appointed Minister for Drought, which did the trick, and, within days, thunderstorms brought heavy rain and flooding. Denis Howell was then appointed Minster for Floods, which also did the trick.[27] Just as the thunderstorms broke a few days later, you could soon feel that a musical change was in the air and a storm was coming. It felt like we'd never be able to lie in a field in the hot sun, drinking cider and listening to a fifteen-minute guitar solo, ever again.

Richard Sale retired as headmaster of Brentwood in 1981, four years after I left. I wrote to him in the year he retired, just after I left Oxford, to let him know what I was doing and planning to do. Characteristically, he wrote a nice reply. He died in 1987, aged 67.

---

[27] *Denis Howell was also appointed Minister for Snow during the harsh winter of 1978-9 but by then he had lost his touch and the heavy snowfall continued.*

God Save The Queen

"Is she really going out with him?" quizzed the lead singer in a spoken word introduction.

The words were familiar, having been the first line of the Shangri-Las' *Leader of the Pack,* but what followed bore little resemblance to the girl group's biker drama. Thunderous primal drums came crashing in, followed by the sort of brutish guitar you rarely got to hear on records around this time. *"I got a feeling inside of me,"* he continued, now singing, but with an urgency and lack of concern for pitching which was unusual. The noise was completely primitive, and not immediately wholly attractive, if you were used to the glossy and manicured sounds then prevalent in 1976. It wasn't a howl of social protest or manifesto for the revolution but a straightforward love song. It was, however, alien and undeniably exciting.

This was *New Rose* by the Damned. It was the first UK punk single, released in October 1976. Two minutes 45 seconds was barely enough time for ELP to inspect the vintage Persian carpet on the stage to confirm it is in accordance with the specifications of their rider or for Rick Wakeman to strap on his cape, let alone commence playing their latest side long spew of drivel. It was, however, the perfect length for a single. It was being played on the sixth form common room stereo by Kim Davis, one of my schoolmates. Kim had eclectic left field musical tastes, which I had always found interesting. He liked things like Steely Dan before anyone else and I attached myself to his musical wagon train and enjoyed the ride. He had lent me a few Kevin Ayers albums a few years earlier and I had grown to love the louche baritone and his gloriously idiosyncratic songs. Every time that success was starting to look like a possibility, Ayers would sabotage it or bunk off back to Ibiza until his wine and weed supply ran out. The high point of his popularity was probably the June 1, 1974 Rainbow concert, where he enlisted the high profile aid of Eno, Nico and John Cale. He prepared for the event by sleeping with the latter's wife, which ensured there was no shortage of artistic tension in the air. It was entirely characteristic that Kim would be the first to catch on to punk. He ultimately became a writer for the NME and was passionate about his music.

We then flipped the record over and found what sounded to be a massive two fingers up to the conservative music establishment, a fantastically rowdy trashing of the Beatles' *Help*. Where John Lennon had wished that the Beatles had recorded *Help* as a slower song, the Damned instead thrashed through it at breakneck speed, with little semblance of melody. It drew some disapproving howls of protest from corners of the common room. I wasn't completely converted immediately, and was certainly not ready to disavow 10cc, but it was a truly startling racket and it was clear that there was something in the air. A few weeks later Kim produced *We Vibrate* by the Vibrators, which was fun but seemed a bit lightweight in comparison, suffering in image terms by being on Mickie Most's RAK label, home to Smokie, Mud, Racey and Herman's Hermits. The B side, *Whips and Furs,* was more like it. There was a strong whiff of fakery about the Vibrators, which got stronger when in the same month they teamed up with old lag Chris Spedding for a shameless punk cash-in (albeit one that caught the wave early), *Pogo Dancing.*

Punk had been brewing for some time. The school bus trip musical entertainment had been upgraded from transistor radio to portable cassette player. The Feelgoods' *Down By The Jetty* was a regular choice, edging out Yes and ELP principally on the grounds of how many tracks we could play during the 25 minute journey. By 1976, the Feelgoods had become mainstream favourites and their brilliant live album *Stupidity* incredibly stood atop the album charts. This was a band with a drive and urgency that was absent in most other music of this era. Eddie and the Hot Rods' *Live At The Marquee EP* carried the baton further, combining the Feelgoods' RnB sound with an amphetamine punky rush. Punk was only a step around the corner. With *New Rose,* it arrived. Within weeks the Pistols had released *Anarchy In The UK* and had their date with Bill Grundy and the whole of the UK knew what punk rock was.

The negotiations for allocation of time to use the various record players available at school had always been complicated and protracted. These were, of course, in the years before we sub-contracted our critical faculties to the algorithm of an automated playlist. Normally everyone was on the same page on style of music and it was just a question of whether you got to play a whole side of *Not Fragile* by Bachman-Turner Overdrive[28] or just *Roll On Down The Highway,* before giving way to Bad Company's *Ready For Love.* I obviously never dared suggest Abba, which would have been howled down by the mob. This dialectic generally produced a reasonable cross-section of mid-seventies rock and prog, with little dissention at the general direction of travel. All this changed in 1977. Whereas before, the occasional voice might have been raised on whether Rory Gallagher's *Irish Tour '74* was a better live album than Wishbone Ash's *Live Dates,* the advent of punk truly divided the house. I would like to say I was at the vanguard of the revolution, bearing the ripped and torn standard at the head of the army. At best, I was a covert franc-tireur in the early stages of the punk war, undecided on where my loyalties lay. Yes, I did like *New Rose* but, on the other hand, the new Manfred Mann's Earth Band album was very good and there was a new Richard Thompson compilation out.

So we still listened to old music in this transitional period before punk swept the rock/prog defending armies aside and we had to swear

---

[28] *Possibly the most ridiculous name for a band ever.*

obeisance to all of its precepts. Richard and Linda Thompson's *I Want To See The Bright Lights Tonight* still got a lot of play on the Sixth Form common room stereo. Such is the censorious absolutism of youth that, had we known then that Linda, the singer of the "*this cruel country has driven me down*" was also the voice of "*Ski – the full of fitness food*", our dreams might also have withered and died. The live version of *Calvary Cross* on the Thompson compilation *(guitar, vocal)* had a searing guitar improvisation that would shortly become outlawed under the new orthodoxies of punk, but was awesome and worth every second of its full 13 minutes.

Were I to accept the concept, Manfred Mann's Earth Band would have been my ultimate guilty pleasure. Their bombastic arrangements owed nothing to subtlety, but Manfred Mann always had a good ear for a good tune. Manfred was also implicated in the "*Ski – the full of fitness food*" aberration as its principal architect. When I heard *Spirit In The Night* on 1975's *Nightingales and Bombers*, I investigated the writing credits on the label, which bore the name Bruce Springsteen. Further investigation showed that the original version was on *Greetings From Asbury Park N.J.*, Springsteen's first album. I bought it and loved it, in a way that I rarely liked any of Springsteen's other work, *Darkness On The Edge Of Town* excepted. Manfred Mann would plunder two more tracks from *Greetings*. Even Alvin Stardust got in on the act with a cover version of *Growin' Up*. I remember being pleasantly surprised that it wasn't a complete abomination. As 1977 wore on and punk took hold, it became increasingly clear that, whilst I could walk around with Springsteen under my arm, Manfred Mann's Earth Band would not be tolerated in the new totalitarian regime. It was only in the early 80s, when the post-punk truth and reconciliation commission was established, that I could dust off my Manfred Mann's Earth Band albums and return them to the turntable. I still prefer their version of *Blinded By The Light* to Springsteen's, but am confident that this is a view not shared by anyone other than Manfred and his close relatives.

One of the highlights of the school year was the school folk and blues club annual concert. 'Folk and blues club' was a historic appellation, and bore little resemblance to the music played, but was probably designed to pull the wool over the eyes of the masters, who fondly imagined that people were wearing Aran sweaters and singing Pete Seeger songs. In 1976 there were lots of versions of Pink Floyd, Groundhogs and Rory Gallagher tracks. We grooved appreciatively. By contrast, the 1977 version featured lots of Ramones, New York Dolls and MC5 numbers, with a sprinkling of Chuck Berry. We grooved appreciatively. Kim Davis and his cohort turned up wearing ripped clothing held together with safety pins. The music was straining the "folk and blues" definition to destruction and some of the pogoing was pushing the envelope of tolerance of the powers that be. Someone wrote a pompous conservative review in the school magazine, condemning the "gullible disciples" of this new music. The folk and blues club concert was banned. I don't know if it ever returned.

I don't really remember much of the jubilee summer of 1977. *God Save The Queen* stalled at no 2 in the charts, strongly rumoured to be the victim of an establishment conspiracy to keep it off the top. Virginia Wade won Wimbledon, but no-one could quite work out how. Perhaps that was also an establishment conspiracy. Elvis died, also now assumed to be an establishment conspiracy. He is, of course, alive and well, mid-way through a residency at Caesar's Palace on the moon. He probably wished for a more rock n' roll ending than death by toilet, occasioned by extreme constipation brought on by an overdose of deep fried peanut butter, banana and bacon loaves. A slightly more rock n' roll death awaited Marc Bolan exactly a month later, as his car crashed into a tree. He would have probably wished it to be on Route 66 between St Louis and Oklahoma City, rather than the B306 at Barnes Common. A month later, Bing Crosby died, not on the road to anywhere but on the walk back to the clubhouse after a round of golf. If you were an establishment conspiracy theorist, you might point the finger at the angel of death, David Bowie, who had duetted with Bolan nine days before his death and with Bing a month before his. Bowie cannot be implicated in Elvis' death as the Thin White Duke stayed clear of Graceland, probably fearing the dietary regime.

It was in the summer of '77 that the idea of buying a guitar began to grow in my mind. I was average looking and, although I have kept a full head of only marginally greying black hair well into my fifties, that was a less notable characteristic at the age of 16. It was clear that if I were to attract girls, I would have to rely on my wits and seek out artificial aids. Playing guitar was obviously a massively cred enhancing activity but, scarred by my piano experience, it had always seemed a bit of challenge. With my lack of application to boring activities like study and practising, there seemed zero chance that I would be able to achieve the level of proficiency required to reproduce *The Revealing Science of God* or its ilk. By the summer of '77, it had dawned on me via the revealing science of God that there was little point in trying. I had always hated all that prog noodling, but now the rest of the world did as well, or at least pretended to. More to the point, however, was that the noise comprising *New Rose,* and what followed in its wake, did sound as if it could have been made by someone who had only just picked up a guitar. *One Chord Wonders* by the Adverts was a paean to incompetent musicianship. Their bass player, Gaye Advert, who was also the girlfriend of the lead singer, had to have chalk marks put on her bass so she knew where to put her fingers. Yet *One Chord Wonders* didn't sound any the worse for it, and was far more tuneful than anything ELP had ever produced, even if it had not just one chord but at least five, as I discovered when I tried to play it later. I had obviously already completed, during my tennis racket years, a lengthy tutelage of throwing the classic shapes and poses of rock guitar, which, having seen Steve Jones in action on television, still seemed to have survived the transition from the ancien regime.

It was time to join the fray.

I cannot recall whether the scarlet piece of wood with which I returned home from the Romford musical instruments shop had a brand, but, if it did, I suspect it is not one usually associated with music. It was, however, very cheap. It was notionally described in the shop window as an acoustic guitar, and it had six strings and some tuning pegs, but the resemblance ended there. It was well nigh impossible to play. The strings were like cheese wire and, even after I had hardened my fingertips with methylated spirit and some practice, you could only just get through the three minutes of *New Rose* without requiring local anaesthetic. I should have stencilled *"this machine kills"* on it.

One of my school friends lent me a copy of Bert Weedon's *Play In A Day* but Bert had not reckoned with my scarlet monster. Nowhere in his classic text did I find instructions on how to hammer the frets back down when they occasionally popped up or a section on remedial first aid to counter the effects of playing for more than ten minutes. I was also dismayed to find that amongst the beginner's practice pieces were *Bobby Shaftoe* and *There Is A Tavern In The Town*. The latter prompted me to go and find one and drink several bottles of Worthington White Shield before dark memories of my piano lessons overwhelmed my soul.

Bert did, however, give advice on posture and amplifier volume. Bert found it helpful to be seated on a wooden stool. This seemed to be inconsistent with my years of tennis racket practice and the methodology of most current guitarists. I don't remember Jimi Hendrix being recumbent on a wooden stool when he was setting fire to his guitar and indeed Pete Townshend would have found it rather an impediment to his amp smashing to have remained seated during the performance. *Anarchy In The UK* did not sound to me like the sort of record where the guitarist had recourse to any sort of seating. Horrible memories of Val Doonican were generated, so I decided to move on and ignore Bert's strictures on playing posture. Funnily enough, Robert Fripp, contrarian that he is, is the only rock guitarist that I know who has followed Bert's advice and plays the whole set seated. I vaguely remembered Bert from his regular slot on children's television programme *Five O'Clock Club* with glove puppets Pussy Cat Willum, Ollie Beak and Fred Barker. Bert Weedon didn't have a name much different from this crew, and was presumably static on his stool, so maybe I thought that he too was a glove puppet. Although it was not strictly necessary to read the section on amplifier settings, as the scarlet monster was an acoustic, I felt compelled to seek Bert's views. Bert informed his pupils that the amplifier should be used with taste and discretion, and volume should be kept to a comfortable level. That didn't sound much fun. I felt sure that little taste and discretion had gone into the making of *Anarchy*. Then again,

Bert was dressed on the cover wearing a very neat blazer and tie, an ensemble rather unlike those adopted by the bands I wanted to listen to. The cover had "Play In A Day" written in a vaguely psychedelic font, but otherwise no concessions had been made to changes in popular music over the preceding twenty years. Bert did help me learn three chords and, as the famous cover of *Sniffing Glue* told us, 'now go and form a band'. It was enough. Not enough for *The Revealing Science of God* but certainly enough for anything that was remotely relevant and fun in 1977.

The only problem was the scarlet monster, which was pretty much unplayable without recourse to regular DIY and medical assistance. I had never really wanted to buy an acoustic guitar in the first place and had obviously wanted a proper electric, but Mum had advised that I should master the acoustic first, which sounded plausible and, being a compliant youth, I followed her advice. I immediately regretted it. I was never going to master the scarlet monster. It was too wild and untamed to take to being saddled by an inexperienced rider and, if I wanted to play guitar without having to be constantly accompanied by a toolbox, Black and Decker Workbench and a first aid kit, I would have to move on.

A return visit to the Romford shop was immediately planned, once sufficient funds from milk rounds, presents and pocket money had been amassed. I also rather hopefully took the scarlet monster with me, in the expectation that I might be able to trade it in as part exchange for its replacement. As is mandatory in all guitar shops, the staff had haircuts a minimum of five years out of date and were widdling away on the guitars, solely vigilant for any visitor attempting to play *Smoke On The Water* or *Stairway To Heaven,* so they might admonish them, but otherwise completely oblivious to any potential customers. That changed once they glimpsed the scarlet monster entering the shop. They bore the fearful shamed expressions of plains dwellers in a cheap western, who have driven some pariah out of town, only to see him return, newly empowered and bent on bloody vengeance. Their look told me that any hope of trading in the beast was clearly a forlorn one. It was clearly not going to form part of any deal. I planted the beast in the corner of the shop, away from the gaggle of assistants. Having extensively researched the pages of Melody Maker and NME, I had determined that a Les Paul was going to be my guitar of choice. Obviously this was nothing to do with how a Les Paul sounded, as I had at this point absolutely no idea of the tonal differences between different guitars. It was purely merit by association – in much the same way that we either like or dislike a name by reference to the people we know with that name, guitars were judged according to the people who regularly played them. The other main contender was a Fender Strat, but I never liked the look of them. I think I traced my dislike of Strats back to when I saw 10cc on Top of the Pops playing them on *Donna,* which I thought was girly and weedy and I hated it. When however they returned with the more beefy and rocky sounds of *Rubber Bullets* and *Wall Street Shuffle,* they were playing the clearly more manly Les Paul. Robert Fripp played a Les Paul. Paul Kossoff played a Les Paul. Eric Clapton practically invented the Les Paul as a modern rock guitar. He then moved to a Strat with the same name as my cat, but I decided to overlook that. That Clapton insisted on sticking with his Strat when Cream reformed, rather than returning to a Gibson, was one of my biggest disappointments with the whole event.

So Les Paul it was. Obviously not a proper Gibson Les Paul, as that was well beyond my wherewithal. Just the cheapest copy I could find. The cheapest copy was branded "Satellite". I've not seen nor heard of a Satellite guitar since and it is safe to assume they left the guitar making business soon thereafter. I tried playing it, desperately trying to ignore the smirking looks that guitar shop staff reserve for any customer who doesn't have the chops of Jeff Beck. It made a noise. I was not experienced enough to judge the quality of the noise. My partner in my band in Oxford, Paul (see later), would no doubt have told me that those were not real humbucker pick-ups but cheap single coils masquerading as the real thing. It really didn't matter. It looked the part and I could play it. I had to have it. This was right at the budget end of the guitar spectrum, so it didn't come with a case. I couldn't afford a case and they wouldn't even take the scarlet monster in exchange for their cheapest case, so it just came in a cardboard box, very difficult to carry when you're also carrying the scarlet monster. The plains dwellers looked relieved as their nemesis left their territory.

The Satellite was pretty defective, impossible to keep in tune, but made a reasonable noise through the Burns combo amp that I had acquired in anticipation of the purchase. The Burns was pretty old but had a great reverb sound. It let me down at its first major test (again, see later) but until then I liked playing through it. It was also fearsomely heavy and a good sturdy seat for those moments when I was complying with Bert's strictures on playing posture. The Satellite may have been a pretty terrible guitar, but believe me, compared to the scarlet monster, it was a finely crafted beauty and served me well for a couple of years. When I took it out of the shop, it felt like that freeze-frame ending of *That'll Be The Day,* when David Essex picks up the guitar that he has just bought in the shop and his life is immediately irrevocably changed forever. Unlike David, I had my A level results to contend with first.

Police and Thieves

'Stephen John Cooke?' asked the police officer standing on my doorstep, whilst my parents looked on aghast.

I had never really come into contact with the law enforcement authorities for the first 18 years of my life. In 1978, they seemed to be all over me like a cheap suit.

O levels had not been a major success. I had reaped the whirlwind of my lack of application and achieved no more than a sprinkling of As, generally in subjects like English Language and Maths which required little or no revision. My A level choices of History, English Lit and French could not be said to be subjects which required little revision. French was a ridiculous choice. I have always been completely crap at languages and French was no exception. Although I was still churning through paperbacks from Bob's Books, the stultifying effect of having to analyse A-level texts until they dropped was a massive turn off. *The Knight's Tale* just didn't have the pull of *The Adventure of the Engineer's Thumb* and, notwithstanding my accidental discovery of Conrad, I hated *Nostromo*.

Television was not notably enjoyable or interesting in the late seventies, but even the most tedious of programmes seemed to be preferable to doing schoolwork. *Z Cars* had morphed into *Softly Softly*, which in turn was rebranded as *Softy Softly: Taskforce* for no apparent reason. They were no longer police car bound, but the results were no more exciting. Colin Welland had long since left for a career as a professional Yorkshireman and Brian Blessed as a professional Englishman. Interest was solely garnered by the fact that DS Harry Hawkins (played by an actor called Norman Bowler) would holiday with his slightly flash speedboat in Solva, the same village in Pembrokeshire where we went. It was as close to celebrity as we or Solva would get to and caused considerable excitement. The Chief Constable in *Softly Softly* seemed a rather malevolent character to have been promoted to such high office in the Police force, but that is probably because I remembered him (an actor called Walter Gotell) from being an unpleasant SPECTRE henchman in *From Russia With Love*. He was shortly to be promoted to head of the KGB in the later Moore-era Bond films.

Far more interesting was *The Sweeney*. 'Sweeney' was a contraction of the cockney rhyming slang for 'Flying Squad'. In case you didn't realize this, the title sequence featured a translation of the phrase, which seemed a touch unnecessary, as total ignorance of cockney rhyming slang was no bar to enjoyment. The themes were familiar – there were still plenty of bad apples around and indeed there was an episode entitled *Bad Apple*, just as in *Dixon of Dock Green* there had been one called *Rotten Apple*. There the similarities ended. *Dixon of Dock Green* had been a favourite with the police, with Jack Warner being made an honorary member of several forces and his funeral being attended by many law enforcement delegations. The police were a bit sniffy about *Z Cars,* not liking the unsympathetic depiction of some officers, so they were never going to warm to *The Sweeney,* where there seemed to be whole crates of bad apples and even the straight policemen bent the rules to get a result. The public, however, myself included, absolutely loved it. The action was unparalleled for a TV police series. Each week there would be lots of shooters going off and at least one police car would get written off during a car chase. Most television series had a formula readily recognisable to viewers. So, for example, in the classic run of *Star Trek,* most weeks Kirk, Spock and Bones would beam down unaccompanied to the latest planet they've chanced upon on their five year mission. Kirk would be looking moody while trying to hold his gut in, Spock would methodically recite tricorder readings and Bones would be muttering bad tempered stuff about Spock. Spock's tricorder readings would generally reveal that the planet was, against all odds, yet another with an atmosphere similar to Earth's, able to support human life but would ominously record some strange anomalies, presaging an unknown danger or threat. Every few weeks, however, they would transport down to the planet accompanied by a few red-shirted security men. It was unclear why on these occasions the trip demanded the presence of additional security, as the anomalies uncovered by Spock's tricorder readings were not noticeably more ominous. All viewers did, however, know that the red-shirted security men had a life expectancy of no more than a few minutes, certainly not beyond the first commercial break. Sure enough, some alien would appear and wipe them all out, fortuitously sparing our regular heroes, who would continue unscathed through another two seasons and seven motion pictures. This was such a common occurrence[29] that 'redshirts' has apparently become a bit of a term of art to denote a stock character who dies soon after being introduced. In *The Sweeney,* our heroes would cruise around in a fleet of spanking new Ford Granada Ghias, probably the result of an early product placement deal with the car-maker. Each week in *The Sweeney* there would be a high-speed pursuit which would inevitably result in at least one of the participant cars being totalled, this being felicitously confined to the vehicular red-shirt of the television automotive world, one of the old, slightly beaten up, sixties grey Jaguars that the blaggers always drove or would occasionally be pressed into service by the squad, their newer Ford fleet being miraculously spared. As soon as the grey sixties Jag appeared, you knew it had an imminent date with the scrapyard. Such were the budgetary constraints of Thames Television. *The Sweeney*'s principal hero, Jack Regan, would ingest breath-taking amounts

---

[29] *In fact, one spod on the internet records that, of the 59 characters killed in the classic Star Trek series, 43 (73%) were red-shirted security men.*

of beer, whisky and cigarette smoke and smash into fornicating villains' bedrooms shouting things like *"get yer pants on – you're nicked"* and *"cover 'em up love – we 'aven't 'ad our breakfast"*, when confronted by the bared cleavage of one of the villains' floozies, which were regularly on display, another major attraction of the series. When there was a major blag in the offing, the squad would tool up – Jack and his partner George with proper shooters, the rest of the team with iron bars, large lumps of wood and other heavy objects. You never saw the *Z Cars* boys carrying iron bars, although when a thuggish Leeds villain was required, Colin Welland was pressed into service, sounding reliably Yorkshire. George Dixon would be turning in both of his graves.

Eventually British television ran out of actual law enforcement units like the Flying Squad and Special Branch to portray, so they had to start inventing new ones. *The Professionals* depicted an organisation known as 'CI5', which seemed to have an extraordinarily wide brief, targeting a huge spread of miscreants from foreign spies and international terrorists, through hit men and racist groups, right down to petty criminals, and even had internal affairs-type responsibilities, rooting out bad apples in a provincial police force. Tough guys Bodie and Doyle would tear around in pursuit of this motley crew of malefactors in a silver Ford Capri, continuing the Ford product placement campaign. You'd never catch Jack Regan driving a silver Ford Capri, which he would probably describe as *"a bloody hairdresser's car"* or something similar. Their guvnor George Cowley got to use a Granada Ghia left over from *The Sweeney*. The reductio ad absurdum of British fictional crime-fighting organisations came in the mid-eighties with the hilariously low budget *C.A.T.S. Eyes,* depicting a crack unit operating in the Medway towns, the eponymous *C.A.T.S.* being the 'Covert Activities - Thames Section', their covert disguise being an all-female detective agency with branches in Gillingham and Maidstone. Their car chases utilised the low to mid-price end of the Ford range, Escorts and Fiestas, whilst their drivers were vigilant not to exceed their regional remit by passing outside the Rochester city limits.

When the A level results came, they mirrored my undistinguished O level performance. The only saving grace was that I had achieved a "1" in English S level, again by the simple expedient of answering questions that required no prior learning or revision, like *"Who contributed more to music, rebels or conservatives?"* or *"Does religion have a future?"*. For the latter, a few clichéd quotes from Karl Marx, Ignatius Loyola, and a less clichéd one from those great religious philosophers 10cc, from their song *The Second Sitting For The Last Supper,* amazingly seemed to be enough to see me through. Notwithstanding my pathetic performance in A levels, the '1' in English seemed to my teachers to be enough for me to try for Oxford in the seventh term in the Autumn of 1977.

In December 1977, I was at school, one of my last days there, when I had an urgent message to call home. As I had never been given a message to phone home before, I had a bit of sense of foreboding. I hoped no-one had died. I tried to recall whether David Bowie had visited our house in the last week or so. Mum answered and, reassuringly, her tone was one of excitement. Ever the dramatist, she milked the moment for all it was worth. A telegram had arrived. This held little in the way of clues for me. I had only ever seen a telegram once before, addressed to my grandmother. Perhaps my father had unexpectedly turned 100. Would it be from the Queen or Sir Keith Joseph's successor?

She continued: *"Congratulations - Stop - Place awarded – Stop - Trend, Lincoln College, Oxford."*

The syntax seemed a little abrupt and I didn't understand the trend bit, not being familiar with the conventions of telegram composition, which obscured the identity of Lord Trend, the Rector of the college, but I got the overall gist of it. It was a great moment, partly because I really wanted to go there and had written if off as a ludicrous long shot, but mainly because I could tell that Mum was absolutely elated and full of pride.

For the nine months until I went up to Oxford, I had to get a job to help pay my living costs, so trooped off down to the Hornchurch Job Centre. I was obviously a student, looking for short-term work, so there was no point in hiding that from the helpful man assigned to me.

'There's some jobs packing paper and stencils in the dispatch department of Roneo Vickers in Barking,' he said.

I gave a positive grunt, signifying interest, as I didn't think I was allowed to be very picky.

'Do you think you'd be able to do that?' he continued.

I was confused by the question, as I couldn't see how anyone other than an amputee, which I manifestly wasn't, could not be able to pack paper. I felt compelled to mention that I was not very good at wrapping presents, particularly the soft ones like jumpers and socks.

He looked at me with a slightly despairing look. It didn't seem to disqualify me from the job. I was told to report at Roneo the next morning.

Roneo Vickers' days were already numbered. It was dedicated to producing office kit destined for the museum, once the age of photocopiers and computers was upon us. They made things like duplicators and typing stencils - the then current method of mass-producing copies of a document. It was the sort of lost cause corporation which my father should have run. Probably, a bit like Kodak, if someone had come in to the office of the head of Roneo and told him that they'd invented the word processor, they would have buried it and hoped that the problem would go away. We worked in a grim warehouse set in a grey industrial estate south of Barking and an eye-opening introduction to the world of work in the late seventies. Work started at 8.30am, continuing until around 9.15, when the breakfast order from the local café arrived. We would then settle down for a 45-minute break and read *The Sun*. Obviously, page three was a regular focal point and the subject of much discussion. The *George and Lynne* cartoon was also scrutinized with care to establish whether either of Lynne's shapely breasts were exposed (generally a 50/50 chance). George was never caught in a similar state of undress and the cartoonist never needed to draw his dick.

Work resumed for an hour at 10, breaking again at 11 for more tea. At 11.30 we had a back breaking stretch of 90 minutes uninterrupted labour until lunch at 1pm, generally returning around 2.15-2.30 for a short burst until our final tea break of the day from 3-3.30 and then an hour until the final bell at 4.30. Walkouts and strikes were a weekly occurrence, generally occasioned by some minor dispute. Within weeks, I had gone completely native and completely identified with my colleagues in their endless battle against the oppression of our tyrannical bosses. What I would have previously viewed as a trumped up petty disagreement over some meaningless detail, had now become a gross affront to the dignity of the working man. Although a bit apprehensive as to how a student on his way to Oxford was going to fit in to what was, by any standards, a pretty rough and ready environment, I soon grew to enjoy it. I was the subject of quite a lot of piss-taking and any airs and graces I arrived with were quickly sandpapered off by the cut and thrust of blue collar life. The London accent which my mother had painstakingly removed, through her own personal elocution lessons regime, quickly returned to form part of my social camouflage.

The workday regime inevitably meant poor productivity and, in an attempt to cure this, Roneo decided to combine the operation with their other factory in Romford. In order to meet the deadline for moving out, we were offered as much overtime as we wanted and a special cash bonus scheme based on productivity in the fortnight before the big move. Unwisely, management gave us advance notice of this bonus scheme and the results were an object lesson in the ingenuity of our fellow men in working around a system and, in particular, the dangers in setting targets by reference to a single metric. The bonus was to be based on the number of 'items' shipped in the fortnight before the big move. An 'item' could be a single pack of stencils, which was relatively time consuming to pack or, at the other end of the spectrum, a palette of 30 boxes which counted as 30 items and just needed labels slapping on them. So, in the weeks before the bonus scheme started, by chance lots of single slow items left the warehouse whilst the large multiple item palette orders piled up in, leaving many frustrated customers wondering where their big orders had got to. In 'item' terms, productivity had fallen to an all time low. As if by magic, as soon as the bonus fortnight commenced, there were few small and slow orders to be despatched, but the big palettes started pouring out of the warehouse. The bosses looked mystified at their clipboards as productivity soared to twenty times the rate of the previous fortnight. A huge, fat bonus became payable. NHS waiting list targets are a good analogue of this. Anyone who'd worked in the Roneo Vickers factory during that fortnight could have told you how waiting list targets would adversely affect hospital behaviours.

I became good friends with a couple of the guys there. Hugh was a few years older than me. He would sometimes give me a lift to work in his old Humber car which he'd done up. I had to endure his tastes in music, which were untouched by punk and generally consisted of AC/DC and little else. I gradually tried to subvert our daily diet of *Let There Be Rock* or *She's Got The Jack* with cassettes of the Stranglers, but we only managed to meet in the middle with Thin Lizzy. We would have a good laugh together. Brad was more downbeat and wore a hang-dog expression. He was a really nice guy and the three of us would hang out together and sometimes go to the Roneo social club in Romford to drink the subsidised beer and play pool badly.

At the other end of the spectrum, there were a couple of people there who were clearly pretty serious hard cases whom you would not want to cross. Ricky, the ringleader, would brandish a flick knife and there was absolutely no question that he would use it without hesitation to inflict bodily harm on anyone who incurred his displeasure. He had a cocky and malign demeanour. I could visualize him stalking funfairs after dark, seeking out softies like me for a beating, or worse. Ordinarily, I would have tried to stay well clear of him, but he was the charge hand in command of my packing group, so I didn't have that luxury. It was difficult to maintain the balance of deference and independence, whilst exuding amiability tinged with quiet resolve, that was necessary to ward off being targeted by the mob. They would scent weakness and natural victims like a pack of jackals circling a wounded deer. Most of the time, the tea boy and general factotum, who had ginger hair and was therefore naturally called 'Ginger', was singled out for the attentions of the wolf pack. He was the subject of relentless bullying and remained desperate to please the mob ringleaders, which of course only made them more brutal and ruthless in their torment of him. On one occasion he was bundled into a large cardboard box, taped up with one small air hole, which was then lifted by a forklift onto the very top level of the warehouse racking, where he was left for over an hour. The foremen, like screws in a nasty prison, stood by whilst this went on, clearly feeling it to be part of the natural order of things. I felt terribly sorry for him. In a movie, I would have confronted them, breaking the cycle of intimidation and submission, but in real life I was not brave enough to intervene and just kept my head down. In a satisfying conclusion worthy of that movie, justice eventually came to Ricky and his gang.

One Monday morning, I arrived at work to find a strangely subdued atmosphere. I noticed that Ricky and five or six other workers were absent. Word soon spread that they had all been arrested that morning and were in custody. It was with a mixture of alarm and sadness that I realised that Hugh and Brad were amongst them. The Roneo warehouse had been the venue for multiple criminal activities. The British Road Services lorry would stop off each day, half way through its daily run, for loading with the Roneo despatches. The BRS driver would be taken off to the works hut for a mug of tea whilst the Roneo palettes were loaded. In fact, what was happening was that a large portion of its existing load was being removed by Ricky and his crew before the Roneo shipment was loaded. The criminal ring were also liberating duplicators and other expensive office equipment. The week before the arrests, a new worker arrived in our midst. He was a pleasant Asian guy, Hari. He kept a low profile and no-one paid him much attention. I used to chat to him as he seemed to be the nearest thing to somebody like me that I was going to come across at Roneo Vickers. He kept his distance, however, and showed little of himself. I thought nothing of it at the time but when he also didn't turn up for work on the Monday of the arrests, it became clear that he had been an undercover policeman. Hugh and Brad were not that different from me, and had just been effortlessly sucked into the criminal milieu, without really thinking about it. In another life, with slightly different influences, they would have had taken a different road. I read in the newspapers later that year that all of them had received custodial sentences. Ginger had been implicated by Ricky using his car to ferry his stash of stolen goods, but fortunately wasn't charged. There were rumours that Ricky had been grassed up by one of the foremen, as revenge for Ricky having an affair with the foreman's wife, who also worked there. If that's true, I would not have wanted to be the foreman when Ricky had finished his stretch. I really enjoyed the six months at Roneo Vickers and it was a huge experience in all sorts of ways. I am, however, still crap at wrapping presents, particularly the soft ones.

1978 was a brilliant year to be between school and university and living in London. There was music breaking out all over the place and loads of places to see it. There seemed to be countless small and medium sized venues where you could see your favourite bands – the Music Machine, the Electric Ballroom, the Hope and Anchor, the Roundhouse, the Lyceum, the 100 Club and, best of all, the Nashville in West Kensington. It's still there, just off the Cromwell Road. It's the Famous Three Kings family pub now, but in 77 and 78 it was one of the best small venues in London. You could see Sting wearing flares there as late as summer 1977. It was right next to West Kensington tube, having the logistical advantage of being on a direct Underground line to home. You had to take seriously the transport arrangements if you didn't want to get stranded in town overnight. There were two options to return to suburbia. Option A was the District Line to Upminster Bridge. This had the disadvantage of being very slow but, on the other hand, if you fell asleep under the influence of excessive beer consumption, the end of the line, Upminster, was only a mile away from home. Option B was the main line service from Fenchurch Street. This was much faster, but the consequences of an alcohol-induced slumber were much more significant, the last stop being Shoeburyness, right out where Essex meets the North Sea, beyond Southend. If that happened, you were faced with a cab ride back home that was well out of the financial reach of an impecunious teenager or spending the night there until the first train in the morning. Eventually, I fell prey to the Carlsberg coma and did my overnight stretch on Shoeburyness Station. From then on, my default option became the District Line.

On a scale larger than the Nashville, the Roundhouse was a favourite venue. We'd seen the Stranglers there and, whilst having a Vibrators-like feel of old blokes faking it, they were an awesome live band with a distinctive sound and some great songs. Lots of people claimed they sounded like the Doors. I have always hated the Doors – a pompous, dull band, who sought to open the doors of perception but only fell through the trapdoor of pretension, with sub-six form poetry lyrics like *The Celebration of the Lizard*. Again affirming the monkeys and typewriters theory of bands, they lucked out with *Break On Through* and *Light My Fire*, the latter being free of any compositional contribution from that bloated buffoon Jim Morrison. Although he did look good in leather trousers in the years when he could still fit into them, and was therefore the model for a million moody and misunderstood lead singers, Morrison is a particular bête noire for me. The only point of interest I have ever been able to uncover in relation to him was not that he got his tackle out on stage once and got arrested, but the manner of his death, which provides an excellent quiz question: what do French revolutionary Jean-Paul Marat, the writer of the original French version of *My Way*, Claude Francois, and the lizard king Morrison have in common? Answer: they all died in a bath in Paris. Marat had a five inch kitchen knife plunged into his chest after he unwisely invited a young female revolutionary into his bathroom to examine his loofah. Francois died trying to change a bathroom light bulb with wet hands standing in bathwater, with predictable consequences. Morrison would no doubt have yearned to have been stabbed by a female fan or even electrocuted, but all he could manage was just to go gentle into that good night in the manner of Elvis, a victim of a heart attack caused by being too fat. The Morrison mythologists, angry at the prosaic nature of their hero's passing, would have you believe he had a heroin overdose and that his body was spirited away from the nightclub where he had been carousing. Anyway, the only point of similarity that I could detect between the Stranglers and the Doors was that they both had an organ player. Even in 1977, the Stranglers already seemed to have written more good songs than the Doors. We'd also seen Dave Edmunds' Rockpile supported by the Motors there in Autumn 1977. It was a fantastic gig, with their Bo Diddley version of *I Love The Sound Of Breaking Glass* being a highlight. Nick Lowe was wearing an immensely cool green suit covered in question marks, like the Riddler from *Batman*.

You could see your favourite bands regularly and they always seemed to have singles out. The album - tour - album cycle seemed to have been dumped with flares, capes and long guitar solos. What's more, giving fans value for money by releasing singles that were not on albums, just like the Beatles and other bands in the sixties, was back in fashion. Some of the best singles in this period, like the Stranglers' *Five Minutes*, Elvis Costello's *Watching The Detectives* and numerous Clash and Buzzcocks 45s were not on albums. Picture sleeves were the norm and you felt as if the bands were really making an effort with each release, rather than just sticking out another album track on an injection moulded single with the B side consisting of a piece of shit that the drummer had just put together while the rest of the band were on holiday, but which you had to own if you were a true fan. Music seemed fun again. You could go out and buy the latest Clash or Jam single, play both sides endlessly, try to decipher the words, examine the artwork and then go and see them at a relatively intimate venue in town, as opposed to waiting for years for Yes or ELP to emerge from the studio with their latest steaming pile of ordure spread over six sides which they would then reproduce in its entirety at Earl's Court or some other enormodrome, which the fans pretended to enjoy, whilst lapsing into unconsciousness during the twenty minute bass solo.

In April 1978 our copies of the NME told us that Rock Against Racism were organizing a march from Trafalgar Square to Victoria Park in Hackney. Me and my mates weren't big on marches. The walk to Upminster Bridge Station was generally enough for us. More importantly, there was to be a free open-air concert in Victoria Park. Even more importantly, the Clash were playing. I had never really got the first Clash album. I liked *Police and Thieves* but the rest of it seemed like a bit of a badly produced thrash, in contrast to *Never Mind The Bollocks,* which was an exceedingly well-produced thrash. The Clash just went into the studio with their soundman and bashed out their set. Chris Thomas, the Pistols producer, encouraged Steve Jones to overdub multiple guitars and achieved an unexpectedly widescreen sound which jumped out of the speakers and into your living room with a vengeance. The Clash album by comparison sounded muddy and flat. The Clash would, of course, get brownie points from the punk cognoscenti for authenticity, but the Pistols sounded better. I often wish that the Clash first album had received the Bollocks production treatment.

However, when *Complete Control* came out in the Autumn of 1977, it seemed to be cut from a different cloth. It seemed more dynamic and well put together than most of the first album and soon became my then favourite punk single. As with most of the records I bought then, I scrutinized it carefully and played both sides endlessly. I didn't know who Lee Scratch Perry was, but he seemed to have done a better production job than the album. I was slightly disconcerted when a guitar solo arrived after the second chorus, guitar solos having been outlawed in the sacred ordinances of punk, but it was ok because Joe Strummer sang *"you're my guitar hero"* during it, validating it as an ironic punk statement. The B side, *City of the Dead,* was also great and featured some unexpected saxophone. I had assumed that the same diktats would have listed the saxophone as a proscribed instrument, redolent of Supertramp, Spyrogyra and the Average White Band. I always disliked the sax as a rock instrument, but the intro to *City of the Dead* was something else altogether.

So I trooped off to Victoria Park with my friends Ian and Mark, stopping off in the pub by Mile End tube station, rather than joining the march. As foot soldiers on the front line of the eternal war against racism and injustice, we were pretty useless. Wearing badges was not enough in days like those, but the badges did look good and my RAR badge became a permanent attachment to my leather jacket for the next few years, signifying a political affiliation that was, other than at the highest level of general principle, pretty fake.

80,000 people turned up to Victoria Park and the crowd was churning. The Clash were on relatively early as they were playing a gig in Birmingham that evening. Patrick Fitzgerald opened. He was that rare thing, an acoustic punk. We'd all bought his EP, *Safety Pin Stuck In My Heart,* one of the most individual new wave records. He was different and the crowd just about tolerated him. X-Ray Spex were interesting, also including a sax player who made a noise of which Supertramp most definitely would not have approved. Next on were Steel Pulse. It would be good if I could honestly say that I was at the Bob Marley and the Wailers gig at the Lyceum in the summer of 1975, but I'm afraid that, like most of my friends who were similarly brought up on the generally lame reggae that made it into the charts[30], we viewed it then as a lightweight passing fad. The ten commandments of punk told us, however, that reggae was cool and we could enjoy it. We therefore skanked hesitantly to *Ku Klux Klan* and liked Steel Pulse. We were having a good time. None of this, however, had prepared me for the Clash. In anticipation of their set, we'd wormed our way down to the front. There was no thought of taking a picnic and staking out our patch of land for the day a la Knebworth. Those were different times. We wiggled our way through the crowd. It was an excellent schooling in the tactics of getting to the front of rock gigs. We approached from the right flank and then made an incisive thrust inwards near the front. We got within twenty feet of the stage. Portions of the Clash set were captured in the *Rude Boy* film and you can see the effect on the crowd that they have. The film gives the impression that they opened with *London's Burning* and the

---

[30] *Check out 'Johnny Reggae' by the Piglets (aka that arch-prat Jonathan King) and anything by Judge Dread for overwhelming evidence of this.*

crowd started furiously pogoing. In fact, that was the second song. They started with *Complete Control* and the reaction was even more manic. I had never felt anything like it in my life. As Mick Jones' opening chords rang out the crowd went absolutely bonkers. We lost any power of independent movement, just pinned within the collective mass, like seaweed floating on a sea. It was scary but wildly exhilarating at the same time. All the other gigs had just been a prelude to this. This was rock and roll.

The Clash played mainly new stuff that I didn't know but that didn't matter. *Police and Thieves* was magnificent; the crowd swayed together to Mick Jones' crunching off-beat. The only low point was when that cartoon punk Jimmy Pursey came on to bellow his way tunelessly through *White Riot,* one of my least favourite Clash songs and not improved by his foghorn contribution. The Tom Robinson Band followed them and were good, albeit made from some suspiciously old school ingredients like Danny Kustow's quasi-metal howling guitar solos and the odd Van Morrison melody. They made a pleasing and sturdily rocking noise, but following the Clash were like a fart in a hurricane.

White Man In the Hammersmith Palais came out the following month. I remembered it from Victoria Park but as soon as I heard it, I knew that *SOS* had finally been eclipsed as my favourite single. *White Man* remains in that position. It seemed a million miles away from the thrash of *White Riot.* Although new wave acts embracing reggae was not a new sound – Elvis Costello's brilliant *Watching The Detectives* (which itself had been written immediately after he listened to the Clash's first album) charted the previous autumn and the Clash themselves had played *Pressure Drop* on their first tour – it still sounded startling. In fact, *White Man* had been in their set since the summer of 1977 when they played the Mont de Marsan punk festival in France. The Police were also on the bill, still then peddling monochromatic punk impersonations. I suspect Sting heard *White Man,* ditched his flares and conceived his reggatta de blanc blueprint then and there. I knew the words off by heart within 24 hours. I parsed every line to extract all of the sweep of the narrative. Of course, the Clash did not at this point provide lyric sheets, so this took multiple plays to decipher the text. It is indeed rare for brilliant words, song and dynamic feel to come into conjunction but *White Man* manages it.

I was in love with the Clash and wanted to be Mick Jones. I needed to see the Clash again. Fortunately that was not then a question of waiting until they were touring their next album or trying to catch them at a summer festival, as it would be now. Bands like the Clash would pop up regularly on short national tours or one-offs in London, irrespective of whether they had a record to plug. The *Clash Out On Parole Tour* was announced shortly afterwards, with a date at the Music Machine in Camden at the end of July. The Music Machine was a fantastic venue, narrow and compact enough for a good atmosphere. It's now Koko and is pretty unchanged. I still worry about how its haphazard bottleneck stair and exit arrangements would work in the event of a fire, but that has never seriously impaired my enjoyment of a gig there. It certainly didn't in July 1978. It was the same gang of us who failed to march in April. To say that we were excited would be a considerable understatement. The venue was throbbing when we got there. First on were the then unknown Specials. I would like to say that we spotted their potential and skanked to them enthusiastically. In fact, we just stood by the bar gassing away. Suicide were on next and we determined now was the time to make our move forwards. By now we were well experienced in the art of getting to the front at gigs. Electing this time for a lightning thrust down the left, we were soon in the melee near the front of the stage. Suicide were really cool but synth duos really weren't in fashion in 1978 and their set became a war zone as a barrage of bottles and any object that wasn't screwed down headed their way. I never saw the axe[31] that Alan Vega says narrowly missed his head that night, but I can well believe it happened.

We were unable to maintain our bridgehead once the Clash had come on, as the crowd reaction was simply too violent and forceful to hold any position. A foaming mass of bodies writhed around. It made Victoria Park seem like seeing Jools Holland and his fearsomely dull Big Band at Kenwood whilst taking cucumber sandwiches and champagne by comparison. We retired to a relatively safe distance.

For the encore of *Janie Jones*, Steve Jones of the Pistols joined the band. Mick, Steve and Janie are not so far as I know related, but the first two were both using Les Pauls, vindicating my choice of guitar. Sadly, the tiresome Jimmy Pursey yet again joined the party for *White Riot* and would be an unwelcome addition to many future Clash gigs. It was a stunning gig, even more exciting than Victoria Park. The Clash had the dynamics of the rock gig absolutely sorted. They looked fantastic – Strummer in the middle, thrashing manically on a generally de-tuned but low in the mix Telecaster, Jones to stage right, the punk Keef, holding the whole thing together, with Simonon on stage left, throwing some fantastically cool rock shapes, an extreme version of which was later to be captured by Pennie Smith on the iconic cover of *London Calling,* and at the back, the fantastically tight human drum machine, Topper Headon, with a brilliant backdrop of WW2 Luftwaffe bombers. It was exactly like a rock band should look and sound. They were also very loud, which always helps, and we emerged onto Camden High Street with our ears ringing in a way that I had never experienced before. They were still ringing the next morning.

We headed to the car. This was a recent acquisition of my friend Mark. It was a bit of an old banger and its MOT had expired a month before. We would normally get the tube to gigs in town but Mornington

---

[31] *A real wood-chopping axe, not a guitar.*

Crescent was a pain to get to from Hornchurch, with the risk of missing the last District Line back, so Mark decided to take a chance of driving without MOT.

We were in the relatively deserted streets on the eastern fringes of the City, when Mark said:

'I think there's a car following us.'

'How do you know?' someone said.

'It's been behind us for the last couple of miles and it's sticking to us like glue'.

'Who do you think it is?'

Before anyone could express a view, the question was answered by the wailing of a loud siren behind us. The car now had a flashing light on top of it. An unmarked police car was pulling us over. Within what seemed like seconds, a police patrol car had joined the party and we were beginning to resemble a major crime scene. This was clearly a major sting operation. We were all rather nervous about the lack of an MOT.

Mark was asked to get out of the car and breathalysed, with negative result, and then assisted one of the uniformed officers from the patrol car in searching his boot. Meanwhile, a central casting bent plain-clothes officer planted himself in the driver's seat and began searching under the steering wheel and fascia panel, clearly looking for drugs. As we knew it would be, it was a fruitless search.

'So where are they?' he scowled at Ian, seated next to him in the front passenger seat.

'Where are what?' said Ian, with a trace of insincerity in his voice, as we all knew what he meant. The officer picked up on it and renewed his search. Rubber gloves and full cavity searches loomed uncomfortably.

He then turned to me, cowering in the back seat.

'What's your name?'

'Stephen Cooke,' I replied. I thought 'Stephen' sounded slightly more law abiding than 'Steve', so adopted my rarely used moniker.

'Ugly fucker, aren't you?'

I hoped that it was a rhetorical question and didn't reply.

He spent the next five minutes trying to bait us into some sort of response that could justify him arresting us. He was thoroughly vicious and unpleasant and seemed absolutely capable of planting some drugs on us if the mood took him. George Dixon would have thought him to be an extremely bad apple. Even Jack Regan would have viewed him with distaste. These were the years of *"George Davis Is Innocent – OK"*, the slogan spray-painted onto railway bridges all over the area in which we had been stopped, reflecting the fitting up of Davis (who was admittedly a career criminal) by the police for a murder he did not commit. George Davis had entered my consciousness a few years earlier, when the Free George Davis campaigners dug up the Headingley pitch on the night before the last day of the Test against Australia, with England poised to win, thereby depriving England of the chance to take back the Ashes. Doug Walters was in bat and he never played well over here. It was clear - we were going to win. No doubt the Aussies saw it differently, but one thing we would have agreed on is that we didn't know who the hell George Davis was, but we were really pissed off with him. When I saw details of the Davis campaign on the sleeve of the Tom Robinson Band's *Power In The Darkness*, I knew I needed to be more sympathetic to George, such was the degree of my radicalisation at the hands of Tom's agit pop.[32] Anyway, if they were prepared to stitch someone up for murder, planting some weed on a bunch of smart alecs like us would be small beer, we reasoned, so we buttoned it and none of us rose to his incessant needling. Eventually, we were reluctantly allowed to continue our journey. We were all pretty quiet for a while after we drove off, having thought that the incident we had just experienced only occurred in Stanley Baker films. Our mood lightened once we realised that his detection methods were not rigorous enough to uncover the only true felony, the absence of an MOT.

The last in my trilogy[33] of 1978 Clash gigs was just after Christmas at the Lyceum, after I'd gone up to Oxford. The Clash were again brilliant. It was after *Give Em Enough Rope* had come out so we all knew the songs off by heart. The sound was better, and the band seemed slicker, than the Music Machine gig but at the cost of a little of their ferocious energy. The Slits were supporting and made an unholy racket, far from the taut, dubby sound that Denis Bovell helped them achieve on *Cut* a year later, which I loved. I don't think they played *Typical Girls* but I may well have failed to recognise it through the scratchy buzzsaw mess. The Music Machine and Lyceum gigs were also captured in the *Rude Boy* film and you can see the progression in stagecraft. All three remain my favourite gigs of all time.

I carried my Clash passion with me to Oxford and was there when *Give 'Em Enough Rope* came out in the Autumn. Although overall a disappointment, the opening blast of *Safe European Home* was a fantastic noise, particularly when played at a volume the nearest I could manage to a Clash gig. The classics tutor below me, did not however appreciate it as an accompaniment to Virgil, which I thought was a bit narrow minded of him. *London Calling* was a better album, which we all devoured hungrily, but the Clash were never again so good live. Clash tour manager Johnny Green

---

[32] *Tom had a thing about liberating Georges - the B side of '2-4-6-8 Motorway' was a version of 'I Shall Be Released', turned into a rallying cry for the release of George Ince, another East End gangland type who been fitted up by the Met. He was previously suspected of involvement in the Mountnessing bullion robbery in Essex, which was certainly the most exciting thing to have happened within a mile of Brentwood within living memory.*

[33] *In fact, I was due to have gone to a fourth, at the Harlesden Roxy in early September, but it turned out that the gig had been fixed by their errant manager Bernie Rhodes without the agreement of the band, and it was subsequently cancelled. It cost Bernie his job.*

describes 1978 as the Clash's "most vital year". After 1978 they became a more diverse band but they had lost a bit of that live edge. Or maybe it's just that I could never hope to replicate the experience of the Clash gigs of 1978. By the time the flatulent indulgence of *Sandinista* came out I had moved on but continued to follow Mick Jones. Big Audio Dynamite were also a brilliant live band, if terribly patchy on record. As he once sang, somehow he stayed thin while the other guys got fat. Shame he didn't keep his hair.

"*What do you call that noise?*" sounded like the sort of question that my father would rhetorically ask after catching me in the midst of some unauthorized use of the stereogram. It was not a phrase I expected to find forming part of the chorus of a pop song.

The flood of listenable music was mirrored on the television. Rather than just your weekly dose of *Top of the Pops* and *The Old Grey Whistle Test*, if you could wrestle control of the television for long enough, there were at least four or five regular programmes featuring music you really wanted to hear – programmes like *So It Goes, Something Else* and *Revolver*. The latter was particularly brilliant, featuring Peter Cook playing the part of the owner of an old ballroom who had reluctantly been forced by dire straits[34] to abandon Edmundo Ross and Victor Sylvester and open his doors to the distasteful racket being made by spotty youths in 1978. His sneering introductions of the bands were superb and it was unlike anything else on television at the time. Predictably, it was too far ahead of its time and was swiftly shunted off to the graveyard slot and canned after only eight episodes.

It was essential viewing and features classic live performances from that era. The very first episode featured the Rich Kids playing *Ghosts Of Princes In Towers* (almost one of the greatest pop records ever made, were it not for it being mired in a muddy Mick Ronson production), the Tom Robinson Band and a rare live appearance by Kate Bush, all punctuated by Peter Cook's character winding up the audience and insulting the bands. The first band to appear on that opening show I had never heard before. They were punky, but a little bit different, with a spiky sound that set them apart. The keyboard player seemed to be playing the bastard offspring of a Vox Continental and upright piano held together with gaffer tape. By the tine the chorus of "*What do you call that noise that you put on?*" came, I was ready for the answer. It was *This Is Pop*. The band was XTC.

It was the beginning of a beautiful friendship. For a start, they had one of the best names for a band that ever was. Very few bands have really good names and you get adjusted to even terrible names if there is enough good music. Witness the Beatles, or right at the end of the awfulness

---

[34] *Economic circumstances, not the band.*

spectrum, Prefab Sprout, brilliant despite their name. With XTC, the name was a good start, which they swiftly consolidated with their product. I bought the single the next day from Downtown Records. It had a wonderful pop art cover, which augured well for the contents. The record was no disappointment. Despite its undeniable catchiness, it's not the greatest song and not my favourite XTC single by any means but it was a wonderful clarion call for pop music. "Pop" had been a dirty word for far too long. You were sneered at if you liked pop. Abba were pop and, prior to their cultural rehabilitation in the court of the style police in the early eighties, were consequently uncool. Were 10cc "pop"? Almost certainly yes but would be categorized as "rock" to avoid this stigma. T. Rex and the Sweet were both pop and spent much of the 70s fruitlessly trying to make the transition to "rock" where their shame could be expiated and musical credibility awaited, but leaving their fan bases behind in the process. When you heard *This Is Pop?*[35], you realised that this wasn't just punk or new wave or whatever, it was pop. This was what pop would sound like in 1978 and it was no longer a shameful label. That survived for twenty years, through the mid-nineties Britpop wave of Oasis, Blur, Radiohead etc. Eventually, pigeon holing and X Factor factory line music production reduced it again to a designation of dishonour and bands once again worry about being labelled as "pop". *This Is Pop?* was my introduction to a band I stayed with throughout their recording career. They never quite captured the spirit of the age for me in the way that the Clash did with that trio of mind-blowing 1978 gigs – I didn't see XTC live until 1980 – but they proved a more durable and entrancing proposition, emerging from their new wave chrysalis to make some staggeringly beautiful music over the years. Who would believe that the band making that brash, spiky noise would one day give birth to *Chalkhills And Children* or *Love On A Farmboy's Wages?* Quite apart from his brilliant songwriting, Andy Partridge is (together with Robert Fripp and Bill Frisell) still one of my favourite guitarists, his angular, individual and never clichéd playing style making him one of the finest and most underrated musicians to come out of new wave.

Practice with the guitar had been a bit sporadic, the stultifying influence of Bert not assisting much, but I could hold down more than three chords and that was enough to write a song and form a band.

My friend Neil had taken up the bass around the same time and lived five minutes away. He was a blues and R n' B purist who hated 10cc and Abba. He embraced punk with some reluctance, generally viewing it as an unwelcome mutation of Dr Feelgood and Eddie and the Hot Rods and preferring to stick with more direct descendants of Feelgood such as the

---

[35] *It had a question mark after it in the title but I wasn't sure why, as this seemed as unambiguous and uncompromising a statement of intent that I had ever heard.*

Count Bishops and the Inmates. He had also adopted the moniker of "Crutch", though no-one could understand its derivation.

'Why Crutch?' you would ask.

'Starsky and Hutch – car keys and clutch – Crutch,' he would reply, as if by way of comprehensive explanatory exposition.

This became a parlour game and we would encourage new entrants to our circle to ask the same question. The reply never differed. The mystery remains. Answers on a postcard, please. Crutch would speak in a ridiculous Thames delta bluesman patois, which, for the most part, no-one could follow. His bass was a white Gibson SG copy which he christened "the Blonde bombshell". He also called his girlfriend's white Ford Capri by the same nickname, which further exacerbated the comprehension gap as we struggled to understand whether he was describing his transport arrangements or a bass line. He also played some rudimentary blues harp, which, when not in use, he would plant in his pint of London Pride, swearing that it improved the sound. To my ears, even with my limited musicality, that was a difficult proposition to sustain. On the plus side, however, he had accommodation at Imperial College in South Kensington, which was a remarkably convenient place to park our bodies, once they had outlived their usefulness after an evening in town on the lash. My friend Ian was the singer. He liked Roy Wood, Phil Spector and Buddy Holly. I also owned Phil Spector's Christmas album and Buddy's *Legend*. This was a strange root-stock of musical influences, onto which I grafted my pitiful first attempts at song-writing. We couldn't find a drummer who was prepared to play with us. Our resulting set was a bizarre mélange of styles. A lumpy plod through John Lee Hooker's *Boom Boom* was followed by *Rave On*, which often had a stuttering opening as we rarely achieved concord on how many *"well, oh well"*s there were meant to be before we came crashing in. *Punky Teddy Picnic* was my very own nursery rhyme homage to Bob Marley's *Punky Reggae Party*. The whole thing was like the Bonzo Dog Band meets the Buzzcocks via Muddy Waters. An unholy mess, we were first called the Albino Bunnies, but it was felt this was not a serious enough name for our weighty project, so we became the Cult Figures. There was later another band by the same name, who only achieved marginally greater success.

Ian and I both loved Jonathan Richman and the Modern Lovers. *Roadrunner* had been the feel-good hit of the summer of '77. We found new resonances in the lyrics, translating Massachusetts to Essex. Ingrave village hall was where endless summer disco parties were held, fuelled by Watneys Party Sevens and Woodpecker cider. Echoing the lyrics of *Roadrunner*, it was also situated out on Route 128 by the power lines – but more prosaically the A128 between Brentwood and Herongate, not the Yankee Division Highway. They had since gone into a more acoustic phase, which we loved, with brilliant out of shape songs like *Abominable Snowman In The Market* and *Here Come The Martian Martians*. I went to see them play at the Hammersmith

Odeon in 1978 and Richman went even more acoustic by singing a new song, *Affection,* completely unamplified, without recourse to the PA. You could hear a pin drop. No-one was chatting to their mates or taking pictures on their phones. The whole audience was totally focussed on Richman playing his guitar and singing to them without any amplification. It was right at the other end of the noise spectrum from the Clash, but was breathtaking. Our favourite Modern Lovers song was *The Morning Of Our Lives,* released as a single in 1978 from their live album. It was a plangent, fragile song of the uncertainties and apprehension of youth and a hymn to how love and comradeship can get you through it. It was a delicate and perfect record. One, therefore, that did not immediately suggest itself to a makeover by the Cult Figures. It just seemed a good idea at the time. The resulting noise removed any remnants of delicacy or pathos, as Crutch's bass tracked the plaintive guitar figure, producing a leaden racket that sounded like Black Sabbath covering Nick Drake whilst on mogadon. Fortunately, we never recorded it.

We were a true garage band but never road-worthy enough to get out of the garage. The nearest we got to playing in front of an audience was the 1978 Windsor Free Festival. You probably don't recall the 1978 Windsor Free Festival. That will be because it never took place. The Windsor Free Festival was a highly illicit festival that took place in Windsor Great Park earlier in the seventies. I was, however, unfamiliar with its history of illegality at this point. When I read in the NME that there was to be another festival in 1978 and bands were invited to come and play, I enterprisingly wrote to the organisers. The NME didn't refer to the illegality of the event, otherwise my law-abiding instincts might have stifled the idea at conception. A rigorous series of rehearsals were organised to hone our proto bluespunk-satire act into a slick audience slaying 25 minute salvo. I visualized ecstatic reviews in the Melody Maker, in the section just before it dissolved into the folk pages and endless loon pants adverts, and the NME, which would probably focus to a greater extent on the political significance of the lyrics to *Punky Teddy Picnic* as a Situationist manifesto.

On the Saturday morning a week before the appointed date for our appearance, there was a ring on the doorbell. Dad was appalled to answer the door to a policeman asking for me. I approached the front door with considerable nervousness. Had the police investigation into the Roneo criminal ring cast its net further and was I about to be fitted up for a lengthy stretch for theft of some stencil ink or correcting fluid? The officer had not asked to come inside to avoid embarrassment with the neighbours, as I had seen happen in the movies. Instead, the interview was conducted on the doorstep. My mother could no doubt visualize the net curtains twitching in the windows of the houses on either side.

'Stephen John Cooke?' the officer asked, consistent with the movie methodology.

A Cult Figures rehearsal, with me (foreground) playing my Satellite Les Paul copy and Crutch (background) on the blonde bombshell. From the look of the fingering, we are lumbering our way in unison through the riff of "Morning of Our Lives".

I stammered an affirmative response.

'Are you a member of the band the Cult Figures?' he continued.

Things were taking a strange turn. Was the blonde bombshell (either version) stolen goods? Was Bob Marley bringing criminal charges for misuse of one of his song titles? Was Jonathan Richman injuncting us from further desecration of his catalogue? I could think of no law enforcement angle to our musical activities. I had (and, incredibly, would continue to have) a clear conscience on the drugs front.

Again I responded positively, this time slightly more confidently.

'Is it correct that your band has been booked to play at a festival in Windsor Great Park next Saturday?'

The arrangements had seemed a little too haphazard and informal to constitute a 'booking', but, now bemused, I again signified assent.

'Were you contacted through your agent?'

The idea of anyone seeking out our ramshackle combo to play, or indeed a professional agency representing us, were truly alien concepts.

'Err…..we don't really have one.'

The officer was beginning to get a measure of the situation. He dutifully read out a warning that to attempt to travel to Windsor with the intention of playing at the festival would constitute a criminal offence and I would be immediately arrested. The fledgling lawyer in me was about to take issue with him over the travel component constituting an offence, but fortunately I thought better of it. Thus ended the live career of the Cult Figures. We thereafter contented ourselves with weaving our magic in the studio, a slightly more high-tech version of the reel-to-reel recorder that I had used for recording from Dad's stereogram. I practised a bit more and the songs got slightly more sophisticated. Crutch left the band, professing, so far as Ian and I could understand, discontent with our lack of musical development. He continued playing endless 12 bar blues jams, complete with lengthy beer soaked harp solos. Ian and I hooked up again at Oxford, doing a set of Phil Spector Christmas Album covers. I played piano in Crutch's blues band a few years later for a few gigs. I couldn't discern any significant musical development from the last time I played with him.

A New Career In A New Town

The conversational skills of most 18 and 19 year olds are pretty limited. Oxford has more than its fair share of dysfunctional young adults with zero social skills. 'So what A levels did you do?' consequently was the question that commenced first contact with other students in about 90% of cases in my first week at Oxford. I dreaded the supplementary '....and what grades did you get?' but only one little spod went there, my answer being greeted by a facial expression generally reserved for signifying detection of unpleasant smells and which screamed 'what right do you have to be here with me in this seat of high learning?' Fortunately, I never saw him again in my three years. He was probably in a library somewhere. There were some very self-confident posh chaps who would open the conversation with a description of the very high quality Moroccan they had back in their room and would I like to try some later? I was slightly taken aback by their forwardness, having never before experienced any invitation to share any form of drug other than paracetamol, let alone so early in a relationship.

Freshers' Week was unsurprisingly a glorious celebration of binge drinking, lurching from college bar to college bar and from one society or club introductory drinks to another. Lincoln College was described in the Oxford alternative prospectus as *"an all-male drinking college"*. That description was entirely accurate and Lincoln was clearly determined to make the definitive contribution to the week of alcoholic excess. It was unclear whether "The Freshers' Blind" (as it was described) was an official college event but, if so, it would now struggle to meet even the most relaxed health and safety standards. It was a simple concept – everyone was herded into Deep Hall (the underground college bar) and then offered strong encouragement to drink huge amounts of beer. This was not fun. Later in the evening, the rugby team (known as the "chaps") would break out into a bout of *"elephanting"* – taking a large swig of beer and holding it in your mouth, raising your arm in the manner of an elephant trunk and spraying the contents of your mouth over your victim. It was a truly bizarre spectacle. The head barman, Ted Busby, looked on with paternal admiration at his flock, in the manner of some tribal leader orchestrating a pagan coming of age ritual, designed to pass on the ancient rites to the next generation. I enjoyed my beer but liked it better when delivered through a hand pump. Women arrived at Lincoln a year later and the elephant became extinct. The tribal ritual became replaced by a more familiar one. No-one other than Ted Busby and a few of his curmudgeonly acolytes lamented its passing.

Arrival at Lincoln had been about a week earlier. It was such a major event that Dad even made a rare appearance, accompanying Mum and me. Mum had decided to buy me a trunk to convey my belongings to Lincoln. I think she must have seen one in *A Yank At Oxford* or *Goodbye Mr Chips*. It was quite large and comfortably capacious enough to hold all my belongings. There was however a certain impracticality in the concept of a travelling trunk in the modern world. In their appearances in the likes of *Goodbye Mr Chips,* trunks are almost always sent on ahead by train by the fabulously wealthy parents of the young darling and accompanied by a posse of bearers to move the fearsomely heavy object to its destination. My trunk was as fearsomely heavy as any fearsomely heavy trunk could be. My record collection alone would have broken the back of a Varsity luggage train sherpa. How we were meant to get the monster into our Triumph 1500 was also unclear. I still have no recollection as to how we got it to Oxford but a strong recollection of having to load and unload the substantial majority of the contents at each end before the thing could be budged an inch, which surely undermined the whole concept of the trunk. Mum's Brideshead-like conception of what an Oxford college would be like was surprisingly confirmed by my accommodation. It was a suite of full Sebastian Flyte-style rooms with separate bedroom and lavatory, overlooking the pleasingly peaceful Grove Quad. She looked approvingly at my name neatly stencilled at the foot of the staircase, just like in the movies. The only downside was that my bedroom overlooked the entrance to Deep Hall and I was regularly woken at 6am by a symphony of beer barrels being rolled down to the bar. This was replicated in my second year at Lincoln when my room was not only roughly the size of my first year lavatory but also overlooked the Mitre pub. The familiar music of rolling barrels was this time accompanied by the percussion of empty glass bottles being thrown into a refuse skip. It often felt like an appropriate and God-ordained punishment for some relatively regular excess the night before.

Conformity to movie Oxbridge stereotypes was also confirmed by the appearance of my "scout", Oxford terminology for someone who would come in daily to make your bed and tidy your room. I could see that Mum was caught between basking in the pride that her son had ascended to the heights of having his own bed-maker and distaste for the idea that I wouldn't be making my own bed and tidying my room at such a tender age. Years of her ruthless enforcement of bedroom responsibility had, however, left its indelible mark on me, and Margaret the scout rarely had to make my bed.

Organising my record collection was my first and most important task. As will be obvious to any woman, men spend a huge proportion of their life organising the different categories of their belongings into a coherent order, whether it be their stamp collections, wine, books, shoes or underpants. Man cannot rest until there is order. One of the most important categories, if not the most important category, for the imposition of order is the record collection. As the segment in the film of *High Fidelity* demonstrates, there are many different approaches to ordering a record collection. The most basic is alphabetical order. This may seem simple, but is in fact fraught with difficulty. One would assume you simply put bands in by the first letter of their name and solo artists under their surname. So Frank Sinatra would be after Simple Minds. So far, so good. Where, however, do you put the Spencer Davis Group? Record shop convention dictates that they would be filed under "S", Spencer himself having had no meaningful solo career. What about the Jimi Hendrix Experience? Should they be filed under "J", whilst Jimi's solo work without the band being put under "H"? Now, ladies, you can begin to grasp the serious issues with which men have to grapple on a daily basis. Once you add the paradox of classical recordings to this – should you file the DG recording of Beethoven's 5th by the Wiener Philharmoniker, conducted by Carlos Kleiber, under "B" for Beethoven, "W" for Wiener or "K" for Kleiber? – the enormity of the problem should be obvious to all.

I rejected a simple alphabetical system for display of the record collection at Oxford. Convention would indicate that numerical names would be placed at the front. That would result in 10cc being displayed prominently at the front. I was anxious to project the right image in my new environment, so this was clearly unacceptable. Banishing numerically named artists to the back of the pack would just result in Abba being in pole position, equally unacceptable. The obvious answer was to order my collection in order of coolness. So, near the front of the starting grid were *All Mod Cons* by the Jam, the Buzzcocks' *Another Music In A Different Kitchen* and *More Songs About Buildings And Food* by Talking Heads. I wasn't sure of the status of Bebop Deluxe's *Drastic Plastic* or Kevin Ayers' *June 1 1974* live album, so they nestled somewhere in the middle. Godley and Creme's *Consequences* triple album boxed set was right at the back and my King Crimson albums didn't even make it out of the trunk. Pole position was, however, reserved for Bowie's *Low* and *Heroes*. They seemed to tick all the right boxes. They exuded an aura of intellectual sophistication and high art. The fact that I really liked both albums and played them incessantly was merely a bonus. The appearance of Robert Fripp's name in the credits of *Heroes* was something of a surprise, and the first indication that King Crimson's confinement within my trunk may not be permanent.

For about a week, I maintained an academic discipline consistent with this seat of high learning. I went to lectures and did lots of reading for my first two tutorials. Roman Law seemed a bit irrelevant but was interesting. I have never needed to know how to manumit a slave or what happens when an island rises up out of the sea (which is rare, Justinian tells us, and that seems to be borne out by empirical evidence). I did, however, find the Roman law insights into the ownership of a swarm of bees which go into your neighbour's garden useful when Mum's flighty queen bee led her flock down the road. My Roman law tutor, Polyvios G. Polyviou, was a Greek Cypriot, possessed of a sharp tongue and brain and quite inspirational teacher. He was soon to leave Lincoln to return to Cyprus. Simon Gardner was my criminal law tutor and was more low key, and less effusive, than Polyviou, but no less effective at generating an enthusiasm for his subject. He tolerated my rather sporadic and haphazard approach to the law and was, in retrospect, a good guiding light.

    The first week turned out to be a flash in the pan. It soon became obvious that lectures were an optional extra. My attendance ceased, at least until the Trinity term of my last year, when the received wisdom dictated that it would give you insight into what was on the examiners' minds. I quickly established an MO for tutorial preparation, which involved little work. This was refined further when I hooked up with my long-term tutorial partner, John McNeil. He always wanted to be known as J.J. but I considered that pretentious rebranding and have always stubbornly called him John on the rare occasions we address each other by our Christian names. Generally we just call each other "Cooke" and "McNeil". It always seemed more natural. Our approach to tutorials was a heuristic technique, based on empirical observation of behavioural patterns of tutors. Take, for example, Polyviou. He never departed from his methodology of getting one person to read the set essay, leaving the other as a passenger who generally got a free ride. He alternated between the two of us with total rigour. The response was clearly for the designated driver to write the essay and then read it out. This worked perfectly until right at the end of Polyviou's tenure, minimising our work to manageable levels. I had written a spectacularly poor Jurisprudence essay on designing your own legal system. It was a predictable cocktail of Hart and Dworkin, with an ill-judged dash of Hohfeld. In accordance with our normal security procedures, I photocopied my essay and gave a copy to McNeil, confident, based on the previous seven weeks, that this was an unnecessary precaution. Our methodology had, however, not taken account of chaos theory and that week Polyviou's unerring rigour slipped and he erroneously turned to McNeil, not me. Maybe it didn't slip, and he was on to us all along and decided to have some fun at the expense of some smart-ass students. McNeil was hideously ill-equipped to read out an essay on the perfect legal system, having done no reading whatsoever and having to decipher my badly photocopied handwriting, which was a challenge in itself, given the speed at which it was written. He stuttered his way through my abomination. It was wince-making to listen to. He finished. Polyviou let out the gentlest of sighs of resignation. This was to be his last tutorial with us before he returned to Cyprus. Had he not managed to teach these dolts anything, I could hear him thinking. Rather than delivering his withering appraisal of the pile of do that McNeil had just read out, he unexpectedly turned to me.

    'Cooke – comment.'

    This rather took me aback, but I was of course ideally placed to deliver a critical assessment of the work, having been its unwitting ghostwriter.

'Well, it wasn't really a coherent construction of a legal system at all,' I started, 'merely a predictable cocktail of Hart and Dworkin, with an ill-judged dash of Hohfeld.'

I continued, beginning to hit my stride, and moving on to a wholesale demolition of the structure and content of the work. Polyviou looked appreciatively at me.

'Cooke – excellent. McNeil – it was an execrable essay.'

With that, the tutorial ended. I hope that I brought a ray of light to Polyviou and that I at least managed to leave him with the impression that at least one of his students knew what they were doing. As I said, it was just an impression, not the reality. If any of his students did, it sure as hell wasn't me.

The empirical observation method was also adopted in our dealings with our tort tutor, John Bowers. He would always start the tutorial by asking if we had any questions on the week's work. Our simple approach was to spend no more than 15 minutes reading a couple of cases in some detail and respond to his opening question by raising a point on those cases. We would then demonstrate detailed knowledge of those cases, which he would naturally, but totally incorrectly, assume was replicated across the whole of the week's work. He of course wised up to our method and by the end of term was firing detailed questions on the facts of random cases at us in a justifiably bad-tempered manner. For goodness sake, it was the summer term of our first year, with exams behind us and no more for another two years. Lighten up.

I was the more responsible of the pair of us, but McNeil was an exceedingly low benchmark to judge oneself by in the responsibility stakes. On one particular sunny afternoon, our weekly tutorial was an hour away, so I wearily announced that we really should interrupt our game of croquet to start our week's work, delivered in the tone of someone who really felt that he was bringing order to the chaos that would otherwise reign. This was a far too constricting regime for McNeil, however, who pronounced ' No, Cooke – we play croquet until a quarter to, then look at the case list'. I deferred to him, satisfied that starting our week's work a good fifteen minutes before the tutorial was a fair compromise between the competing demands of leisure and education.

I can't remember where the idea of hitchhiking around the country during term time came from, but it seemed a good one and neither of us could see anything to detain us in college. There weren't any competing leisure activities demanding our presence in Oxford that week. Our studies were briefly considered for form's sake, but not found to present an insuperable obstacle, so long as our schedule returned us to Lincoln a quarter of an hour before our next tutorial in five days time. I think we had probably both recently read *On The Road* and visualized a trip to California to hang five in the surf. Cornwall was the nearest feasible equivalent for the cut price Paradise and Moriarty. McNeil was an experienced hitchhiker and counselled white shirts and jeans to project an image of wholesome cleanliness to potential rides. I had never hitch-hiked, having heeded my mother's dread warnings of the fate that had befallen innocent travellers, a sub-category of the talking to strangers section of her standard homily on life's hazards (the others being the perils of riding motorbikes and smoking). We determined that we would go where our rides took us, with no fixed destination, and that we would always sleep under the stars. Since we didn't have a tent with us, that was a rash pronouncement. Preparation was minimal. We slung a few pairs of underpants and our toothbrushes into our bags and hit the road - the A420 via the Botley roundabout. We foundered at Swindon, at a particularly barren junction on the M4, forcing us to abandon our surf odyssey and to strike out east to London, then onto Leeds, back down to Cambridge for a student party and then back to Oxford. The skies remained clear and we stuck with our rule of sleeping under the stars, unpunished for our lack of a tent. Timing discipline was maintained and indeed we arrived back at Lincoln a full two hours ahead of the tutorial deadline, allowing us to sunbathe on Lincoln House roof until we resumed our studies at a quarter to.

 Undeterred, we determined we were going to try again for Cornwall during the summer vacation. This time we had more luck on the M4. After a brief episode with a bunch of squaddies in an army land-rover, first crossing the Severn Bridge four times trying to locate an army depot and then unwittingly rendering the vehicle immobile by filling it up with petrol when it took diesel, we made camp for the night, sleeping rough under the motorway somewhere west of Leigh Delamare services. The next morning, we had a stroke of luck and were fortuitously picked up by an American Express rep with a surplus of luncheon vouchers, who bought us full cooked breakfast at Bristol Gordano services. Adapting to the mood of each ride was a skill in itself. We would take it in turns to sit in the front. The front seat rider was expected to gauge the mood of the driver and assess whether the driver wanted to chat or not. Usually they did and we felt obliged to repay the driver with some erudite and witty conversation – or at least our approximation of it, which was neither erudite nor witty, but which seemed to suffice in repaying our side of the bargain. By the end of the second day, we were in St Just, right at the western end of Cornwall. We had determined that we would strike camp at Cape Cornwall, right on the western tip of the county and just a mile or so from St Just. Sensible travellers would have noticed the deteriorating weather and continued on the winding and occasionally hazardous path to Cape Cornwall whilst the light was still good, hitching our tent before night fell. As you may have gathered, reader, sensible was not part of our collective mind-set. Rejecting the wearisome conventions of this approach, we instead elected to stop for refreshment at the inn in St Just. Entering the pub was a bit like the bit in *An American Werewolf In London* where the eponymous werewolf-to-be enters the pub on the Yorkshire moors. The hostelry fell into a hushed silence and everyone stared at us as if we had just arrived in a flying saucer from the third moon of Kepler 9b. We tried to make polite conversation with the landlord, but he was having none of it, and just eyed us with suspicion as he pulled our pints. Four hours later, tensions seemed to have eased, so we moved on to some rather strong bottled beer, which we managed to convince ourselves was being mistakenly sold at 1930s prices. In fact, it was such a bargain that we determined that we should carry a stock of it with us to our lodgings for the night off Cape Cornwall. And so it was, laden with our backpacks full of bottles of old speckled peculiar goat ale, that we emerged from the pub into the thick fog and drizzle which had fallen during our refreshment break. It is unclear how we drunkenly stumbled through the zero visibility to our spot on Cape Cornwall without mishap. The vigorous inebriated unfurling of our tent pack (for we had decided to allow ourselves the luxury of sleeping under canvas) resulted in all the tent pegs being scattered far and wide in the darkness, but miraculously we managed to erect our quarters for the night and stumble into our sleeping bags. The next morning we awoke in blazing sunshine to find ourselves a mere five yards from the cliff edge, with raging thirsts but with nothing to slake them with other than a week's supply of the sickly barley wine-like strong ale in which we had invested so heavily the previous night. In the distance along the coast we could see Sennen Cove, the surf capital of west Cornwall. It didn't look that far. Surely we could get there within the hour? This proved to be a hopelessly optimistic assessment, even without our alcoholic weight burden, which we stubbornly refused to abandon. By the time we reached Sennen, three and a half hours later, we felt like the parched survivors of some Saharan disaster movie. We ran along the half-mile beach at Sennen to get to the pub. The four pints of cold soda with lime cordial we gulped down never tasted sweeter. We never drank the old speckled peculiar goat.

The Band That Time Forgot

'The single is called "Calling All The Shots", the band are The Stereotypes – have a listen and see what you think,' said Peter Powell from the radio.

It was summer 1980 and the radio was sitting next to my workbench at McCarthy's Pharmaceuticals in Romford. McCarthy's was my regular holiday job since I had started at Oxford. I worked in the maintenance department and had to mend just about anything that was broken. I can't recall exactly what pharmaceuticals they manufactured, with the exception of denture cleaner. I can remember this, as I accidentally fell into a vat of denture cleaner during my tenure there. There were no adverse side effects but I did feel clean and fresh tasting for the rest of the week. More importantly, Peter Powell was the king of daytime Radio 1 and he was playing my record.

Rewind almost two years.

'Paul – Steve, Steve – Paul. You need to form a band,' said Nick Moncrieff, thrusting me in the direction of this dark-haired bloke who was lingering uncertainly on staircase 15.

This was only the third day of my new life at Lincoln and I had only met Moncrieff the day before, so it felt a bit presumptuous for him to be marching around college introducing people he barely knew. Moncrieff is, however, one of the world's glorious networkers. We never called Moncrieff "Nick". He was always known by his surname. We now know him as the College Stalker, for his extraordinary ability to keep tabs on the exact whereabouts of a huge number of people from our lives at Lincoln. The apogee of this must be his encounter with the very same Paul (more of him shortly) some twenty years after we left Lincoln. Paul was, at that stage in his life, an immigration officer at Heathrow and Moncrieff was returning to London from one of his regular glamorous overseas television industry trips and was about to pass through immigration, when his finely tuned networking senses alerted him to the presence of a potential target. One would have thought that an immigration officer would be a racing certainty to recognise an old friend whose passport he is examining, before the old friend recognized him. He is, after all, required to examine the passport, look at the name and compare the likeness in the photo with the face of the person standing in front of him. That would be reckoning against the abilities of the College Stalker. Before Paul was even close to identifying Moncrieff and designating him as a potential subversive for immediate rendition and waterboarding, Moncrieff startled the immigration man by announcing "Paul Galley!" at the top of his voice. This was an unexpected reversal of roles. Further conversation was difficult without incurring the ire of the passport queue.

Paul Galley was indeed the person who Moncrieff had just introduced me to. Moncrieff had obviously spent his first two days of college on a tireless round of enquiry about people's A level subjects and other social niceties, gathering personal data and relevant social touchpoints. By the third day, he was ready to spin his web. He had discovered that I played guitar and that we had both been at the Hammersmith Odeon Jonathan Richman gig, when had sung *Affection* without a microphone. He lived on Victoria Park Road, but unaccountably had not been at the Clash gig in Victoria Park, missing the most essential music event of 1978 when it was right on his doorstep. That was very unlike Moncrieff. He had the urban cool that came from living in Hackney, rather than suburban Essex. He would suggest that we go to late night showings at the Penultimate Picture Palace (the "PPP") to see films we had never heard of, like *Texas Chainsaw Massacre* or *Eraserhead*. The former, he reliably informed us, we would only be able to see at a cinema club like the PPP, as it had been refused a certificate by the censors and would not be shown in normal cinemas. How did he know this stuff? He also seemed to be a well-travelled man of the world. I remember him returning from a holiday in Mexico with a huge bottle of tequila, not a drink that was as readily available then as it is now. The two of us proceeded to drink it in one sitting. Moncrieff had procured some salt and lemons as accompaniments. His learnings from Cancun had not, however, included the precise order in which to ingest the tequila, salt and lemon. The entire session was therefore accompanied by a debate about the correct sequencing. The last words I remember him saying, just before we parted company with our consciousness, were "the great thing about tequila is that it doesn't give you a hangover". This demonstrated he was not as on top of some of the details as it appeared. The resulting physical wreckage the next morning was not only extremely uncomfortable, but at the same time faintly reassuring as it reminded me that Moncrieff was not as colossus-like in bestriding the modern world as his confident exterior seemed to suggest.

He had an impressively obscure record collection. Whilst we all had *My Aim Is True* and *This Year's Model,* Moncrieff had the Costello bootlegs *50,000 Elvis Fans Can't Be Wrong* and *Live At El Mocambo*. For every XTC and Television single I played, Moncrieff raised me an obscure Postcard single by Orange Juice, Josef K and Aztec Camera. Even when I got out my battered copy of *Pretzel Logic* to stress the breadth and sophistication of my tastes, Moncrieff called me with a copy of the ultra rare *Rotoscope Down* Dan bootleg. Incredibly, by day three, the ganglia of his network were developed enough for him to be able to pair me up with a bass player and drummer. Paul was the bass player. Jeremy Brill was the drummer. We didn't think that "Jeremy" was a very rock n roll name. His middle name was Max, so we renamed him "J. Max" on the sleeve on our record. Paul didn't seem that cool and was wearing a very sixties looking suit and a tie, which I thought was strange. He looked as though he'd just come from an audition for Gerry and the Pacemakers. Jeremy had a green, yellow and red rasta hat and used to sprinkle each sentence liberally with "I and I" in place of "me". I didn't understand this at all, but it seemed endearing. Jeremy had a love of fiercely unapproachable reggae. When he got very excited about some Tapper Zukie or Dillinger 12" he was playing in his room, he would shriek "I and I in-a-Babylon", which I understood even less and was marginally less endearing.

Paul and I were soon strumming guitars together in one or other of our rooms. Two things quickly became apparent. Firstly, our musical tastes didn't overlap much. Overlapping with Paul's musical tastes was like trying to hit a goal crossbar from the half way line. He loved the Beatles and the Stones and old style rock n roll like Chuck Berry, with a dash of Dylan, and that was about it. That is inevitably a bit of an exaggeration as I seem to recall that he had a Patti Smith poster in his room and he definitely wanted his bass to sound like J. J. Burnel of the Stranglers, but you get the drift. As far as the Beatles went, I was still severely scarred by the Alan Haven experience and had limited myself to the red and blue compilations, although I had a tape of *For No-One* taken off Radio 1. I didn't know quite how it began, as I had to wait for Ed "Stewpot" Stewart to stop gabbling inanely over the intro before I could press the record button. It remains my favourite Beatles song. Paul seemed relatively untouched by punk and would flip through my record collection with a look of concern on his face. Sadly, he was diligent enough to make it beyond the cool front section, through the intermediate tranche of Bebop Deluxe and Kevin Ayers and onto the deeply incriminating back markers, sighing when he got to the likes of Abba, 10cc or Manfred Mann's Earth Band. He curled his lip when he saw not just one, but two, Chic albums. Second, he seemed to be a real musician, who knew lots of different chords and had actually recorded his songs in a proper recording studio. I was just a spoofer who knew four chords and had written a couple of terrible songs. Paul played me some of his demos. One of the songs, *Nostalgia,* had a really good tune and had some minor chords which sounded cool. I knew I had a lot to learn, but at least I had a battered leather jacket with a Red Army Faction badge permanently pinned to it and looked like Keef.

We began the process of negotiating a set list. This established the familiar tug of war between Paul and me, which sometimes produced rancour and conflict but more often some interesting and occasionally great musical collisions. The set was liberally sprinkled with Paul's Chuck Berry favourites, like *Don't Lie to Me* and *Talkin' Bout You*, which at least had the advantage of only utilising three of the four chords then in my repertoire. I brought along the Standells' *Dirty Water* and Nick Lowe's *Heart Of The City*. I had heard the former played by the Inmates at one of the many gigs of theirs that I went to with Crutch in 1978 and then sought ought the original on a copy of *Nuggets,* the US garage punk and psychedelia compilation put together by Lenny Kaye. The fact I had an original 1972 Elektra copy, rather than the Sire re-release, impressed Moncrieff and Jeremy enormously. We substituted *"Oxford"* for *"Boston"* in the last line of the chorus, which sounded a bit lame. We met in the middle at Buddy's *Rave On,* a rare convergence of our musical avenues. The introduction of *Police and Thieves* into our set was a point of some contention. Paul was not keen. He didn't really like the Clash and liked reggae less. Jeremy of course had the original Junior Murvin version and was enthusiastic. It was in and I got to sing it. The band was hewn from chunks of rock left over by the Clash, Beatles and Bob Marley.

Paul was a much more confident singer and sang most of the songs in our set. I think he didn't really mind having a guitarist who sang the odd song, a bit like Keef, so long as his ascendancy as band front man wasn't challenged. Turbulent waters lay ahead.

We knew we needed a second guitarist, but even Moncrieff's burgeoning network had failed us. Eventually word reached us that there was another guitarist in college who might be interested in joining us. We invited him down to one of our rehearsals in Deep Hall, the college bar. I had visualised a wasted looking Tom Verlaine/Steve New type with a shock of fair hair, a low-slung Les Paul and a cigarette hanging out of the side of his mouth. Paul probably wanted a mop-top sporting George Harrison lookalike who played tuneful solos you could hum along with, or maybe a Brian Jones wayward guitar genius who would play unconventional lines and master any instrument slung at him. Jeremy would inevitably hanker after a Peter Tosh type, chopping out great chunks of off-beat metallic skank axe. In fact, any of these would have been great. Expectations were high. Disappointingly, a moustache entered. We all fell silent. The moustache was Martin Pailthorpe. "PT" for short. He reminded me of one of the three burgundy-clad sidemen in Middle of the Road. As Paul once said, PT once came first in an Oliver Reed lookalike contest, narrowly defeating Ollie himself. Now, to be clear, Oliver Reed was a great man. His autobiography *Reed All About Me* (a worthy entrant to the autopunography pantheon, and a cleverer title than it appears if you don't know that Oliver is dyslexic) is a fantastic book, heavily featuring photographic coverage of our hero minus his trousers. It remains a staple on the bookshelf in my recording studio for use by Russell (my long-standing music partner) or me to relieve the boredom when the other is labouring for too long over a take. Notwithstanding that he would hang out with Keith Moon and drink 60 pints of beer in under 24 hours and then hang a beer mug from his erect member, Oliver's hell raising uber-male image has never been one that fitted in well in the world of rock n' roll. Once we had recovered from the shock of the moustache, we noticed that he was wearing a large knitted cardigan of the type sported by Paul Michael Glaser in *Starsky and Hutch* and some flapping flares. It was not a good look. Beggars could not be choosers, however, and we meekly accepted him to our bosom. Things took a worse turn the next day when he suggested that he play a screwdriver solo at the beginning of *Nostalgia*. We were rather mystified, not having come across the use of a screwdriver in a musical context. Maybe, he too had mistaken Rod Stewart's mic stand for a hammer and been inspired to explore the possibilities of the rest of the tool-box. It turned out that he would run the screwdriver over his guitar strings with some phaser applied, like a primitive version of Godley and Crème's Gizmo. We indulged him for a while. He played us tapes of his old band when he was at Harrow. They were called Husky Frog and had a song called *Strut*, which sounded pretty much as you'd expect it to. There were lots of long guitar solos.

    Our first band photo has the disparate nature of the individuals on full display. On the left is Jeremy, wearing a skinny leather tie and Rock Against Racism and Virgin Frontline fist badges. Then me, all in black with my trusty leather jacket, leather thong round my neck a la Hugh Cornwell, a cigarette in my hand and looking suitably wasted in the Mick Jones/Keef tradition. The cigarette was, in fact, a piece of shameless fakery, as I never smoked, bearing in mind my mother's entreaties. I was not really cut out to be a rock n' roll rebel. Paul was a smoker and originally held the cigarette, but our photographer (Moncrieff) pronounced the tableau insufficiently realistic and transferred the gasper to me. Mum saw the photo and took a bit of convincing that I hadn't turned smoker. Paul has a cream jacket, collar turned up, with a Pleasers badge attached and a slightly shiny nylon shirt, which is difficult to place as being a la mode in any particular period. Next to him is PT with a cream cricket sweater, a stripy shirt with white collar and his old school prefect's tie. Now, old school ties were faintly fashionable in this period, when hung very loosely round the neck, better still paired with a t-shirt bearing an anti-establishment slogan, to create an ironically contrapositionary ensemble. The pairing with a David Steel-style shirt and cricket sweater went in entirely the wrong direction. These were, however, the days before Photo-Shop and we just had to live with it. PT used to hang out with the 'chaps' who were at the centre of the beer elephanting initiation ceremony. To be fair, he was a very nice guy. Paul, Jeremy and I were a bit of a gang and spent hours discussing the band and plotting our platinum future. It always felt as if PT would drop in at rehearsals on his way to his next rugby practice.

    Moncrieff, of course, became our manager. For some reason I cannot recall, it was determined that we should have a Kit Lambert/Chris Stamp style managerial pairing and an Old Etonian called Marcus Keppel-Palmer became our co-manager. He also wore cricket sweaters but it seemed to matter less and he looked the part of the slightly eccentric posh manager. *Spinal Tap* and the cricket bat wielding Ian Faith were still several years away at this point.

I think Jeremy came up with the name "The Stereotypes". I don't think we had a long list of alternatives and there wasn't much debate. It just seemed to be accepted. It's a pretty awful name, not quite in the Prefab Sprout league, but certainly on a par with the Beatles. It soon became part of the woodwork. Paul and I spent a lot of time together. Just sitting in each other's rooms, playing records, drinking cups of coffee with lumps of powdered milk floating on the top and, in his case, smoking. We would just sit there, taking it in turns to play each other one of our favourites. I knew not to even attempt playing King Crimson or 10cc, but XTC, the Buzzcocks and the Only Ones were worth a shot. In turn, I would hear Beatles and Stones stuff that I had never heard before because it wasn't on the red or blue compilations or *Rolled Gold*. Paul lent me a copy of *With The Beatles*, probably so I could learn *Money*. I thought it was a bit of a mixed bag, but it was my first introduction to brilliant Beatles' songs that I really should have known, like *Not A Second Time*. It was also a reminder of those fantastic sleeve notes that they used to write on sixties albums, in this case penned by Beatles' publicist, Tony Barrow. In keeping with the style of the time, Tony felt he had to sell the album like soap powder which was now in an extra-value 1lb pack. Thus, the record had no less than *"fourteen freshly recorded titles"* crammed into *"two generously filled sides"*. Later in this classic text Paul and John *"put their heads together to pen a special new number for their fierce throated drumming man"* and *"the result is a real raver"*. I had never thought of Ringo as fierce throated or indeed much of a singer at all. That was the great thing about vinyl – you could pore over the sleeve and the lyrics for hours to accompany your endless replays of your latest purchase. I remember a couple of years later chuckling over Stan Cornyn's sounds-like-your-dad notes to Sinatra's *Strangers In The Night* album[36], where, albeit in some wonderfully florid and beautifully written prose, he dismissed all pop music with a sweep of the pen: *"If the guitar were dis-invented tonight, a few thousand singers would be out on their amps. But not Sinatra. He defies fad. He stayeth. You can't sing the way he does until you've been belly to belly with reality a few times"*. I doubt in 1963 the Beatles had gone belly to belly with reality as much as Sinatra, but they seemed to make a good noise. Paul gave me a copy of *Rubber Soul* for my birthday. It's still one of my favourite Beatles albums, narrowly behind *Revolver*. Gradually, we forged a musical understanding. We wrote a few songs together. It was the beginning of a partnership. My contributions were pretty underwhelming and it was Paul's song-writing which was the foundation for this early version of the band. When he freed himself from his Chuck Berry anchor, he wrote beautiful soaring melody lines. Although at times deeply frustrating, he was a truly inspiring musician to work with. Competitive as I was, I knew I had to do better.

---

[36] *For which, apparently, he won a Grammy. I never knew there was a Grammy for best sleeve notes. Were there also ones for best pressing plant and distribution?*

Christmas 1978 came and went. We were tiring of the rehearsal room and wanted to take on the world. We had a ramshackle set comprising mainly covers, sprinkled with a few originals. Our joint managers got to work on arranging our global debut. February 2, 1979 was the 20th anniversary of the death of Buddy Holly[37]. It was also the date of our live debut. We decided to include *Rave On* in our set. The gig was in one of the rooms at Lady Margaret Hall. A reasonable crowd had gathered, with lots of our mates from Lincoln making the trip up to Norham Gardens to see what we were made of. We opened with *Money*. Surprisingly, it sounded good. I found myself wondering whether the crowd would think the same. They seemed to like it. Things seemed to be going well. Even PT's screwdriver solo was greeted with more favour than expected. The great chunks of primitive rhythm from my Satellite Les Paul copy combined pleasantly with PTs more refined phased lead, Paul's trebly bass and Jeremy's frenzied thrashing behind us. Our harmonies seemed in tune. What could go wrong? The crowd were in the palm of our hands. We were set fair for mega-stardom. I mentally computed our natural trajectory and my calculations confirmed a headline slot at Knebworth by summer 1981. It was at that moment that my Burns amp decided it had had enough and suddenly there were no more loud chunks of primitive rhythm. Like a raw recruit who had served his time through basic training, but faltered when ordered to go over the top of the trench, it had marched through rehearsals, only to let the platoon down when the big push came. We all huddled around the smoking wreck of an amplifier.

'Looks like the valves have blown,' I opined, despite having zero knowledge of the internal workings of a guitar amplifier.

I did know, however, that my amp had valves in it, so it seemed a reasonable supposition. The anniversary of the day the music died suddenly seemed horribly appropriate.

'Yeah – it's bad,' nodded Paul gravely.

PT concurred. Jeremy nodded agreement and then returned to bashing his snare drum, which is what he did at all critical band moments, including when the other three of us were trying to tune up or Paul and I were discussing the structure of a song. I since discovered that this was not just an individual idiosyncrasy of Jeremy, but a standard setting for all drummers. It was indeed a huge advance when the Linn drum arrived, equipped with the sort of manual override that we hankered for when Jeremy was bashing away. When the A.I. version of a real drummer arrives, fitted with a volume control and on/off switch, that will be an advance that will be received gratefully by all other musicians. We looked around for assistance from our roadies, then realised we didn't have any. Moncrieff was

---

[37] *Although it was 1am on February 3 in Clear Lake Iowa, it was still February 2 in the UK when the Beechcraft Bonanza carrying Buddy, the Big Bopper and Ritchie Valens crashed, killing them all.*

too busy working the crowd to notice the slightly longer than normal pause between numbers. God knows what Keppel-Palmer was doing. This was our first gig. We didn't have a contingency plan for malfunctioning equipment. We were out there, in the nervous white light of the stage, without a net and falling fast. After a few seconds, which felt like several years, during which we could feel the audience's attention ebbing fast, I noticed that Paul's bass combo had a spare input.

'I'll plug into Paul's WEM and hope it's loud enough,' I ventured.

The band sparked back into life, disaster averted. The crowd continued jumping up and down, seemingly oblivious to the sonic downgrade and happy enough with the thumping noise coming from the stage. I mentally adjusted our natural trajectory to a headline slot at the Rainbow, to take account of setbacks that, unlike this one, we were unable to deal with.

We discovered the next day that Sid Vicious had died. People seemed to think it had been inevitable and his destiny. I hoped that our rock and roll destiny wouldn't involve any death, and this seemed unlikely when you caught sight of PT's cricket sweater. We weren't sure what Buddy would make of Sid when he arrived in the celestial concert hall for the great gig in the sky.

The rest of the spring term of 1979 was a bit of a write-off. We had played a gig the night after the LMH debut in Lincoln Deep Hall, which passed without incident. Many of PT's chap friends turned up to see what all this rock n' roll fuss was about and looked a bit bewildered when they saw that no-one was elephanting. Soon after that gig, probably as a result of rehearsing in the freezing Lincoln cricket pavilion, I went down with an appalling flu, which knocked me out for three weeks and rendered my voice a hoarse croak for the rest of the term, precluding further gigging. A diet of Benylin and Lemsip for the rest of the term was the nearest I got to Sid's lifestyle. My etiolated pallor increased. Moncrieff marked my birthday with the touching present of a Clash bootleg. He presented it to me – *Clash White Riot Tour '77*, badly stencilled onto a white label. The track listing was nearly all of their set, with *Pressure Drop* and the mandatory mis-spellings that all bootlegs seemed to have – *London's Buzzing*. I was hugely excited. Where did Moncrieff get hold of all these rare bootlegs? I soon found out the answer. I slapped it on the turntable. Instead of the sturm and drang of the Clash, came the tame burbling of something resembling Crosby, Stills and Nash. It was a cruel wind-up. It turns out that *London's Buzzing* wasn't a deliberate master touch, but a mistake when the fellow student whom Moncrieff had enlisted to type the track listing couldn't read his handwriting and *London's Burning* inadvertently became *London's Buzzing*. Evil bastard.

Had you asked us where we would have liked our debut London gig to be, it is fair to say that Dingwalls, the Nashville, the Electric Ballroom and the Red Cow would have been in the mix, but Harrow School would not have made the cut. That was, however, the rather improbable venue for our maiden London appearance. PT had been at Harrow (a fact we were keen to airbrush out of our bio, together with the moustache) and his father was still a housemaster there. We were offered the opportunity to play there on a Sunday evening in late March. Paul and I looked at each other, each thinking that this sounded like a very bad idea. It certainly didn't fit with my image of the band.

Someone suggested it would be good to play in London.

'Harrow's not really London. If that counts, we could tick the London box by playing in my garage in Hornchurch,' I said surlily.

Besides, ever the pragmatist, I foresaw the logistical nightmare of getting all our kit to Harrow on a Sunday. For our first two gigs, we had used a trolley to ferry our amps to and from the venues. That seemed a mite impractical for Harrow. Talk of a substantial fee was, however, enough to dispel our concerns on the street credibility front. A parental car was appropriated to solve the transport issues.

We got to Harrow mid-afternoon to discover that, rather than playing the Harrow main stage, we were in fact headlining in the school gymnasium. This seemed rather an absurd idea. We weren't supported by a puppet show but it felt similarly ridiculous. Worse still, Jeremy and I had both recently begun dating two girls from St. Anne's and they'd come along to witness our glorious London debut. We were keen to impress. This was not what we had in mind.

It was certainly one of the strangest gigs I have ever played. The audience, whilst not wearing their gym kit or practising on the parallel bars while we thrashed through our set, were all in school uniform and plimsolls. There had clearly been an ordinance that soft-soled shoes should be worn to avoid damaging the gym floor. This did, however, assist them in pogoing, rather self-consciously but very vigorously, reaching heights that their gym master would have no doubt considered satisfactory effort. We played well and the judges awarded us 9.5s across the board for stylistic content and execution and an encore of *Dirty Water*. We left Harrow with our honour satisfied and our relationships with the St. Anne's pair intact.

The Lent term during the lay-off from gigging had not been wasted. Paul and I would get together almost every day to try and write something. I could tell that he thought that my song-writing efforts were not in the same league as his. He was right but I was determined to seek promotion in my first season. His own songs were generally clever, with good tunes, but normally went astray at the middle eight with some mind-bending lyrical and melodic swerve, which I assumed was his bid for some artistic credibility. To me, they just sounded stupid. He wrote a brilliant song called *Too Many Morons,* which had an infectious fast chord sequence but, as you got to the chorus, it veered off into a strange key as he sang *"they've buried the intellectuals"* multiple times, while the listener rued the fact that they seemed to have missed one. Another had a chorus proclaiming *"I don't mind, cardboard can't hurt me"*. Paul was always writing songs with titles like *The Coastguard's Fifth Dream* with lyrics about queuing for quicksand. I saw it as my job to expunge all such fripperies from the band and to refurbish his middle eights and choruses so that they could be enjoyed by the world outside the Captain Beefheart fan club. Paul clearly saw this as a grotesque corruption of his artistic vision and tended to vacillate between (often enthusiastic) acceptance of the merits of collaboration and, on the other hand, rejection of any compromise of the purity of his original vision. Our first joint efforts didn't stay in the set long but gradually we got better. *Moving Away From The Shadows* was one of the few Galley/Cooke originals from our first six months to survive more than a couple of gigs. Its title was a mash-up of Buzzcocks and Stranglers tracks, with words on loan from Strummer and Jones, complete with sten guns in Knightsbridge and references to the IMG[38]. Despite its overwhelming dash of Clash, it worked as a song and tended to go down well.

---

[38] *The International Marxist Group, not the Mark McCormick sports representation organization, although a song featuring the latter would be a challenge but, for the moment, we had decided not to go down the Half Man Half Biscuit route.*

We obviously spent a long time discussing whether our song-writing credits should be Galley/Cooke or Cooke/Galley. Alphabetical order favoured me. Paul reasoned that Galley/Cooke sounded much better than Cooke/Galley, just like Lennon/McCartney. I pointed out that the songs on *Please Please Me* (which Paul had also lent me, this time to learn *I Saw Her Standing There* for our set) were credited McCartney/Lennon. There was a brief impasse before I conceded, partly because I agreed that Galley/Cooke did sound better, but mainly because he was clearly the senior partner and a proper songwriter, while I was just an ambitious chancer who was tagging along for the ride.

Don't Treat Me Like A Coat was originally a song Jeremy had from his school band. Jeremy sang it to me one day in his room, but couldn't really remember the words, apart from the chorus. I thought at first it was called *Don't Treat Me Like A Goat*, which I thought was quite interesting, and frustrating that he couldn't remember the words, as I was curious to know what treatment as a goat might entail. Jeremy couldn't hold a tune to save his life so I had to approximate it and make up some chords. The words were a grisly pun-fest:

Don't treat me like a coat,
Putting me on and wearing me out.
You said you loved me, now you don't,
Do you ever wonder I get so hung up?

You took me to the cleaners
And treated me like dirt.
You kept me in your closet
And darling that really hurt.

Couplets that could indeed have been written by Basil Brush and lacking the sort of emotional charge that is engendered by true loss and dislocation. This was shortly to arrive.

On arriving back in Oxford after the Easter vacation, my first port of call was up the Banbury Road to see St. Anne's Girl, from whom I'd been apart for two weeks. This was the sort of deprivation I could have barely imagined six months ago. She'd come to stay in Hornchurch for a few days during the vacation. I thought it went well. Mum, however, noted that she had a ruthless streak, finishing Mum off in their last game of chess when my mother (who considered her an inferior player) had graciously gone lightly on her and not pounced on her many tactical errors in the previous games. My years of similar ruthlessness in repeatedly scholar's mating Mum in five moves seemed to have been forgotten. This observation had, in fact, probably been made after I told Mum that we had split up, supportive soul that she was, but who am I to upset a good narrative? My return visit to her house in Chepstow was not such a success. I had made a mental note not to play any member of her family at chess or any other competitive sport, now realizing the unexpected pitfalls that lay there. Despite my personal embargo on board games with her relatives, I managed to fall out with her father almost immediately on arrival. He was called Roydon, was a domineering bully, and clearly didn't welcome my presence in his daughter's life. He was a rabid Welsh independence supporter, although apparently mainly as a mechanism for keeping blacks and Asians out of Wales. As a white Englishman, I was only marginally more acceptable. He was also keen on expounding his repellent views over the dinner table. I was only able to maintain silence for a matter of minutes. A significant row ensued.

'My boy, you're nothing more than a communist,' was his closing statement, shortly before he exited the room, red-faced.

I wasn't, but had been wearing my Rock Against Racism badge for long enough to know that what I had heard was pretty abhorrent. Matters took an even more negative turn when a routine search of St Anne's Girl's bedroom by Roydon - apparently a common occurrence in the household - revealed her contraceptive pills. The kitchen of St. Anne's Girl's house was not a good place to be, as Roydon brandished the packet as irrefutable evidence that his lily of the valleys had been defiled by some infidel from the wrong side of Offa's Dyke. The fractious atmosphere soon became too much and, by mutual consent, I was off to the station, deported back to England. I hoped that we might navigate our way through this minefield, but my heart told me that a black cloud had descended upon our relationship. I hoped that blue sky might soon return, but my experience of holidays in Wales told me that the black cloud was unlikely to disappear for a while and likely to rain down bad stuff for a considerable time. I looked out of the train window at Newport Station as she waved goodbye in a manner that seemed to evince emotional uncertainty and shed a tear. She was my first real love and I was in deep. I told myself to harden my heart and be more distant from the epicentre of the potential explosion. This is something I have never managed to achieve, then, since or now. If it came, I was going to be right in the middle of the blast zone.

I had hoped that the hiatus of a fortnight might draw a line under this hiccup in our relationship. There was, however, a certain frostiness and distance to her manner when I got to her room, which, even for someone as inexperienced as me in the ways of love, rang alarm bells. A dumping was coming. I could feel it. The fact that there was a general election going on, the first in which I was eligible to vote, was a mere sideshow to the emotional turbulence I was feeling. A delay in execution of the blow by St. Anne's Girl of about 24 hours cruelly allowed me to briefly believe that my instincts had been awry and that she was just in a bad mood.

The hammer blow came and it hurt. Like a true pro, she did it in my room in Lincoln, rather than her room in St. Anne's, so she could terminate the encounter at her time of choosing. That old ruthless streak again. I headed for Jeremy's room and sought male companionship. As usual, he was playing some reggae that I'd never heard before. If I'd ever felt like accepting a spliff in my life, it was then. Fortunately, he had some scotch, which took the edge off the Delroy Wilson 12" he was playing, as well as helping ease the emotional turbulence I was feeling. Jeremy inhabited the John Le Carre room, named after its former occupant, the famous author. I had truly come in from the cold and Jeremy debriefed me in a way that George Smiley would have been proud of, sensitively extracting each detail, to build up a picture of the doomed relationship, interrupting the interview only to replace Delroy with *Garvey's Ghost*. It was enormously comforting. He definitely had a future as a psychotherapist. It was only later, once the whisky had worn off, that I remembered that he was still going out with St. Anne's Girl 2 and the current inhabitant of the John Le Carre room was clearly a mole, albeit one clad in a dubby disguise that the SIS would not have the creativity to adopt until many years later.

When I woke up the next morning, my baby had gone. She treated me bad, she done me wrong. I had the blues. I also had a hangover. I assumed that if Robert Johnson were available, he'd attest that the two often went hand in hand. I picked up my guitar. Rather than singing *Love In Vain*, with Burning Spear still lodged in my brain and it being a warm, sunny morning in May, I turned more naturally to reggae, and found myself plucking the chords of *Don't Treat Me Like A Coat* and mouthing the comedy words Jeremy and I had penned. A new, less Brush-like, verse soon emerged:

> *I kept you warm, you thought I was useful,*
> *You only needed me now and then.*
> *Your feelings change with the weather.*
> *Guess I'll have to wait 'til it's cold again.*

They seemed a bit more real and heartfelt than the rest of the song. So there was a silver lining to that big black Welsh cloud.

I managed to get myself together to go to the polling station and vote on election day. John Patten, the Tory candidate, won the seat. I voted Labour. It was the start of almost twenty years of fruitless exercise of my franchise. I followed Talking Heads' advice and tried not to worry about the government, but it proved increasingly difficult.

The summer of 1979 was a brilliant time for the band. My last set of exams for two years had passed without incident, with the help of some notes borrowed from one of my friends, Dave Graham. I pleaded incapacitation through illness, when in reality indolence was the true story. He was acquiescent in a saintly way. I tried to repeat the trick in the following term but he wasn't playing ball, having got the measure of the indolence issue, notwithstanding that my cough still lingered. There was nothing to do except play croquet, cricket and music. For once in the life of the band, we were united around a common liking of a single record, Graham Parker's *Squeezing Out Sparks*. We all bought it and agreed it was a brilliant. Moncrieff had the Japanese import, of course, which included *Mercury Poisoning,* GP's searing indictment of his own record label, which was understandably excised from the UK version. We all trooped off to Gants Hill Odeon in the Easter vacation to see them live. We noted the way that Brinsley Schwartz and Martin Belmont's guitars played off each other and filed that away for future reference.

Moncrieff suggested that we start a regular residency at the Cape of Good Hope. The Cape was a rather down at heel pub on the Magdalen bridge roundabout. It had a bad name with bands, mainly on account of its rather unpleasant landlord and the difficult set of steps, up which you had to lug your PA and kit. The landlord, Fred, didn't really like students, viewing them, with some justification, as layabouts who had never done a decent day's work in their lives. We certainly didn't do much to dispel his prejudices. A little bit of law having already rubbed off on me during my sporadic studies, I did wonder whether, with him having taken up residence in England's oldest university town, this might have led one to conclude, as Lord Denning once said, that he had come to his nuisance and should just shut the fuck up and quietly subsist on the proceeds of students drinking in his godforsaken hostelry. To be clear, Lord Denning never said that last bit. Fred also instructed us not to admit any "Winstons or Pakis" and had a fearsome dog, which looked quite vicious. I remember it to be a pit bull, but this is probably canine stereotyping on my part. None of us wanted to stroke the dog and Paul was particularly nervous of it. We deputed Moncrieff to conduct all business dealings with Fred. Moncrieff as usual did so with a cocky London charm, ignoring Fred's apartheid mandates as he collected money on the door. He even collected money off Patrik Fitzgerald, who came to see us after his gig at the Oranges and Lemons. Normally, no-one would have recognised him, but that was reckoning against Moncrieff's extensive minor celebrity mental database. Patrik also seemed to expect that he should be admitted for free. Perhaps he knew I'd seen him for free the previous year in Victoria Park. Moncrieff wasn't having any of it, and extracted the full price of admission from the acoustic punk poet. We played at the Cape most weeks, honed our act and started to build an audience. The same faces started to appear each week and they weren't just our mates from Lincoln.

The college ball season did not offer us much credibility, but what the hell, we were a student band from Oxford, so there wasn't much credibility to be had in the first place, and balls were fun. What's more, Elvis Costello was playing at Teddy Hall ball so it must be ok. We could be supporting the likes of him. Who knows, we might get to meet Jake Riviera and get signed to his new label. It is fair to say that, in the universe of bands that we would wish to support and hang out with, Dave Dee, Dozy, Beaky, Mick and Titch were not high up the list. They were one of the crappiest bands from the sixties and the fact that they were still an operating unit was almost certainly completely unknown. They were headlining the Lincoln Ball and we had been signed up to support them. There was no sign of Jake Riviera. In fact, it wasn't Dave Dee, Dozy, Beaky, Mick and Titch, as Dave Dee had cleared off years before for a career as an A&R man, and they were now just Dozy, Beaky, Mick and Titch. Dave Dee had been the lead singer, so his absence pushed them to the top of "band missing a critical member" leader board, narrowly beating the Sensational Alex Harvey Band (without Alex). I doubt, however, that any member of DDDBM&T could be considered critical.

According to Wikipedia, they have continued to gig. Various members have retired and they are on their third Beaky and Mick and second Titch, substituted just like pet goldfish and dogs. Dozy was never replaced. Even with my anal knowledge of music, I wasn't sufficiently well-versed to know whether the DBM&T appearing at Lincoln were the originals or their replacements. I did wonder, however, which idiot on the Lincoln Ball committee had made the decision to hire them. Probably one of the elephanting chaps. DBM&T's set seemed to go on forever. They started off trying to be a serious band, covering the Band's *The Shape I'm In*, but soon descended to donning their capes and cracking whips during *The Legend of Xanadu*. It is a reasonable rule of thumb that any song with "Xanadu" in the title is going to be crap[39] and this was no exception. Despite a tepid audience reaction, they played endless encores of *Bend It* and *Zabadak*. By the time we went on, it was three in the morning. We, and the audience, had peaked several hours before. Even though we were playing on the biggest stage on which we had ever been, it was a dispiriting experience.

The next day everyone was in a bad mood. Paul was grumbling about there being too many of my songs in the set. I was moaning about no-one helping me shift the kit after the gig. PT wanted us to play *Sultans of Swing*, which no-one else thought was a good idea. Instead we tried his other suggestion, Tom Petty's *Breakdown* but Paul and PT argued about what the chords were. Jeremy just thumped away on his snare drum during these discussions until someone (almost certainly me) shouted at him to shut up. It was a fractious atmosphere.

I can't remember exactly who walked out first but by lunchtime the band was no more.

---

[39] *The offerings by ELO/Olivia Newton-John and Rush with this title confirm the soundness of this theory.*

Groovy Times

It was the briefest of splits.

The next day I was sitting in my room thinking about what I would do instead of rehearsing and writing songs with Paul. Maybe I'd play more cricket. I could always watch *Emmerdale Farm* or *Crown Court*. The fact that I was attending a seat of high learning obviously did not prompt me to consider more studying as a plausible way of filling the void left by the demise of the band. The nearest I would get to feeling the pressure of my academic surroundings was by watching Carl Sagan's *Cosmos* rather than *Blake's 7*. In reality, I would not watch *Cosmos* so I could marvel at the wonders of the universe, but rather at Carl's mangling of his vowels and how many times he would say "uman" - as in "the uman race" or "umanity" - during a single programme. Never mind the rings of Saturn and the crab nebula, it was a true wonder how someone could get to present a primetime television programme when they were barely comprehensible to most of the population.

There was a knock on my door.

It was Keppel-Palmer.

'There's been an interesting development,' he said, mysteriously.

'What?' I grunted.

He always liked to over-dramatise everything and involve himself in personal intrigues, so I suspected that it wouldn't be in the least bit interesting. It might not even be a development.

'I had a call today.'

I could see it was going to take a while to drag the salient facts out of him. I affected a disinterested look.

'Yeah?'

'We've been asked to play a gig.'

'WE don't exist any more,' I countered.

'That's a shame, because it was the organisers of the Bicester Rock Festival wanting to know if we could play on the main stage,' he said smugly, while closely scrutinizing my face for a reaction.

I didn't know where Bicester was or, indeed, that it held any musical events of note, but the words "rock festival" and "main stage" got me very excited indeed. It was a bit like getting the news that *Sex Farm* has gone top ten in Japan and a tour is on the cards, except that hadn't happened yet.

'Does Paul know?' I asked.

'Moncrieff's talking to him.'

By lunchtime, we had agreed to reform.

There was one snag. PT had committed to spend three months water skiing in the South of France, or something like that, and couldn't play at Bicester. Band solidarity should have demanded that we turned the gig

163

down immediately, but PT's moustache and cricket sweater precluded that kind of band solidarity. There were various derogatory comments about water skiing. Paul mentioned that the Beatles had used Jimmie Nicol when Ringo had got tonsillitis just before their Australian tour in 1964. This seemed a weighty and relevant precedent. We decided to take the gig. PT accepted the news with his usual equanimity and returned to his reveries of Riviera. French, not Jake.

The search for a replacement for PT didn't take long. Jeremy said he knew a guitarist from his old band. No-one had a better idea. He was in. We gathered in a rehearsal space under the railway arches by Hackney Downs station in the week before the gig. His name was Steve Critoph and he looked the part. He had an Ibanez Les Paul copy, generally had a cigarette hanging out of the corner of his mouth in the classic tradition, and played with the sort of Keef-ish attitude that both Paul and I liked. He wasn't as new wave as I would have wanted, but he brought a punkish energy to the band that was good. The week that we spent in that rehearsal space was some of the best fun that we'd had. The band sounded better and we did a lot of jamming for recreation, rather than just rehearsing. Being in a proper London rehearsal space made us feel more like a real band than some Oxford students playing at pop stars. We went to the pub over the road and joshed like a proper group. There were four of us, rather than three of us and another bloke who turned up to rehearsals. It felt more like the sort of band that I wanted it to be. I think Paul felt the same.

The Stereotypes on stage at the Bicester Rock Festival. Paul would probably have preferred not to have been singing from behind a piece of scaffold.

There was quite a bit of excitement around us about our first outdoor festival appearance. My sister Laura and one of her friends tagged along. We were hardly expecting Woodstock, but by the time we got to Bicester, we were half a dozen strong. The weather that summer had been hot and dry, and that held for the Saturday of the festival - it was a beautiful sunny day, so no-one told us that if we thought really hard we could stop the rain, but there was lots of brown grass. Someone told us there were about 10,000 people there. We had no idea if that was right, but there was a crowd big enough to make us quite nervous. Our time in the Hackney rehearsal space was well spent and we were well drilled with a set list that we knew backwards. Half our songs, half cover versions. The 45 minutes we were on stage seemed to pass in about 5. It was a fantastic feeling. The crowd, whilst not being ecstatic, were reasonably appreciative and we came off-stage on a massive high. We would never again play live to so many people.

It was time to go into a recording studio. In truth, we probably all would have liked to go into the studio with Steve Critoph, rather than PT, but no-one suggested it. It just felt too disloyal. The experience of Bicester with Critoph gave us a taste of what we could be, but we just weren't ruthless enough. We gathered at Jeremy's house in Woodford, near to the studio he had booked.

Except he hadn't.

It was unclear why the studio hadn't been booked and there were some raised voices, mainly mine, I imagine. As Viv Albertine says in *Clothes Clothes Clothes Music Music Music Boys Boys Boys,* in every band there is a member who does all the organizing and who takes the pain and the losses of the band to heart. In the Beatles, it was clearly Paul McCartney. You only need to look at the footage of the *Let It Be* film to see that, and the friction it causes in the band, in particular the classic grump of George Harrison. In the Stereotypes, it was me. I had never been particularly organized before in my life, just another shambolic teenager who never knew which day it was. I turned into something else once the Stereotypes had started. I was ambitious for the band to succeed and, when I set my mind to something, it's a pretty immovable force. Paul would later observe that I was a bit like his dad and was too bossy. I never met his dad, but I'm sure Paul was right. I wanted to get stuff done and had little time for the niceties of how I communicated that. Not much has changed since. I had little tolerance for organizational failings elsewhere. Again, not much has changed since. When Jeremy looked blank about the studio booking and we then established it was already booked by another band, I cannot recall exactly what occurred, but there would certainly have been some cross words exchanged. As I reached for the nearest Yellow Pages to locate a replacement, I probably had a look on my face which said "If you want something doing….."

It is fair to say that no noisy rebellious music has ever emerged from Ingatestone in Essex, nor is it ever likely to. Ingatestone was quite near to where I went to school and I had a couple of friends who lived there. It is the ultimate sleepy commuter haven. A by-pass of the A12 around Ingatestone was built in the late 50s and, since then, the rest of the world has pretty much left Ingatestone to itself. The nearest Ingatestone has come to being on the rock n roll map is Ian Dury's *Billericay Dickie*, the eponymous town being a mere five miles away. Ian Dury never recorded any songs about Ingatestone. "Pussycat Tracks" in Ingatestone was, however, the only studio we could find which was free. It did not have a name that inspired confidence. No doubt the Ingatestone and Fryerning Musical and Operetta Society are still doing good works, but I knew that Ingatestone would not be a great environment for our maiden recording. It was about an hour away from Jeremy's house. It was our only choice.

The engineer, Ray Durrant, was very old school, but not in a good way. He was clearly from the Bert Weedon *Play In A Day* camp where you used your amp with taste and discretion. Consequently, we weren't allowed to turn our amps up to five, let alone eleven. He probably thought we should sit on stools. He looked apprehensively at my leather jacket and Red Army Faction badge. Aside from the occasional argument in the Rotary Club, political unrest was not a big feature of Ingatestone. He suggested we enunciate our words more clearly. We recorded four songs. *Nostalgia* probably came out the best, as it had a lighter feel more suited to Ray's MOR leanings. We excised PT's screwdriver solo from its intro, which he was grumpy about. Ray didn't like it when Paul sang "last time now" before the final chorus, which we thought gave it a rough and ready live-ish feel. Ray didn't want a rough and ready live-ish feel. *Lovers of the Future* was one of my St. Anne's Girl breakup songs, with a title and guitar intro shamelessly copped from two different Only Ones songs. Ray put a stupid effect on my voice on *Don't Treat Me Like A Coat,* which made it sound as if I was singing through a megaphone. It chugged along inoffensively but didn't sound anything like reggae. I wanted us to sound like the Clash, but it came out like an Eagles tribute band. We made sure it wouldn't happen again. Given that the day had started so unpromisingly, we were happy enough to have been inside a recording studio and captured four of our songs, albeit in a manner which seemed to bear no relation to what we actually sounded like.

I spent the rest of summer 1979 writing songs and working at McCarthy's Pharmaceuticals. The Clash were relatively quiet, releasing just a single EP of new music, *The Cost of Living.* It was a bit of a curate's egg, but we gobbled it up hungrily. *I Fought The Law* was a brilliant cover version, but there was some alarming acoustic guitar on *Groovy Times.* Clash fans would have to learn to be more broad-minded about their musical stylings in future. Paul and I would exchange cassette tapes through the post. Sometimes I would write some music and send it to him for the words or write some words for him to do some music. Sometimes I would just reconstruct one of his bizarre middle sections. I had decided that my Satellite Les Paul copy needed to go. It was a pretty awful guitar, which just wouldn't stay in tune. I decided I needed to work to buy an Ibanez Les Paul copy like Critoph's. At some point during the summer, the plan morphed into buying a real Gibson Les Paul. By mid-September I had the £380, which I knew was what was needed to go to the shop I had identified in Denmark Street and get myself a Les Paul Standard, cherry sunburst finish.

Straight Outta Ingatestone. An unlikely setting for our first recording date.

The guitar shops in Denmark Street were even more forbidding places than the guitar shop in Romford. They had the usual collection of long-haired shop assistants sitting around noodling on their instruments, rather than serving anyone, but everyone looked even more serious and competent than in Romford. This was where real rock musicians bought their instruments. Eventually I managed to catch the attention of one of the dimestore Blackmores, interrupting a 15 minute rendition of *Highway Star*. Punk had still not arrived in these places. He handed me the instrument to try. It was much heavier than I expected. My Satellite felt as if it had been made out of balsa wood in comparison. It was a completely different instrument.

Unfettered by any Weedon-like strictures, I even got to turn up the Fender Twin Reverb they had plugged me into and marvelled at the sustain I could get. I almost sounded like a proper guitarist. In reality, it didn't matter what it sounded like – I wouldn't have known good from bad – I had set my heart on it. I handed over the banker's draft and it was mine. Obviously the first hour or so when I got home was spent examining how it looked on me in the mirror. It felt good. It had a thick, meaty sound, which was much louder than my Satellite. As I got to know guitars better later, it became clear that a Les Paul is not a weapon of choice for all situations (in particular, when I played in a jazz band in the eighties), but for the Stereotypes in 1979 it was perfect.

When I got back to Oxford in late September, word got around that I had bought a real Gibson. People would come to my room to examine it as if it were some holy relic. Paul didn't share my enthusiasm for it. He was pleased that I had a guitar that wasn't constantly going out of tune, but probably wondered why I hadn't bought a Rickenbacker or an Epiphone Casino like the one Lennon used in the Rubber Soul period. He's never liked the sound of a Les Paul and still doesn't. I didn't care. I was one step nearer Mick Jones.

Temporary Kings

I don't remember exactly what Mr A. P. Horn of Barclays Old Bank on the High Street looked like, as I only met him once. He was my bank manager at Oxford and later in my time there we had a spirited correspondence about my habit of running unauthorized overdrafts, which culminated in him writing to instruct me to destroy my Barclaycard immediately. I visualize him as looking like Richard Wattis, with small round national health specs and a stiff collar, but that is probably projection from watching too many Ealing comedy portrayals of bank managers. He was also the Stereotypes bank manager, as we had an account there. It never seemed to have any money in it. Certainly not enough for him to contact us with creative investment ideas, possibly tax exile or diversification into plastics, or even just putting the funds into an interest bearing deposit account. The finances of most students were a pretty haphazard affair, and I was no exception. I was always running an overdraft by the end of term and would work each vacation to build up some funds to squander the following term. The fact that we didn't use real money at Lincoln didn't help. We lived entirely on plastic money. Not credit card plastic money but real plastic money – plastic tokens that you signed for and were put on your college battels (as Oxford college accounts were quaintly named) bill. It was like living inside a strange board game, rather divorced from reality. When you got your battels bill at the end of term, it generally came as a nasty shock, pretty much an irrefutable record of how many pints of beer you had drunk.

The occasion of meeting A. P. Horn was when Paul and I went to see him to seek funding for a Stereotypes business venture. Paul often wore a suit and tie (in a sixties retro sort of way, but not as retro as A. P. Horn), so looked quite respectable. I can't remember what I wore. I didn't own a suit or tie that I would wish to be seen around in. I briefly considered borrowing Jeremy's skinny leather tie, but decided that it wasn't going to achieve the desired effect. We were quite hopeful. We had lent and entrusted our funds to A. P. Horn for the last year. It was his turn to return the favour, we reasoned. Paul did the talking. I may not be able to remember exactly what A. P. Horn looked like, but he definitely did have a look of boredom and complete disdain on his face. In all fairness, our proposition did lack the sort of detail that any responsible bank manager would require before green-lighting a loan. We were doomed to failure. It didn't take long for A. P. Horn to dispatch us from his premises, empty-handed.

The winter of '79 was not remotely like Tom Robinson had predicted it to be in his song of the same name two years earlier. A pint of beer was still only 30p in the college bar, not ten bob, National Service didn't come back in and the SAS didn't come and take our names. One can't help thinking

Tom was being a bit alarmist. His football forecasting was no more accurate. Spurs didn't beat Arsenal, the Gunners winning 1-0 at Highbury on Boxing Day. Typical. I could have predicted that. His career as a soothsayer, as well as a musician, was over, Tom having also failed to predict that the Tom Robinson Band's second album would be a real stinker and would completely bomb.

When we gathered for our first rehearsal of the new term in October 1979, Paul and I brought along a clutch of new songs. They were a step forward from our previous efforts and most of them were destined to stay in our set for the rest of the life of the band. The next few months was a period of great development. If this were a film, there would be a montage sequence at around this point, showing Paul and I writing together, the band tirelessly rehearsing, kicking out many of our old Chuck Berry covers and replacing them with our own songs, with the audiences growing and more appreciative. There would be shots of our posters getting more professional looking and showing the venues getting bigger. We needed to take it to the next level.

The business venture that A. P. Horn had rejected was making our own record. It was around the beginning of 1980 that this idea emerged. It seemed the obvious thing to do. A fruitless round of sending demo tapes to record companies had driven us to it. We had put together a demo tape, including some of the tracks from our Ingatestone venture, mixed with some live recordings to show how we really sounded. Sending demo tapes to record companies is truly a soul-destroying experience. If you believe A&R men, they don't care about the quality of your recording or how well produced it is – for they are the consummate professionals with golden ears, able to discern that kernel of true talent from even the most crudely produced and badly presented recording. Don't believe that for a moment. You should assume they are cloth-eared dolts who are unable to appreciate anything unless it sounds exactly like they expect the finished product to sound. So when you get a letter back from them saying something like *"We have carefully listened to your tape. Unfortunately it is not for us. It is not our policy to return demo tapes."* they mean *"having listened to the first 15 seconds, we noticed it had been quite badly recorded and didn't sound like the current number one so we threw it in the bin."* Or sell it as a job lot with every other demo tape they've received that week: a few years ago Paul found one of our demo tapes for sale on eBay. We received a good variety of rejection letters, with some creative variations on the theme that we were not for them. Stiff told us we had narrowly missed joining the Stiff artists roster. The cynic in me assumed that was what they said to all the girls. One label even told us that they couldn't sign us as they were closing down. That sounded a bit of an over-reaction to our under-produced demo tape. We had a band meeting to discuss the record project. Paul and I were enthusiastic. Jeremy leaped and down a bit which seemed to indicate he liked the idea. PT was lukewarm, particularly when it became clear that we would have to put our own money into it. The band cash call brought to the surface the difference in commitment that had always lurked since we began. PT was quite fair about it. We were always keener on the band than him, he said, and he didn't want to spend his grant money on our record. He probably had his eye on a new pair of water skis. This had been coming for a while.

Things had taken a turn for the worse the previous Autumn, when he wanted us to play one of his songs. Up until then he'd been happy just to play guitar and the Galley/Cooke song-writing partnership had no George Harrison to upset the delicate balance of power. We could see trouble on the horizon. The song was called *Adults of the 80s*. Paul and I didn't like it. It had tacky words and was not really us. To be fair, we weren't the most objective judges of other people's songs, particularly when they were being presented to our band. We agreed to play it. PT couldn't sing so one of us had to. For once, Paul was happy for me to take the lead vocal. I wasn't.

'I've got another song,' said PT.

Paul and I looked at each other. One song was just about fine, but any more were out of the question. We had to draw a line, otherwise next thing you know Jeremy would be wanting to have his own song and as history shows that would be a disaster. We would be one step away from an Alan White or Carl Palmer solo album. However good this next song was, it was clear that we were going to hate it. Fortunately, it was truly awful and we rejected it with a clear conscience.

By the end of the meeting, we were short of one guitarist and no nearer to making a record.

'I know a guitarist,' said Jeremy. 'He's called Eric'.

He wasn't, in fact, called Eric. He was called Stuart and he was from Liverpool, which was a plus in Paul's eyes. I still don't know why he was called Eric. Someone said it was because he played guitar like Clapton. He didn't play guitar remotely like Clapton. His surname was Donaldson so maybe Jeremy had been playing *Cherry Oh Baby* and made the leap from there. In any event, the name Eric stuck. He had rather long hair, which I gave my views on. He looked a bit like the guitarist in the Ruts, whose hair was also a bit too long for my tastes. He was however wearing skinny black jeans and had a cigarette in his hand. He had a haunted nervous look about him. He didn't have a moustache. Visually at least, this was a huge improvement. We didn't really hold an audition, we just met Eric. It was assumed he could play the guitar well. Fortunately he could. We were back in business.

'There's too much shit on the tape, Eric. We need to get the shit off the tape,' said the slightly exasperated engineer as Eric attempted his fifteenth take of a guitar solo.

The engineer was Larry Wallis. Not the Larry Wallis who was in the Pink Fairies, was a founder member of Motorhead and made that great single *Police Car*. Not him, but his father. Larry Wallis senior ran a dingy little studio in South London called Duffy's. That was where we were attempting to record our single. Senior didn't have a wild mane of black curly hair or wear shades and a leather jacket 24/7 like junior did. He had a cardigan and a pair of comfortable slacks. We found the studio through our new manager, Pat Fish. Pat Fish had entered our lives around the time that Eric joined the band. Pat Fish's real name was not Pat Fish but Patrick Gerard Sibley Huntrods. He was also a wannabee rock star and that was not the sort of name that was compatible with his self-image, so Pat Fish he became. His self-image was a wasted member of the Velvet Underground, MC5 or a band like that, ingesting chemicals on a regular basis and hanging out with a very cool crowd. He was in fact very posh, and the rumour was that his mother was the mayor of Northampton. If this was true, he was keen to downplay it and affected a nasal cockney-inflected whine, when making his regular Delphic pronouncements on the state of the world. My mother had done her best to remove all residual estuary English characteristics from my speaking voice. Patrick had been moving in the opposite direction. He had been around for a while, studying Greats at Merton, and saw himself as the godfather of Oxford rock, even doing a Pete Frame style family tree detailing his involvement in the nascent scene. To his credit, he kept at it and when we'd all given up, he did achieve cult success as *the Jazz Butcher*, recording albums with titles like *The Jazz Butcher in a Bath of Bacon*. He just carried on as he was at Oxford, maintaining his persona of being an anarchic rock rebel, while we all got jobs as lawyers and civil servants. I remember seeing him on *The Tube* one Friday night, when he played his new single *Hard*, a typical tuneless strum-along, and laughing when Jools Holland took the piss out of him for leaving his guitar feeding back against the amp at the end, a characteristic piece of Patrick minor league anarcho-posing. In retrospect, we were cut from very different cloth. He was most comfortable in discomfort and liked to be unpredictable to an extent that was predictable. We didn't have much in common, music wise. He was even more wilfully obscure than Moncrieff and didn't really like anything that had sold more than 100 copies. Our only common musical reference point was Kevin Ayers, although his second Butcher album was called *A Scandal In Bohemia*, so I assume he was also a Sherlock Holmes fan. He did seem immensely cool and well connected in the Oxford music scene, so we hung out with him. Jeremy embraced him enthusiastically, I did so with some hesitation and Paul never liked him. I think Eric thought he was a bit frightening. Moncrieff and Keppel-Palmer had been tiring of the management role (and probably fed up with me doing all the organizing when that was their job) and had resigned some months before. We decided that we should ask Pat to be our manager. He liked the idea of extending his

The Morning of our Lives / Steve Cooke

173

McClaren-like empire and said yes. He already managed another Oxford band, *The Sonic Tonix*. In his estimation, we were clearly the Bow Wow Wow in his stable, to the Tonix's Pistols. He adored the Tonix and was constantly suggesting ways that we might be more like them. Endless hours were spent in his room at Merton listening to his anecdotes about the glory years of 77-79 and how the Tonix blazed their trail. I was the wedding guest to his ancient mariner as he droned on about the glory days of Oxford alt-rock. *"You boys just need to take more speed and turn your amps up all the way. That's why the Tonix sound great." "I remember when the Tonix supported the Only Ones. John Perry kept asking if we had any chemicals." "I was so close to the Tonix that we used to share each other's socks"* were typical sentences.

    We didn't actually want to sound like the Tonix, and we definitely didn't want to share their socks. Their single, *Don't Go Away,* was the catchiest of their songs (a low benchmark, as most of their set was composed of tuneless dirges with titles like *Mutants Club* and *Dinosaur*) and had been recorded at Duffy's. It sounded good, mainly due to some infectious lines played by their young lead guitarist, Simon Mawby, who ended up a few years later in the House of Love. Duffy's therefore seemed the obvious place for us to make our record. *Lovers of the Future* was originally going to be the A side but Paul came up with a new song *Calling All The Shots*. The verse was very catchy. Jeremy told us that it was the same as Iggy Pop's *The Passenger* and my Dad said that it sounded like *Puttin' On The Ritz*, but we didn't care. As usual, Paul's first version came equipped with an odd-sounding chorus with lyrics about buried intellectuals and a man behind a console that didn't seem to fit his verses. I wrote a chorus and some words for the other verses. It sounded good. We started working it up. In the past, working up a song just meant both guitars chugging along, playing pretty much the same thing, with a wall of buzzsaw guitar and then a guitar solo after the second chorus. With *Shots,* for pretty much the first time, we arranged the guitars to play complementary parts. I picked the intro around the chords and then Eric would play some harmony arpeggios. Very quickly it sounded a lot better than everything else we were playing and got promoted to the short list for the single and later to the A side. We started to work on all of our material in the same way, rearranging so that the two guitars were bouncing off each other. We were starting to sound a lot more interesting.

    Patrick escorted us to Duffy's on a rainy Saturday morning. It was agreed that he would co-produce the record. We didn't actually know what producing a record involved but assumed that Patrick would be able to do it in his sleep. We got the basic tracks and vocals down pretty quickly and then it was time for Eric to do his guitar solo. This was much less straightforward. Eric was nervous and didn't react well to six increasingly impatient faces staring in at him through the control room window. If Patrick or anyone else had really known how to produce a record, they might have suggested that we all bugger off and leave Eric to it, to take the pressure off him. I think Patrick quietly suggested that Eric partake of some of the huge plastic bag of weed that he was as usual carrying around. It might have been a good idea, but I growled something disapproving. I never took drugs and didn't like them and, already adopting some civic responsibility, I thought it was unfair to put Larry in a difficult position by using them in his studio. Besides, he might not be as broad minded as George Martin and, rather than taking us up to the roof for some fresh air, he might just simply kick us all out. Larry was patient for a while, but after Eric fluffed take 15, he told him he was going to wipe all his previous takes and start afresh "to get the shit off the tape." This seemed to do the trick and focus Eric. Patrick skulked off to work on the contents of his bag.

Once Eric had got his solo down, our recording day was finished. Mixing started on the Sunday morning. I sat beside Larry at the desk, keen to learn from him. Paul and Eric sat behind us. Patrick was nowhere to be seen. Reasoning that the two guitars, with their intertwined distinct parts, might sound good panned left and right, I asked Larry if we could mix in stereo.

'Boys, if you want to mix in stereo, you got to record for stereo,' he replied.

Since the two guitars were on separate tracks and I could see on the mixing desk that each had a pan control on it, I didn't understand what he meant and still don't. Besides, if you need to record for stereo, why didn't he ask us whether we wanted to record for stereo. I was a bit grumpy and probably showed it. There was an uneasy rustling from the row behind me.

'I'll put some ADT on the vocals,' Larry ventured, in an attempt to mollify me, having sensed trouble brewing.

I didn't know what ADT was – I thought it was what Dad put on the roses to keep the bugs down – but it sounded convincing. There were murmurs of approval from the back row. Our single was destined to remain in mono. Paul didn't mind this. It had a reassuring retro Phil Spector feel. He was probably worried that if we mixed in stereo, all the vocals would be on one side and the backing track the other, like those early Beatles stereo mixes. Maybe that's what Larry meant.

We'd been mixing for a couple of hours, starting to edge towards a reasonable mix, when Patrick reappeared, ready to assert his control over the proceedings. Our ears were all getting tired so we welcomed fresh input. His instructions however were even more obscure than normal and seemed to consist of an early version of Eno's oblique strategies, but more oblique and less strategic. It soon became clear that he was temporarily lodging on the second moon of Jupiter, as he moved knobs at random and invoked the spirit of Captain Beefheart every few seconds. In theory, this sounds like a cool approach. In reality, it was not. For every accident in the recording studio that produces a wild and brilliant new groove, there are another 99 that result in a crap sound. We were not in the one per cent and soon had a heavy, heavy, monster sound, which sounded truly awful. Jeremy was deputed to accompany Patrick to Pluto, and distract him with chat of Augustus Pablo, while we restored the mix to a semblance of sanity. Patrick had been about as useful as a Bolivian naval attaché. So that was how you produced a record.

Larry was clearly relieved that the session was over and didn't say "Congratulations, gentlemen, you have just made your first number one record." It didn't dampen our enthusiasm.

It's funny what you remember and what you completely forget. I have a pretty good memory, but the ensuing comedy of errors in getting our record pressed fell into the latter category and I have Paul to thank for reminding me that it actually happened. Patrick was entrusted with the master tape, as he was in charge of the pressing arrangements, having done it before for the Tonix. The following week came the news that Patrick had mislaid the tape, having stopped off on the way to the pressing plant at a party on Neptune and was a bit hazy on what had happened. This never happened to *Trout Mask Replica*.

A replacement master tape having been obtained, Paul and Eric went up to London to pick up the boxes of singles. While they were there, they decided to drop in on John Peel at Broadcasting House. Paul blagged his way in and convinced the uniformed commissionaire that he was a close confidant of the veteran DJ and, incredibly, was allowed to phone Peel in his studio while he was still on air. Even more incredibly, Peel answered the phone and, gamely, came down to reception at the end of the show and accepted a copy of the single. He even offered Paul and Eric a lift, which they unaccountably rejected.

We would maintain a nightly vigil, as we sat in my room, applying a John Bull printing set to the labels and scoring, cutting and sticking covers together, listening to Peel for that moment he played *Calling All The Shots*. We had to sit through hours of dull industrial post-punk, all the time trying to keep Jeremy away from the glue, lest the whole of our output meet a sticky end. Eventually, one night, just before the end of the show, when it was clear that yet again we weren't going to be played, Paul got fed up with listening to the latest 12" by Dislocated Diagram from Sheffield or something like that.

'I'm going to phone him,' said Paul, emboldened by his previous telephonic contact with Peel.

He put down the pot of Copydex, as Jeremy eyed it covetously, and headed for the door. It was the sort of mad idea that Paul would have, and which permeated all aspects of his life, including song-writing, but which often gave rise to some marvellous inspiration. We all laughed. We all laughed even more, when a couple of minutes later, Peel closed the show by saying "Have to go now – the phone's ringing!" Yes, Paul had again

The Morning of our Lives / Steve Cooke

managed to get through to Peel, who was very apologetic about not playing the record and promised that he would.

We'd only taken delivery of 650 of our 1,000 singles, as the pressing plant had gone into receivership.

'That's not our problem,' I said to Paul.

Enough of my legal studies had sunk in for me to know that our contract for recording and pressing 1,000 singles was with Larry and he'd just have to sort it out.

Paul phoned Larry.

'Don't worry. You boys will get your singles,' he said.

He said the same thing a week later, when Paul phoned him again, but we never did.

The legal principle of sanctity of contract was trumped by the fact that Larry already had our cash, so we had to go whistle. We would just have to make that run of 650 count. I didn't have the figures to hand, but suspected that any chance of us going platinum had disappeared. On the plus side, it meant that we had 350 less records to apply our John Bull printing set to and stick covers together for.

Eventually, Peel kept his promise and played it. It was one of the most exciting moments of my life. My record was being played on Radio 1. He played it a couple more times and there were rumours that Anne Nightingale had also played it and that Kid Jensen was playing it on his daytime show. It was difficult to establish if any of this was true without a round the clock Radio 1 monitoring team, which was beyond our patience. It was, therefore, by pure luck that the radio was turned on at McCarthy's Pharmaceuticals during our lunch break, when Peter Powell eulogized about this great new record he was going to play – *Calling All The Shots* by the Stereotypes. I couldn't believe it. Nor could the guys at work, until he read all our names out, dispelling any lingering doubts in the workplace. Even more miraculously, Laura, who bought into our whole apprentice rock star thing with massive and touching enthusiasm, had clearly been maintaining the kind of 24/7 radio vigil that we couldn't manage ourselves. The result was that she had taped the whole of the Peter Powell eulogy. I still have the recording and indeed it appears on our retrospective that is on the iTunes music store. Laura has my undying gratitude.

We had a record out and it was being played on daytime Radio 1. We were on the verge of a breakthrough. Now for the big push.

At least we went in guns blazing. We must have visited most of the important record shops in London. The Virgin Megastore took five on a sale or return basis. We even found a copy in the Beggars' Banquet shop. God knows how it got there. We harassed radio stations. We sent copies of the single to all the major record companies. In our highly limited terms, the summer of 1980 was, as Neil Tennant terms it, our imperial phase, albeit on a massively smaller canvas than that to which that phrase is usually applied. People in Oxford were hearing that our record that was getting played on Radio 1 and there was a real buzz around us. We played live on Oxford High Street on Mayday morning and our performance was captured on a local BBC programme. We were interviewed by the Oxford Daily News. Paul sent a copy of the single to the Queen as a birthday present, but one of her ladies in waiting returned it with a polite rejection letter. She had a promising future as an A&R man.

We gigged away, playing loads of summer balls. We headlined the Unknown Heroes Festival outdoors at Balliol. The quad was packed and the crowd was really up for it. We felt as if we were on the crest of a wave. We were asked by Linacre College to headline their ball. Did that mean we were now more famous than Dave Dee, Dozy, Beaky, Mick and Titch (without

BUCKINGHAM PALACE

1st May, 1980

Dear Paul,

    The Queen has commanded me to thank you very much indeed for your message of birthday greetings.

    Your offer to forward a copy of your record to Her Majesty is appreciated, but I have to explain to you that it would be contrary to The Queen's rules in such matters to accept a gift from people who are not known personally to her.

    I am sorry to send you a disappointing reply.

Yours sincerely,

Susan Hussey

Lady-in-Waiting.

Paul Galley,
Linoln College,
Oxford.

Even the Queen sent us a rejection letter.

Dave Dee)? More importantly, they asked us to play for two hours. We only had an hour's worth of material rehearsed, but took the gig anyway. I think Paul suggested dusting off our old Chuck Berry repertoire, but no-else was keen on that, so instead we turned into Jefferson Airplane for the night and populated each song with long psychedelic improvisations. We had followed Patrick's advice and turned our amps right up so that we had to play less and feel the holes in the music. He was right. It sounded great. The two guitars were ringing out, nicely separated, the bass and drums locked together and the vocal harmonies tight and clear as a bell. We even got some coverage in the national music press when *New Music News* covered an Oxford battle of the bands competition, judged by John Peel. Peel remembered our record and we got an ecstatic review from the *New Music News* reporter, who went by the name of Johnny Bordello. I'm guessing that, like John Peel, that wasn't his real name.

We even got some fan mail. Well, a single fan letter from someone who had chanced upon our single in a London record shop. We also received a pompous letter from another band, called the Reluctant Stereotypes, suggesting that we might like to change our name to avoid confusion. They offered to meet our costs of changing our letterhead. This momentarily made us feel a bit inadequate as we didn't have any Stereotypes letterhead. Then we noticed that they hadn't written their letter on a Reluctant Stereotypes letterhead, so nor did they. Confidence restored, I wrote back letting them know that we'd decided to change our name to the Reluctants. Come to think of it, that's a better name than the Stereotypes.

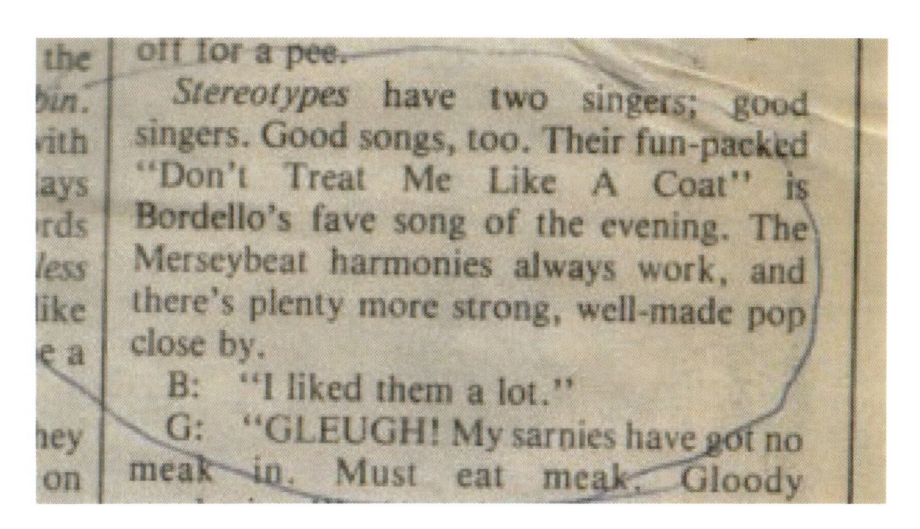

> *Stereotypes* have two singers; good singers. Good songs, too. Their fun-packed "Don't Treat Me Like A Coat" is Bordello's fave song of the evening. The Merseybeat harmonies always work, and there's plenty more strong, well-made pop close by.
> B: "I liked them a lot."
> G: "GLEUGH! My sarnies have got no meak in. Must eat meak. Gloody

The full extent of our coverage in the national press. That's it.

The high point came, when amongst all the usual rejection letters, we received one from Pulsar Records offering to re-release *Calling All The Shots* on their label, with national distribution. We had never heard of Pulsar Records and indeed couldn't recall having even sent them a copy, but they seemed to be a record company. We started salivating at the thought of national distribution and planning the track listing for our first album. We went into Oxford Radio recording studios to record eight tracks in anticipation. Pulsar Records promptly went bust. We didn't know it at the time, but being played by Peter Powell on daytime Radio 1 was destined to be the high-water mark of the Stereotypes.

Ashes To Ashes

In summer 1980, inflation was at 21% and, Thatcher having worked her magic, unemployment had risen to 2 million for the first time since 1935. She visited Harold Hill, a mile away from home in Hornchurch, to hand over the keys to the 12,000th tenant to exercise their rights under the right to buy scheme. The neighbours didn't take to her. The arrival of Cruise Missiles was announced. Major Tom was back at number 1[40] in Bowie's *Ashes To Ashes*, followed by the *Scary Monsters* LP, Bowie's last great album. I played it a lot. Robert Fripp was all over it, playing some extraordinary guitar. His rehabilitation seemed complete, signalling clearance for retrieval of my King Crimson albums from the trunk. I had moved into a ground floor flat in Leckford Road, just off the Woodstock Road in North Oxford. Ten years earlier, Bill Clinton lived a few doors along, when he was a Rhodes Scholar. At the end of my second year, I started to look for somewhere to live, as nearly all of us had to live out of college in our last year. I had got back together with St. Annes' Girl in the autumn of 1979. We had a relatively stable and happy nine months together, although I never chanced another visit to Chepstow and avoided all contact with the rebarbative Roydon. She introduced me to another St. Anne's student, Russell, who was also a musician, playing in a band with the amusing name of Eric and the Ominoes. Well I thought it was funny, anyway. He was also looking for somewhere to live and she said that we'd like each other. She was right. We had a similar sense of humour and hit it off immediately. Our friendship and musical relationship has endured to this day. For the last thirty years, he has been writing the *Alex* cartoon, first in the ill-fated *London Daily News* and then in *The Independent* and *The Daily Telegraph*. He received the MBE in 2002, but in 1980 was certainly the last person I would have expected to have received an honour from the Queen. We moved into Leckford Road with an old school friend of his who was at Mansfield, Robert Saunders. Saunders had a highly irritating air of pretension about him, fancied himself to be a bit of an auteur and generally talked shit most of the time. Russell and I took the piss out him relentlessly. Fortunately, he wasn't around much and eventually, after Russell had detonated a smoke bomb in his bedroom, leading to the arrival of the fire brigade and a forensic scientist specialising in arson, Saunders left altogether. We were pleased to see the departure of his turgid record collection. Fashionable as it was to like them at that time, Russell and I both hated Joy Division and were relieved to see Ian Curtis' droning vocals and pompous lyrics leave our abode.

---

[40] *Having featured in Bowie's only previous number 1, Space Oddity. He might have been strung out in heaven's high, hitting an all-time low, but he was a good luck charm for Bowie.*

Leckford Road became a bit of social hub. In the flat below were three guys from Mansfield who seemed to be the centre of OUCA, the University Conservative Association. Kevin Steele was from London and a lively, wild-eyed type, who seemed slightly unhinged and was often mistaken for the Marquess of Blandford, to whom he bore a striking resemblance, both facially and in behavioural terms. Simon Edwards was always about to collect his grant cheque and could he borrow a fiver? Bashir Ahmed had some gloriously 1977 disco clothing, with some fabulous extravagantly tailored white suits and gold medallions. He was also a big Prince fan a good two years ahead of the rest of the planet, and delighted in playing to us Prince's anthems to incest and deflowering under-age girls. We didn't really get it until the rest of the planet did. Their basement flat was a bit dingy, so they seemed to spend most of their time in ours. This was a fevered time in Conservative politics, when groups with names like One Direction were right wing think tanks, not boy bands. William Hague and Guy Hands, both serious OUCA hacks, were regular visitors to Leckford Road and the air seemed to be thick with political conspiracy. It was only a bit later, when Hague was convicted of electoral malpractice by OUCA, that we realised that this was not just an illusion. Hague went on to lead OUCA, the Oxford Union and the Tory party. Hands became the UK's biggest pub landlord and later attempted to bring private equity discipline to rock bands when he acquired EMI. This was not a success and Chris Martin showed little interest in meeting Guy's prescriptive timetable for the delivery of the next Coldplay album. The Rolling Stones, Radiohead, Paul McCartney and others left the label in droves. Hands was a big music fan and this was the world's biggest vanity purchase. In his own words, he looked a "chump". Maybe he should have stuck with politics. Kevin Steele became a director of QPR and was given a 5½ year jail sentence in 2012 for his part in a £17.5m fraud. Bashir is a lawyer in Dubai. We still keep in touch. I'm not sure what Edwards is doing but is probably still trying to borrow a fiver.

The Stereotypes rehearsed and wrote in Leckford Road for most of that summer. Paul was writing some brilliant songs. The competition between us was intense, but in a good way, and we came back after the summer with six or seven really good songs. Eric and I spent some time together arranging the guitars. I co-opted Russell's Vox Continental organ and a Wasp synth and retrieved my ten year old memories of piano lessons to double on keyboards. Paul looked at the synth suspiciously. A synthesizer had definitely never featured in his musical plans and probably never has since. He prefers his music to be put together from more wholesome and simple ingredients. By the end of August, we had a new well-drilled set. The disappointments of the summer were forgotten and we were ready to start a new campaign. Lurking in the back of my mind was the coming storm - the end of university life in nine months' time; finals for which I had done little work; the thought of having to apply for jobs. A real apprentice rock star would have just shrugged and carried on playing his guitar, roll a spliff and have another crack at writing that brilliant song that would change the world, forever in search of the lost chord. That's what Pat Fish would have done. Indeed he did do it, and is still doing it, almost forty years later. That wasn't me. So instead of buying a pair of leather trousers, I hedged my bets and went for a terrible flared pinstripe suit, bought from Mr Byrite on Romford Market, which I could wear for law firm interviews.

It was characteristic of my indolent and disorganised approach that I only applied to three or four firms. My selection from the sheaf of papers that I had casually snatched up at the university careers office seemed to be entirely random. My first interview was at a two partner firm in Bloomsbury, called J. Tickle & Co. I was interviewed by Mr Tickle himself. He seemed entirely bemused that I was applying to them and spent most of the time asking me why I was interested in them. I didn't have a convincing answer. They offered me a job anyway. My next interview was at Slaughter and May. Neither before nor since has anyone entered the hallowed portals of the City's most blue-blooded law firm wearing such an awful suit. Slaughter and May seemed to have a lot more partners than J. Tickle & Co and also asked me why I applied to them, but it seemed to be posed in a much more rhetorical way than Tickle. Two partners interviewed me. A good cop and a bad cop. The good cop asked me simple questions like whether I had any brothers and sisters. I managed to answer them without any mishaps. The bad cop fixed his glare on the flapping lapels of my appalling suit and fired some difficult questions about the rule of law. I blundered my way through 45 minutes, barely escaping with my life. Maybe I had watched too much of *The Sweeney* but I liked the bad cop better than the good cop. To my amazement, they offered me a job. The bad cop, Michael Pescod, went on to be my boss, mentor and later one of my best friends.

The Stereotypes had a full autumn schedule of gigs. At one college bar gig we were informed that we could not encourage the audience to dance as they did not have a licence for dancing. We had never encountered this prohibition before and wondered if we were the subject of a practical joke. Would there be a groove inspector with a white coat and clipboard who would cut us off if we played anything faster than 100 BPM? The gig seemed to pass without incident and the crowd moved in time to the music without impediment or any legal intervention. We played a regular residency at a rather nasty disco/night club in the Westgate Centre called Scamps. It didn't have much going for it, other than clarity that they had all the requisite authorisations in place for the audience to jump up and down as much as they liked. We supported Chicken Shack outdoors in Exeter main quad. The highlight of the gig was accidentally being shown into Chicken Shack's dressing room and our entourage rapidly drinking and eating all their food and drink, before we were turfed out and shown to the correct

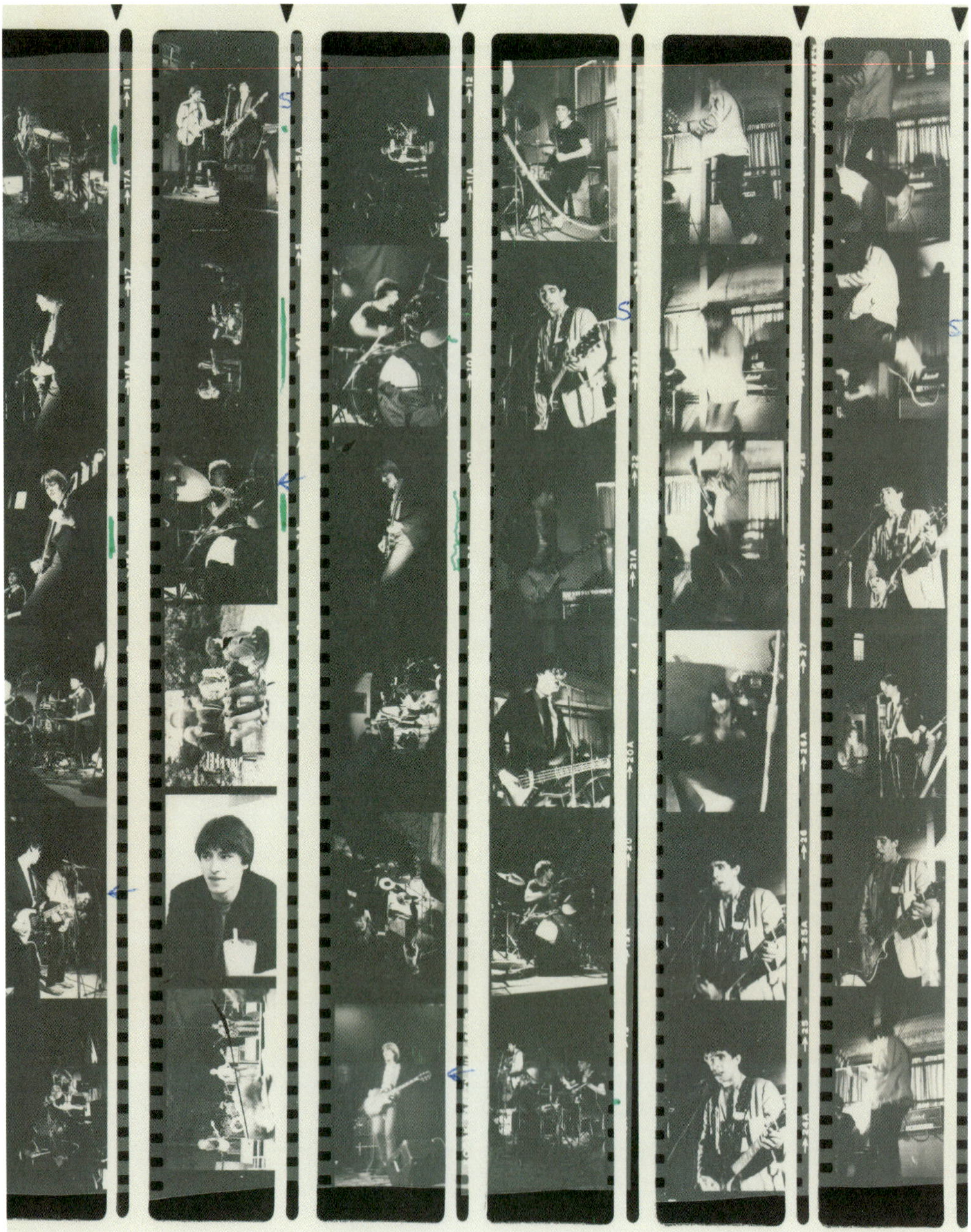

dressing room, containing our more modest food and beverage rider.

Robert Saunders fancied himself as a fledgling rock impresario and promoted a Stereotypes gig at his home village of Blewbury. Word went round shortly before the gig that the Didcot skins would be coming. This was at the height of Sham 69 gigs being appropriated by BNP and National Front supporting skinheads, chanting *Seig Heil,* throwing Nazi salutes and generally screwing things up. We never thought that they would turn their gaze to the Stereotypes. We were, however, probably the biggest band that had ever played Blewbury. This is obviously a relative concept, but we were big enough to attract the attention of the Didcot skins. I had never heard of the Didcot skins, but their name was said by locals in the sort of hushed terms that indicated a degree of trouble. Half way through our set, that trouble arrived. There was some routine thuggery and violence in the crowd. I introduced our song *You Don't Know A Thing About Love* with a dedication to those in the audience who didn't. I don't know if the Didcot skins grasped the full implications but clearly apprehended that this was a slight intended for them. There then ensued a preliminary bombardment of the stage with all the hall fire extinguishers, followed by a full stage invasion. We fought with axe and drumstick but soon had to concede the stage as they broke through to the left of the keyboard rig. It didn't seem that scary at the time, but it was our only first hand experience of mindless, ignorant violence. For the first time, my Anti-Nazi League badge seemed to mean something.

Machiavelli said that *"Wars begin when you will, but they do not end when you please".* The same is true of bands, for entirely different reasons. Bands start with the consensus that is unnecessary for wars, but end when that consensus expires. Things had started to get a bit more fractious in the band. The failure to make a breakthrough must have taken its toll. Paul and I started grumbling about Jeremy. Paul and Eric spent some time together in Leckford Road probably grumbling about me. Then Eric and I spent time arranging the guitars and synth and grumbling about Paul. I grumbled about always having to chivvy them into helping me put up posters and get our rig back after a gig. Paul grumbled about me being bossy like his dad and was going through one of his periods when he felt that he had compromised too much of his artistic vision.

We didn't know it at the time but our gig at the Balliol Lindsay Rooms on 25 October 1980 was to be our last. It was also our best ever gig. We were supported by a bunch of Joy Division copyists called Strangers To Romance. Their posters had a graphic of someone hanging himself, which, given that Ian Curtis had done just that earlier that year, seemed a little tasteless. Their lead singer, Jimmy, was a real tosser and insisted that they remove our backdrop of posters while they were playing their support set. They wittily put them all back up upside down when they had finished.

There was a smug self-satisfaction about them and Jimmy actually said "Follow that!" to us after they had finished their droning set. So we did. Our collective irritation with them temporarily mended the fissures in the band and cemented a new common purpose – to bury the tosser Jimmy. We played the best we had ever done. It was a tight set with all of our best songs. We had incorporated one of our Jefferson Airplane psychedelic jams onto the end of one of them. Some nights it worked better than others. This time it was awesome. I remember as we hit the last chord there was an awed silence from the crowd. The response after the gig was absolutely tremendous. Jimmy and his cohort skulked off.

A month later, the band was no more. Paul came down with glandular fever and sold the WEM bass amp his dad had bought him. Fractiousness returned. We had one last big argument and that was it. Ashes to ashes, punk to punky. A week later, John Lennon died and I split up with St. Anne's Girl for the third and final time. Musically, it felt like a bad time. The new broom of punk had gone a bit stale. The Clash released the bloated monstrosity of *Sandinista* the following week and the charts was full of dreck like Shakin' Stevens, that poundland Elvis Preselli [41]. A. P. Horn's unreasonable demands for me to settle my overdraft forced me to sell my beloved Les Paul. It felt like the end of innocence of youth and the beginning of the age of reality of adulthood. Ou sont les neiges d'antan? It was time to settle down, start taking my law course seriously and prepare for the world of work. It seemed the natural thing to do at the time and I don't regret it. Mum was relieved and Patrick was disgusted. I never left music behind, moving to synthesizers, a jazz band and ultimately television soundtracks, but never again did I have the faith that it was going to be the main part of my life and harbour the illusion that I was going to be a proper rock star. Come children, let us shut up the box and the puppets, for our play is played out.

The Stereotypes never played together again on the same stage.

    I was with the College Stalker Moncrieff when we were driving together on the M4 in the late 1980s, when conversation turned to people from college.

    'What's PT doing now?' I said.

    'He's working as a reporter for one of the west country local TV stations,' he replied instantly, as ever having the precise movements of every alumnus of Lincoln college at his fingertips. Within seconds, we hit a massive traffic jam and were stationary in a sprawl of cars. We'd only sat there for a few minutes, when glancing round to the car next to us, Moncrieff noticed a familiar moustache in front of the steering wheel. It was PT. Even by the College Stalker's standards, this was an extreme piece of networking. Continuing the conversation through the open car windows in the slowly crawling traffic was a bit testing. We decided not to continue the liaison all the way to Bristol and came off at the next junction. We later saw him reporting a fast-moving breaking local news story about a cow escaping from a field.

    In 2009, on the 30th anniversary of our first gig and Sid Vicious's death and the 50th anniversary of Buddy Holly's death, Paul, Jeremy, Moncrieff and I met for dinner in Oxford. It was the first time we were together in the same place since 1980. At around the same time, it transpired

---

[41] *For those not expert in the geography of Shaky's homeland, the Presellis are a range of hills in South Wales. Boom boom.*

that my elder son Harry was working in a pub less than 50 yards away from Jeremy's coffee shop *Brill* in Exmouth Market, whilst younger son Charlie was living two streets away from Paul in Headington and was working in the Cape of Good Hope. Landlord Fred and his dog are no longer there.

Paul brought the news that the Stereotypes were, if not big, respectably moderately proportioned, in Japan, with copies of *Calling All The Shots* changing hands on eBay for well north of £100. We half expected Moncrieff to announce the offer of a lucrative engagement at the Budokan, in the manner of the last reel of Spinal Tap. Jeremy mentioned that he had licensed both sides of the single for a couple of new wave compilation albums[42]. Paul wondered what had happened to our royalties. Jeremy sheepishly admitted he'd spent them. It is 2009. Heritage rock is the thing. Shed Seven and Toploader have whole evenings dedicated to playing the whole of one of their classic albums. There is a Jags box set. Can we, the Stereotypes, not get our snouts in the trough? If Dave Rowntree of Blur can renounce life as a mega-platinum rock star for the thrill of the chase as a lawyer, surely there is room in the rock firmament for me to make the opposite journey? Ever honest to our art, we eschew simply rattling through *Don't Treat Me Like A Coat* and *Nostalgia* in Asian enormodromes, instead electing to attempt some new recording. The Turl Street Irregulars eventually track down Eric. He is nervous about all of us being in the same recording studio. I have a cup of coffee with him in Starbucks on Highbury Corner. It's nice to see him again. He wires me the guitar parts for a couple of songs.

As ever, drama was not far behind. Eric suffers a stroke and his parts (guitar that is) have to be pieced together with cornflake packets and sticky back plastic. The resulting album *Midnight In The Botanical Gardens* is still on the iTunes store and Spotify and does a brisk business with the orient.

Sherlock Holmes once said: *"I consider that a man's brain originally is like a little empty attic, and you have to stock it with such furniture as you choose. A fool takes in all the lumber of every sort that he comes across, so that the knowledge which might be useful to him gets crowded out, or at best is jumbled up with a lot of other things, so that he has a difficulty in laying his hands on it. Now the skilful workman is very careful indeed as to what he takes into his brain-attic. He will have nothing but the tools*

---

[42] *If you can get hold of them, check out "Powerpearls Vol. 8" where we're there with proper heroes of the era like Fingerprintz, Jilted John, Rudi and the Shoes and "Messthetics 2", accompanied by the TV Personalities and the Terraplanes.*

which may help him in doing his work, but of these he has a large assortment, and all in the most perfect order. It is a mistake to think that that little room has elastic walls and can distend to any extent. Depend upon it - there comes a time when for every addition of knowledge you forget something that you knew before. It is of the highest importance, therefore, not to have useless facts elbowing out the useful ones." Reader, I am that fool. As you will have gathered from the preceding pages, my mental attic has been populated without discrimination, housing an extensive collection of bric-a-brac that my mother would not have tolerated, had she had the tools to clear out that particular space with her customary rigour. I hope, however, that you have enjoyed navigating your way through all the antique ornaments and trinkets that clutter up this reverie of a past that was truly a foreign country. In a place far away from anyone or anywhere, I drifted off for a moment.[43]

---

[43] *If I couldn't start this memoir with a line from one of my favourite books, I was damn well going to end it with one ('The Wind-up Bird Chronicle' by Haruki Murakami, translated by Jay Rubin).*

IN LOVING MEMORY

OF

Barbara Cooke

Died 11th June 2000

Printed in Great Britain
by Amazon